"One of the great regrets of history occurred in the [...] of science and religion between Galileo and the chu[...] without this split we would have had better science and better religion. Heidi Russell not only offers us the best of science and religion of the twenty-first century but recasts for us their whole relationship. Instead of contending their truths, she engages the rich analogies that each has to offer in the pursuit of relationality/love. This is an utterly pastoral approach to science and theology, 'rejuvenating what it means to be the body of Christ as inherent connectedness to all of creation impacting our understanding of social and environmental justice.' "

— Bob O'Gorman
Professor Emeritus
Loyola University Chicago

"Heidi Russell's book *Quantum Shift* is an engaging, informative, and often profound glimpse into the way in which the worldview produced by quantum physics can alter and invigorate our conceptions of God and creation. Charting a course between innovation and tradition, Russell offers novel vocabulary and fresh perspectives for theologians, pastoral ministers, and other persons of faith seeking to navigate the implications of the new sciences for religious belief. Eminently readable and replete with examples to concretize sometimes abstract concepts, Russell's work is sure to whet the reader's appetite for more science and to slake the reader's thirst for the more expansive and dynamic insights into God and the God-world relationship afforded by this scientific worldview. *Ephphata*—and enjoy!"

— Gloria L. Schaab
Barry University

"In *Quantum Shift*, Heidi Russell provides an insightful look into the implications of contemporary scientific research for theology and ministry. This work helps to advance the important idea that it is possible to be a deeply committed person of faith and still appreciate contemporary scientific inquiry. The pastoral application of scientific and theological insights that she offers are also a particularly valuable contribution for both theologians and pastoral ministers and stands out among other recent works on the relationship between theology and science."

— Theodore James Whapham
Dean, School of Ministry
Associate Professor
University of Dallas

"In his revolutionary encyclical, *Laudato Sì*, Pope Francis called everyone on Earth to conversion at the level of conscience to a connected way of being and acting, because to do otherwise is to live in a false reality: 'Everything is connected' (90). In this book, Heidi Ann Russell builds on the important academic premise, as articulated in the foreword, that 'there is a universal basis for our understanding and, since that basis cannot be self-contradictory, the understanding one has from one discipline should complement that which one has from all other disciplines.'

"Russell's work is exemplary in that she models this converted way of thinking in every chapter. In so doing, she opens compelling new insights into traditional tenets of the Christian faith. In her hands, complex concepts of science—quantum mechanics, chaos theory, modern cosmology, etc.—are made accessible and the portal of entry into dialogue with the Christian tradition. Russell's engaging, dynamic, infectious dialogue draws the reader toward religious renewal that supports a connected lifestyle. It is a must-read—for the sake of God's people and the planet!"

— Dawn M. Nothwehr, OSF
Erica and Harry John Family Endowed Chair in
Catholic Theological Ethics
Catholic Theological Union
Chicago, Illinois

Quantum Shift

Theological and Pastoral Implications of Contemporary Developments in Science

Heidi Ann Russell

Foreword by
George V. Coyne, SJ

A Michael Glazier Book

LITURGICAL PRESS
Collegeville, Minnesota

www.litpress.org

A Michael Glazier Book published by Liturgical Press

Cover design by Monica Bokinskie. Illustration courtesy of Thinkstock.

1   2   3   4   5   6   7   8   9

Library of Congress Cataloging-in-Publication Data

Russell, Heidi, 1973–
    Quantum shift : theological and pastoral implications of contemporary developments in science / Heidi Ann Russell.
       pages   cm.
    "A Michael Glazier book"
    ISBN 978-0-8146-8303-3 — ISBN 978-0-8146-8328-6 (ebook)
       1. Religion and science.   2. Pastoral counseling.   I. Title.
    BL240.3.R8765   2015
    261.5'5—dc23
                                                          2015006950

For Daniel James Damarion Russell,
the center of my universe

Contents

Foreword

The supposition that underpins this book is that there is a universal basis for our understanding and, since that basis cannot be self-contradictory, the understanding one has from one discipline should complement that which one has from all other disciplines. One is most faithful to one's own discipline, be it the natural sciences, the social sciences, philosophy, literature, theology, etc., if one accepts this universal basis. This means in practice that, while remaining faithful to the strict truth criteria of one's own discipline, we are open to accept the truth value of the conclusions of other disciplines. And this acceptance must not only be passive, in the sense that we do not deny those conclusions, but also active, in the sense that we integrate those conclusions into the conclusions derived from one's own proper discipline. It is that active integration of science with theology that characterizes this book. Such an integration is of particular importance when we are addressing fundamental and ultimate questions and their meaning for our Christian faith. Does the existence of intelligent beings in the universe have any significance for understanding the universe as a whole? Does our knowledge of God depend on our understanding of the universe? In fact, a very strong piece of evidence that there is a universal basis for understanding is the persistent drive of the human being for meaning. This is seen clearly from the very dawn of human history where, with even a very primitive collection of data, our ancestors sought for the meaning of life in the physical universe as well as in the events of their personal lives and those of society in general.

Our modern society is one in which science, and not just technology, is dominant. In fact, technological progress is almost always a result of progress in fundamental science, in our understanding of the physical universe in which we live and to which we are intimately related. And yet there is a persistent widespread attitude among religious believers that much of science is in conflict with their religious tenants. This book not only jumps into that fray but turns it upside down by actively showing that the results of science, correctly understood, can become a source of enrichment for religious beliefs. It succeeds because, on the one hand, it presents a correct and clear summary of some of the principal areas of modern science and, on the other hand, it preserves the independence of religious belief and science while employing the latter through the use of analogy to enrich our theological understanding. Analogy is the key to the author's bold pursuit at integrating these two dominant areas of modern culture without conflating them.

By analogy we attempt to get some rational understanding of God and our relationship to God, who is ultimately mystery, by the use of images drawn from our lived experiences that may give us a glimmer of the divine. In a masterful way, the author uses images drawn from a vast array of the fields of modern science to bring about a deeper understanding of some of the principal areas of Catholic theology. In so doing, she avoids the persistent temptation of the religious believer to make God primarily a source of explanation rather than a source of love. For many, God becomes the tool to try to explain things that we cannot otherwise explain. How did the universe begin? How did we come to be? We seize upon God, especially if we do not feel that we have a good and reasonable scientific answer to such questions. God is brought in as the Great God-of-the-Gaps. In fact, the author does just the reverse in seeking a deeper meaning of religious beliefs through an understanding of science.

The science presented ranges from the notions of space and time, through quantum mechanics and chaos theory to modern cosmology and attempts to unify our understanding of gravity in general relativity and quantum mechanics. This adventure through science results in a number of challenging new insights into classical theological themes, such as: the human as body and soul, as free, sinful, and redeemed; death and resurrection; cocreators in a universe of which we have been born and to which we are intimately related; the future of the universe and Christian eschatology. The fundamental theme that unifies the various chapters is the unity of the cosmos, that no element in the universe from the micro to the macro can be understood except as a part of the whole. And the whole is more than an assembly of parts. It is rather a dynamic and future-directed creature of a loving Creator who continues in us his loving care of the whole. The pastoral implications of such a vision are breathtaking and, although they are not the principal intention of the author, they always lie in wait to call us to action.

To journey with the author through this book is a rather heady endeavor as to both the science and the theology, but it is masterfully written for a general audience. It is directed, as the author says, to "the people in the pews." The effort of those people to venture into this intellectual adventure will, I am convinced, be very well rewarded.

George V. Coyne, SJ
McDevitt Chair in Physics
Le Moyne College
Director Emeritus
Vatican Observatory

Acknowledgments

A book is never the work of one person alone, and I am so grateful to be a part of the network of relationships that enabled this book to emerge. I truly do believe that God works in and through our relationships, and I feel so blessed to have experienced God's love in the interconnectedness of my life with countless others.

I owe a great debt of thanks to all of my family and friends who have supported me and encouraged me through the writing process. First and foremost, I am grateful to my son DJ who kept me both grounded and inspired. I am indebted to my mother, Janie Russell, who patiently read through drafts of every chapter, offering extremely helpful questions, suggestions, and corrections. I am thankful to my father, Dan Russell, who was a science teacher and wanted me to be more interested in science when I was young. Hopefully I have made up now for my lack of interest then! From my parents, I learned to see God in and through the beauty of creation and the interconnectedness of love.

I am very grateful to Fr. George Coyne, SJ, who graciously agreed to read this work and write the foreword for it. I am thankful to my colleagues from the Institute of Pastoral Studies at Loyola University Chicago who talked through some of these ideas with me at research seminars. I am especially thankful to Bob O'Gorman and Tim O'Connell who read through early drafts of chapter 2 as it went from being a CTSA talk to an article in *Theological Studies* to the chapter in this current volume. I am thankful to the science and theology group at the Catholic Theological Society of America for listening to papers I have presented, asking helpful questions, and offering key insights through our discussions. I am deeply thankful to the late William

Stoeger, SJ, who always took the time to talk with me at CTSA, encouraged me in my work, and was a wonderful mentor.

I would like to thank our IPS research assistant, Layli Carsi, who painstakingly edited the footnotes for several of the chapters, looking up citations when I did not have the complete information recorded. All of my students at IPS have also contributed to this book by keeping me excited about theology and engaged in the world of pastoral ministry. I would also like to thank my friend John Mand for his interest in science and religion and our great discussions. John also read through the entire draft of the book, catching many typos and grammatical errors that needed to be fixed while offering support and encouragement for the project with each chapter he read.

Finally, I would like to thank the people at Liturgical Press: Hans Christoffersen for enthusiastically supporting the project, Lauren L. Murphy for patiently answering all of my questions, and Patrick McGowan for being a wonderful copy editor.

Introduction

Theology is the art of bringing our religious tradition into dialogue with our changing or evolving worldviews. The early Christians grappled with Greek philosophy. Aquinas engaged the newly rediscovered works of Aristotle. The transcendental Thomists of the twentieth century brought Aquinas into dialogue with the philosophies of Kant, Hegel, and Heidegger, among others. Twentieth-century theologians also engaged the positivistic worldview of the scientific and industrial revolutions. Liberation and contextual theologies of the current time have since embraced a postmodern worldview that focuses on the particular rather than the universal and trades the optimistic worldview of the modern era for the reality of oppression that resulted from industrialization and colonialism.

To all of these developments in theology, we see today another dynamic engagement—the dialogue between science and religion. There has been a new movement in science in recent decades aimed at helping people who are not scientists understand the vast revision of our worldview that has occurred through scientific research. For example, books by scientist Brian Greene became PBS *Nova* specials *The Elegant Universe* and *The Fabric of the Cosmos*. The Carl Sagan *Cosmos* series was remade into the new series featuring the astrophysicist Neil DeGrasse Tyson. At the time of the writing of this book, Tyson is doing a live tour, "An Evening with Neil DeGrasse Tyson," to sold-out crowds. We see posts and re-posts from popular Facebook pages such as "Science Alert," "Everything Is Physics," "Science Cosmos," "Science Is Awesome," "I f*&#ing love science," etc. The last of these pages currently has 19,677,440 "likes" on Facebook.[1]

---

[1] "I f*&#ing love science," Science Website, Facebook, https://www.facebook.com/IFeakingLoveScience (title edited).

People today are cognizant of developments in our scientific world-view, and if theology and pastoral ministry fail to engage these developments, we run the risk of becoming irrelevant in the contemporary world.

Klaus Nürnberger declares:

> Experts are laypersons in fields other than their own. Physics, especially, has become too complex and inaccessible for the untrained layperson to understand. Fortunately excellent popularizations have been written that unlock these mysteries, at least to some extent, for the nonexpert. Similarly, much of academic theology presents, to the nontheologian, a conceptual and logical jungle that is extremely hard to penetrate. Because of its lack of critical thought, the vast devotional literature does not make things any easier. As the example of the new atheists demonstrates, puzzlement easily turns into dismissal and contempt. We owe our contemporaries a lucid and consistent account of "the hope that is in us" (1 Pet. 3:15).[2]

We lose a critical point of engagement with contemporary society if we leave this conversation to fundamentalist Christians and fundamentalist atheists such as Richard Dawkins and Lawrence Krauss. People's image of the relationship between science and religion too often comes from newspaper headlines about yet another creationism and evolution debate by a local school board. The superficial and false image of the relationship between science and religion is often caricatured by the icon of the Catholic Church's condemnation of Galileo.

At the same time, however, in most mainstream, nonfundamentalist denominations of Christianity, theologians have been taking part in a very serious dialogue with scientists to understand the implications for our theological tradition of a radical revision of our understanding of all that exists. In a letter to George Coyne, SJ, the director of the Vatican Observatory at the time, Pope John Paul II wrote:

> If the cosmologies of the ancient Near Eastern world could be purified and assimilated into the first chapters of Genesis, might

---

[2] Klaus Nürnberger, "Eschatology and Entropy: An Alternative to Robert John Russell's Proposal," *Zygon* 47, no. 4 (December 2012): 273.

not contemporary cosmology have something to offer to our reflections upon creation? Does an evolutionary perspective bring any light to bear upon theological anthropology, the meaning of the human person as the imago Dei, the problem of Christology—and even upon the development of doctrine itself? What, if any, are the eschatological implications of contemporary cosmology, especially in light of the vast future of our universe? Can theological method fruitfully appropriate insights from scientific methodology and the philosophy of science?[3]

Yet somehow that call for theology to incorporate new insights from contemporary scientific developments is still not reaching the people in the pews. While science is more accessible than ever due to the ability to look things up online and the existence of a vast amount of popularized literature available everywhere, there nonetheless seems to be a disconnect between science and people of faith. "The MIT Survey on Science, Religion, and Origins" summarized:

> We find a striking gap between people's personal beliefs and the official views of the faiths to which they belong. Whereas Gallup reports that 46% of Americans believe that God created humans in their present form less than 10,000 years ago, we find that only 11% belong to religions openly rejecting evolution. This shows that the main divide in the origins debate is not between science and religion, but between a small fundamentalist minority and mainstream religious communities who embrace science. The fact that the gap between personal and official beliefs is so large suggests that part of the controversy might be defused by people learning more about their own religious doctrine and the science it endorses, thereby bridging this belief gap.[4]

---

[3] John Paul II, "Letter of His Holiness John Paul II to Reverend George V. Coyne, SJ, Director of the Vatican Observatory," Libreria Editrice Vaticana, 1988, http://www.vatican.va/holy_father/john_paul_ii/letters/1988/documents/hf_jp-ii_let_19880601_padre-coyne_en.html.

[4] Eugena Lee, Max Tegmark, and Meia Chita-Tegmark, "The MIT Survey on Science, Religion, and Origins: The Belief Gap," MIT (February 11, 2013), http://space.mit.edu/home/tegmark/survey/survey.pdf; cites Frank Newport, "In US, 46% Hold Creationist View of Human Origins," Gallup, June 1, 2012, http://www.gallup.com/poll/155003/hold-creationist-view-human-origins.aspx.

Theologians and ministers have a responsibility to the faithful to make sure they first and foremost understand the teaching of their own religious tradition. The survey notes that "the Roman Catholic Church endorses evolution, but nonetheless, no more than 58% of US Catholics believe that evolution is the best explanation for life on Earth."[5] Americans also tend to perceive hostility between science and religion (55%) even when they don't feel it conflicts with their own personal religious beliefs (61%).[6] Perhaps most disturbingly, "whereas Gallup reports that 18% of Americans believe that the Sun revolves around Earth, 0% belong to religions supporting this view."[7] While the religious institutions are clearly not at fault for this ignorance in the American public, how much are they actively doing to help alleviate it? The study also positively correlates a high level of religious observance with likelihood of seeing science in conflict with religious beliefs and notes:

> About four-in-ten (42%) of those who attend religious services at least once a month say the clergy at their place of worship have spoken about science or scientific findings; more than half (56%) say the topic has not been raised. . . . A smaller share of Catholics (35%) say science has been raised at church. Of those who say their clergy occasionally speak about science or scientific findings, three-in-ten (30%) say the clergy at their church are usually supportive of science, while 11% say they are critical of science. A majority (52%) say the clergy's references to science are neither positive nor negative.[8]

[5] Lee, Tegmark, and Chita-Tegmark, "The MIT Survey," 1. Cites The Pew Forum on Religion & Public Life, "US Religious Landscape Survey" (February 2008), http://religions.pewforum.org/pdf/report-religious-landscape-study-full.pdf.

[6] David Masci, "Public Opinion on Religion and Science in the United States," Pew Research Center (November 5, 2009), http://www.pewforum.org/2009/11/05/public-opinion-on-religion-and-science-in-the-united-states/. Masci notes, "More than half of the public (55%) says that science and religion are 'often in conflict.' Close to four-in-ten (38%) take the opposite view that science and religion are 'mostly compatible.' Yet the balance is reversed when people are asked about science's compatibility with their own religious beliefs. Only 36% say science sometimes conflicts with their own religious beliefs and six-in-ten (61%) say it does not."

[7] Lee, Tegmark, and Chita-Tegmark, "The MIT Survey," 7.

[8] A. Kohut et al., "Scientific Achievements Less Prominent than a Decade Ago: Public Praises Science; Scientists Fault Public, Media," The Pew Research Center for the People & the Press (July 9, 2009), http://www.people-press.org/files/legacy-pdf/528.pdf.

This book is an attempt to bridge that gap. It will take the insights from the scientists trying to make science accessible to the average person and match that effort with a theological exploration that is grounded in academic theology but made pastorally relevant. This book also attempts to offer the people of God a more sophisticated theology that can stand up against the claims of writers such as Richard Dawkins who tend to build up a straw man of religion as the enemy of science that can be easily torn down. Rather than seeing science as a threat, theology can engage science in such a way as to help us to develop our theological insights, look at the healthy challenges these insights offer our religious worldview, and think about God and our religious tradition in new and exciting ways.

Furthermore, this book is meant to be a resource to theologians, ministers, and laity to open up new frontiers of thought in terms of spurring our theological imaginations to contemplate God in new and marvelous ways. I am indebted to Fr. George Coyne, SJ, for the way in which I have thought about this project. On November 17, 2011, Fr. Coyne gave the Albertus Magnus lecture at Dominican University in Chicago, Illinois.[9] In that lecture, he talked about the fact that science does not prove the existence of God. We do not come to believe in God because of what we learn from science. He went on, however, to note that if we believe in God, and if we believe that God is Creator, science can tell us something about the God in whom we believe. Herein lie Bonaventure's vestiges of God in the Book of Creation. In a similar text available online, Coyne elaborates:

> I have never come to believe in God, nor do I think anyone has come to believe in God, by proving God's existence through anything like a scientific process. God is not found as the conclusion of a rational process like that. . . . I have never come to love God or God to love me because of any of these reasoning processes. I have come to love God because I have accepted the fact that he first made the move towards me. If that is the case, why should I not use my best knowledge of science to try to get an idea of what God is like? It will be only a glimmer, a shadow, but it is the one thing I have to go on, and I have a passionate desire to want to know more about this person who loves me so

---

[9] George V. Coyne, "Children of a Fertile Universe: Chance, Destiny, and a Creator God" (Albertus Magnus Lecture, Siena Center at Dominican University, River Forest, IL, November 17, 2011).

much. And that is what I am going to try to do now. I am going to try to present in broad strokes what I think is the best of our modem understanding of the universe, and then ask the question at the end: What does this say about the God who loves me and who made this universe?[10]

The physicist and Anglican priest John Polkinghorne makes a similar point:

> Theology has often to proceed by careful appeal to analogy, making use of, and seeking to extend, concepts formed in the course of human experience, in order to guide and control its attempts to use finite human language to speak of the infinite reality of God. What is being suggested here about hints of the Creator discerned in the form of creation encourages the belief that human descriptive language is not totally powerless to convey something of the nature of God. Images drawn from science, such as mutual entanglement, may provide a modest analogical resource, however pale they may be in comparison with the brightness of divine reality. The discourse will be qualified by the warnings of apophatic theology concerning the inaccessible mystery of the divine, but surely something must be said, even if human language is necessarily being used in some open and "stretched" sense when it is applied to God.[11]

Inspired by Fr. Coyne, this book will try to look at our modern understanding of physics and cosmology and ask what it might say to us about the God who loves us and created the cosmos of which we are a part. Even more so, the insights of the sciences can give us new ideas about humanity and our relationships with one another and the God who created us. Jesuit theologian Karl Rahner has an axiom that theology is anthropology and anthropology is theology. In other words, we never say something about God that does not also say something about what it means to be human, and we never talk about

---

[10] George V. Coyne, "The Dance of the Fertile Universe," 6, Universidad Interamericana de Puerto Rico, AAAS Dialogue on Science, Ethics, and Religion (DOSER), Public Lecture, March 27, 2006, http://www.metro.inter.edu/servicios/decanatos/academicos/documentos/HandoutCoyne.pdf.

[11] John C. Polkinghorne, "The Demise of Democritus," in *The Trinity and an Entangled World: Relationality in Physical Science and Theology*, ed. John C. Polkinghorne (Grand Rapids, MI: W. B. Eerdmans Publishing, 2010), 11–12.

what it means to be human without implicitly saying something about the God we believe created humanity. What we believe about God has implications for the way we live our lives; the way we live our lives says something about the God in whom we believe.

In unexpected developments, whether in science or in our lives, one finds exciting opportunities to learn something new. Mystery has a depth that is inexhaustible. We experience that depth of mystery in the explorations of science, in human life, and in God. In both science and theology, every answer leads us to new questions. Rather than try to fit what we know and discover of the world into a predetermined idea of God, we need to let what we discover teach us new things about God, creation, and our relationship to both. In order to do so, we must adopt an openness to scientific discovery rather than defensiveness. Science offers theology no threat. Indeed, it offers the possibility of further revelation.

The Changing Landscape

The development in physics in the twentieth century involved a major shift in worldview that was as significant as the Copernican revolution leading to the understanding that the earth revolved around the sun instead of vice versa. As Brian Greene notes, "Newton's rigid and unchanging scaffolding of space and time collapsed into Einstein's unified whole that warps and curves."[12] The physics of Isaac Newton, which has proven to be incredibly successful in describing the world in which we live and move on the scale of our own experience, understood the world to be a static background against which the drama of our everyday lives played out. The universe was understood to function like a clock with all of the pieces working together in perfectly designed harmony. If we just had enough information, we would be able to plug that information into the proper formulas and predict the movement of every single atom in that universe. Atoms were understood as the individual building blocks that collectively made up everything that exists, the components of the machine, so that our entire view of nature was based on

[12] Brian Greene, *The Fabric of the Cosmos: Space, Time, and the Texture of Reality* (New York: A. A. Knopf, 2004), 10.

a fragmentary view of reality.[13] The universe and everything in it was understood in terms of the sum of its parts.

One of the key revolutions of the twentieth century in both relativity theory and quantum theory is that the world can no longer be understood in the fragmentary way. Instead, we now have a view of reality that is entirely relational. In relativity theory, we come to understand time and space, or rather space-time itself, to be something that is not an absolute void or a static scaffolding but rather relation itself. In quantum mechanics, atoms can no longer be understood as individual parts but rather are understood in the context of fields and as aggregate systems. John Gribbin explains, "Such truth as there is in any of this work lies in mathematics. . . . And what those mathematical laws describe are fields of force, space-time curved and recurved back upon itself in fantastic complexity, and a reality that fades away into a froth of virtual particles and quantum uncertainty when you try to peer at it closely."[14]

The understanding of materialism[15] breaks down in a world governed by quantum mechanics, relativity, and field theory, yet most

---

[13] Panos Ligomenides, "Scientific Knowledge as a Bridge to the Mind of God," in *The Trinity and an Entangled World: Relationality in Physical Science and Theology*, ed. John C. Polkinghorne (Grand Rapids, MI: W. B. Eerdmans Publishing, 2010), 75.

[14] John Gribbin, *The Search for Superstrings, Symmetry, and the Theory of Everything* (Boston: Little, Brown, 1998), 52.

[15] Philip Clayton, "Unsolved Dilemmas: The Concept of Matter in the History of Philosophy and in Contemporary Physics," in *Information and the Nature of Reality: From Physics to Metaphysics*, ed. Paul Davies and Niels Henrik Gregersen (New York: Cambridge University Press, 2010), 38. Clayton explains the concept of materialism as follows:

Materialism consist[s] of five central theses:

(1) Matter is the fundamental constituent of the natural world.

(2) Forces act on matter.

(3) The fundamental material particles or "atoms"—together with the fundamental physical forces, whatever they turn out to be—determine the motion of all objects in nature. Thus materialism entails determinism.

(4) All more complex objects that we encounter in the natural world are aggregates of these fundamental particles, and their motions and behaviors can ultimately be understood in terms of the fundamental physical forces acting on them. Nothing exists that is not the product of these same particles and forces.

(5) Materialism is an *ontological* position, as it specifies what kinds of things do and do not exist. But it may also become a thesis concerning what may and may not count as a scientific explanation [e.g., excluding top-down causation].

people still live in a world conceptualized by the myth of matter.[16] What we think of as reality is not reality. That is to say, things are not the way they seem—at least not the way we experience them in this world. That statement holds true both on the quantum level, the level of the very small, and on the level of cosmology, the level of the very large.

Each chapter in the book will outline various new theories and developments in science and then explore the possible theological and pastoral implications of those theories. As an important caveat, this book is not an effort at dialogue—it is not a reciprocal endeavor. I am limiting myself to discovering the insights we can gain from science as theologians, ministers, and believers. I am also not trained in any scientific field, so I am very dependent on those scientists who have popularized scientific concepts for the masses. I have made every effort to stay true to the science and not draw theological conclusions based on scientific evidence. As such, the theology presented here primarily uses the scientific images as analogies and metaphors for theological concepts. In other words, the new images of reality taken from a contemporary scientific worldview give us new images for thinking about God, humanity, sin, grace, and other theological concepts. I am not equating any of these theological concepts with the scientific concepts being articulated.

Chapter 1 will delve into the developments in our concepts of time and space from the time of Einstein's theories of special and general relativity. From the perspective of the block universe, one can understand a unity to all that exists and will exist, even while we live out our lives and decisions on a day to day and moment to moment basis. The understanding that we live our lives into the future becoming the people we were created to be will then be discussed in light of the contemporary debate between pluralism and relativism. I will suggest that the framework of relativity and relationality provides an alternative perspective.

Chapter 2 outlines the development in quantum mechanics known as particle-wave complementarity and the results of the double slit experiment. Using the analogy of particle/wave, we will ask what

---

[16] The phrase "myth of matter" is taken from Paul Davies's book, *The Matter Myth: Dramatic Discoveries that Challenge Our Understanding of Physical Reality* (New York: Simon & Schuster, 2007).

it means to be body/spirit. We will reimage the human person as having infinite potential that is lived out in actualized choices conditioned by probabilities based on freedom, grace, and sin. We will also briefly examine the meaning of resurrection in light of a world that is less material than we might have imagined.

Chapter 3 further investigates the world of quantum mechanics through the phenomenon of entanglement, also known as nonlocality. With the new understanding of the inherent relationality of nature and a view that looks to particles as part of a larger unified system, we will rejuvenate our understanding of what it means to be the Body of Christ. When one understands the Body of Christ in a way that encompasses the inherent connectedness of humanity and then connects humanity to creation itself, the practical implications of that connectedness impact our understanding of social and environmental justice.

Chapter 4 enters the world of chaos theory. It looks at concepts such as fractals and strange attractors to discover the emergence of life and complexity on the edge of chaos. In light of these theories, we will explore the idea of creation out of chaos and the complexity in our human lives. Can we image God as a strange attractor inviting us to live on the edge of chaos and find within the deeper complexity a new fractal sense of beauty?

Chapter 5 moves us into the realm of cosmology. There we will explore the origin of our universe in the big bang. In looking at how our universe began and how it evolved, we will continue to discuss the concepts of creation and causality. On a personal level, our understanding of our utter dependence on God for our very existence and a belief in a God that sustains us even when we do not see a way forward is at the core of our spiritual lives.

Chapter 6 investigates the question of a possible multiverse. What are the implications for theology if our universe is not the only one that exists? How do we understand our relationship with God if there are possibly infinite other universes out there? For insight we turn to the stories of Scripture and the pattern of how God has worked in salvation history in and through the least and the smallest.

Chapter 7 turns from the beginning of the universe to its possible end. What does science say about the end of our universe? Given the rather grim outlook for the universe, is there a place for hope? Some scientists suggest that new universes might be born in and through the death of our universe. Theologically we have a concept for understanding new life emerging from death—the concept of resurrection. We will explore the possible resurrection of the universe itself in the context of our hope in the re-creation of a new heaven and a new earth.

Finally, chapter 8 will investigate some of the most intriguing ideas that attempt to reconcile relativity and quantum mechanics in string theory and loop quantum gravity. String theory envisions a world of possibly eleven dimensions, a world where we live on a three-dimensional "brane" (think membrane) oblivious to the existence of these other dimensions. Loop quantum gravity envisions a world where space itself emerges from the relationship between events and processes occurring in the universe. The image of hidden dimensions can give us a way to think about God as the hidden incomprehensible mystery who nonetheless encompasses and influences our lives. As science grapples with the inability to have certainty or definitive proof of these theories, so too do we grapple in our lives with the inability to have certainty. As in science, preconceptions must be let go (for example, the idea that there are only three dimensions) in order to make progress developing new theories. So also in our lives must we let go of preconceived images of God when they no longer help us understand and make meaning out of the often tragic events in our lives. When we do so, we find that like the spatial network of loop quantum gravity that creates nonlocal connections, love is what holds us together. Love is the inherent relationality of the world that connects us to the God who is Love and to one another.

While each of these chapters stands alone, common themes thread them together. The major underlying theme is relationality—from the microcosm to the macrocosm, from the triune nature of God to the core of what it means to be human. All of the recent developments in physics and cosmology seem to indicate that reality, in its most fundamental form, is not about individual objects but rather relationships and interactions. These relationships and interactions thus give reality to and tell us something about that which is relating and interacting. John Polkinghorne explains the balance one must maintain:

> The physical world is not so atomized that we can understand it fully by an examination conducted constituent piece by constituent piece. Nor is it so inextricably relationally integrated that

until one is able to comprehend the totality, one cannot understand anything at all. Physical science needs to wrestle with the issue of how it may both acknowledge the substantial degree of relationality manifested in phenomena such as quantum entanglement and the mutuality of space, time, and matter, while at the same time being able to do justice to our everyday experience of a significant degree of separability between objects in the macroscopic world. Like theology in its different sphere, science has to struggle with the problem of reconciling unity with diversity. In fact, all theoretical engagement with issues of relationality has to find some way of combining connection with separation, since it is only to the extent that one can recognize a distinction between two entities that one can also speak of their being in mutual relationship.[17]

Such a shift in our understanding of reality itself as inherently relational must have an impact on the way in which we image our God who is triune relationality and how we understand what it means to be human in this vast and mysterious cosmos that God created.

---

[17] Polkinghorne, "The Demise of Democritus," 13.

Chapter One

Relativity and Our Understanding of Space and Time

Scientific Developments—Relativity

What is space? What is time? Augustine famously says of time: "We surely know what we mean when we speak of it. We also know what is meant when we hear someone else talking about it. What then is time? Provided that no one asks me, I know. If I want to explain it to an inquirer, I do not know."[1] Space and time form the context of our entire lives, but when we try to put into words what we mean by space and time, the concepts can defy definition. To further complicate matters, the scientific understanding of space and time has changed drastically since Einstein in a way that few of us can truly comprehend. In Newtonian physics, space provides the background, the stage, on which everything that exists plays out its history (time). Space and time are understood as absolute and unchanging.

With Einstein's theories of relativity, there is a shift in scientific thinking from the idea that space and time form some type of rigid scaffolding on which everything is built to the idea that "space and time no longer provide a fixed, absolute background. Space is as dynamic as matter; it moves and morphs. As a result, the whole universe

[1] Augustine, *Confessions*, trans. Henry Chadwick (Oxford: Oxford University Press, 1991), 11.14.17.

1

can expand or shrink, and time can even begin (in a Big Bang) and end (in a black hole)."[2] Einstein's theory of special relativity deals with the fact that the speed of light is constant and, therefore, all other motion is relative.[3] In other words, what does not change is the speed of light. Length can contract (called Lorentz transformations) and time can slow down (called time dilation), but the speed of light stays constant.[4] Our frame of reference affects our measurement such that two people with different frames of reference will not get the same spatial (length) and temporal (duration) measurements.[5] Within different frames of reference, space-time is experienced differently. Einstein's theory of special relativity, however, did not take gravity into account, and so he later developed the theory of general relativity which does account for gravity. General relativity has to do with the fact that not only is space-time not an absolute static reality but also that it can actually curve like a fabric due to the mass of objects.[6] To think of space and time as dynamic rather than constant, as relational and relative rather than fixed, can boggle our minds because in our day to day experiences, we generally share the same frame of reference (the earth) and move at speeds much slower than the speed of light. Consequently, we do not notice the dynamism of space and time. To us, they do seem to be constant and fixed.

One of the key lessons of relativity is the importance of our frame of reference. Our frame of reference impacts both our experience of time and our experience of space, particularly our sense of "now" and our perception of motion, due to the dynamic and relational nature of space-time. Lee Smolin points out that these concepts about

---

[2] Lee Smolin, *The Trouble with Physics: The Rise of String Theory, the Fall of a Science, and What Comes Next* (Boston: Houghton Mifflin, 2006), 4.

[3] Sean Carroll notes that what is important is not the fact that light travels at this speed, but the fact that there is "unique preferred velocity," a speed limit, that cannot be exceeded. It just so happens that light travels at that speed through empty space because photons do not have mass. Sean M. Carroll, *From Eternity to Here: The Quest for the Ultimate Theory of Time* (New York: Dutton, 2010).

[4] Ibid.

[5] Note that the reference frames involved must be traveling at a constant velocity, and so they may also be referred to as inertial frames. George F. R. Ellis and William R. Stoeger, "Introduction to General Relativity and Cosmology," in *Quantum Cosmology and the Laws of Nature*, ed. Robert J. Russell, Nancey C. Murphy, and Chris J. Isham (Vatican City: Vatican Observatory, 1993), 2.

[6] Brian Greene, *The Fabric of the Cosmos: Space, Time, and the Texture of Reality* (New York: A. A. Knopf, 2004), 46–47.

time and space as dynamic arise in part due to the relationship between reality and observation. In science, reality is described as that upon which all observers agree.[7] It turns out that one of the things observers need not agree on is the concept of "now" in the sense of whether or not two events are happening at the same time. This concept is called the relativity of simultaneity.[8] Smolin explains, "What Einstein showed is that our natural intuition that it's meaningful to talk about what's happening right now far from us is mistaken. Two observers who move with respect to each other will disagree about whether two distant events are simultaneous. . . . Thus, there can be nothing objectively real about simultaneity, nothing real about 'now.' "[9] Whether or not we observe two events as simultaneous depends on our frame of reference. Two events that may be simultaneous in one frame of reference may not be simultaneous from another frame of reference.

This lack of agreement about the concept of "now" is related to another issue that observers do not agree about: motion. If you and I are both moving at a constant speed, it is impossible to say who is in motion relative to one another. Picture yourself sitting in an airplane. From your frame of reference—the constant speed of the airplane—you are at rest (so long as there is no turbulence which would cause a change in speed). As you look out your window while flying over Chicago, you are sitting still in your seat watching my office building move past you. From your frame of reference, you are at rest and I am in motion. From my frame of reference—the constant speed of the earth—I am at rest sitting in my office. As I look out my window at your plane flying overhead, I am at rest, and you are in motion.

Were we to agree on a common frame of reference, say the earth (which of course, we generally do), we can then both agree that you are moving, and I am sitting still. If we do not share a common frame of reference, however, there is no objective way to determine who is in motion and who is at rest. There is no objective way to determine which observation, yours or mine, constitutes reality. Both observations are correct in their respective frames of reference. Resist the temptation to think, "But we *know* the airplane is *really* in motion."

---

[7] Lee Smolin, *Time Reborn: From the Crisis in Physics to the Future of the Universe* (Boston: Houghton Mifflin Harcourt, 2013), 56.

[8] Ibid.

[9] Ibid., 57–58.

We only know that from the frame of reference of the earth. From the frame of reference of Mars, a Martian would say that both of us are in motion and she is sitting still with me moving past Mars on the earth and you moving past Mars in the earth's atmosphere.

When we think of motion, we tend to think of motion through space, but space and time are interconnected. When you stand still in space, you are still moving in time.[10] Einstein's theory of special relativity taught us that they have an inverse proportion. The more you move through one, the less you move through the other. Matt Tweed explains, "Everything is moving at the speed of light. We are hurtling through time at light-speed even if sitting reading a book. If we start to move through space, our velocity through time slows to make the combined space and time velocities still equal to the speed of light."[11] If your movement through space increases, your movement through time decreases. Brian Greene explains this relationship with an analogous illustration. Imagine you are traveling north at 60 mph. If you turn northwest, going the same speed, suddenly some of your northward motion is diverted westward; you will not get as far north now.[12] Similarly, Greene tells us, motion through time is diverted by motion through space so that the more you move through space, the less you move through time. The speed of light is the constant, so that "the combined speed of any object's motion through space and its motion through time is always precisely equal to the speed of light."[13]

[10] Note that technically, you cannot sit still in space; we are moving all of the time. As a Facebook post on September 4, 2013, on the page "Universe Amazing Facts" noted: "Right now you are simultaneously hurtling around the sun at 66,600 mph while sitting on a rock that is spinning at 1,070 mph. On top of that, our whole solar system is rocketing through space around the center of the Milky Way at around 559,234 mph. On top of that, our galaxy is hurtling through space at around 671,080 mph, with respect to our local group of galaxies. On top of that, for all we know, our entire universe is hurtling through some unknown medium at some other ridiculous speed." https://www.facebook.com/UniverseAmazingFacts/posts/3598380741 48471. We can directly observe this motion of the earth when we watch the sun rise and set, appearing and disappearing over the horizon.

[11] Matt Tweed, "The Compact Cosmos," in *Scientia: Mathematics, Physics, Chemistry, Biology, and Astronomy for All*, ed. John Martineau (New York: Walker Publishing, 2005), 366.

[12] Greene, *Fabric of the Cosmos*, 48. In addition, see the PBS *Nova* Special based on the book online, http://www.pbs.org/wgbh/nova/physics/fabric-of-cosmos.html.

[13] Ibid., 49. Conceivably, if you were able to move at the speed of light, which you cannot do because your mass would increase requiring an infinite amount of energy

Therefore time passes more slowly for someone in motion when compared to someone standing still. The key phrase in that sentence is "when compared to," because the person who is in motion does not experience time as moving more slowly. It is only in the comparison of the two frames of reference that a difference is measured. The key insight about the relativity of time is the fact that the experience of time depends on one's frame of reference. Time is not absolute.[14] Remember that in our day to day experiences, we do not notice the effects of special relativity because we move so slowly through space compared to the speed of light that we do not directly experience the impact our motion has on time.

Greene explains, however, that we can understand the fact that time is a relative concept even without experiencing this phenomenon known as time dilation when moving near the speed of light. Greene uses the historic example of trains, which he notes influenced the young patent clerk Albert Einstein. Initially, cities all set their own times based on when the sun was at the highest point in the sky. But that time was different for different cities depending on their geographical location. Trains ran on the time of the city from which they departed. Coordination became necessary when trains started using the same tracks because cities in different geographical areas, today

---

for you to move, time would actually stop for you. While a photon (a particle/wave of light) may take eight billion years to travel from a distant star to earth from our frame of reference, from its own frame of reference, it took no time at all. Note that photons can travel at the speed of light because they have no mass.

[14] The famous example of this phenomenon known as time dilation is the twin paradox. Consider twins, where one twin travels on a rocket ship at a speed close to the speed of light, while the other twin remains on earth. When the traveling twin returns home, she will be younger than the twin who remained on earth. Having moved through greater amounts of space, she will have moved through less time than her twin, and so she will not have aged as much as the twin who remained on earth. To put it another way, time passed more slowly for the twin who was in motion than it did for the twin who remained on earth. Her motion through time was diverted by her motion through space. Again, think about the fact that there is an inverse proportion, so as someone's movement through space increases, his movement through time decreases. Someone standing still has decreased her movement through space, so her movement through time increases. These effects, however, are not noticeable unless one is moving at very great speeds. Traveling at near the speed of light not only causes time to slow down but also causes length to contract in a phenomenon known as Lorentz transformations. As mentioned above, the speed of light stays constant and time and space shift in order to maintain that constant velocity.

called different time zones, did not experience noon at the same time. Einstein realized that everyone has his own time; time is relative.[15] Avoiding train wrecks required communication and coordination.

In 1915, Albert Einstein proposed his general theory of relativity which incorporated the concept of gravity into the relationship between space and time. He suggested that space-time is not passive, absolute, and unchanging but rather is like a fabric (only three-dimensional rather than two-dimensional) that warps around objects based on their mass and thus affecting the motion of the objects moving through space-time.[16] The two-dimensional image frequently used to illustrate this concept is that of a stretchy piece of fabric. Stretch the fabric taut and roll a marble across it. The marble should roll in a relatively straight line across the fabric (albeit causing a slight indentation in the fabric due to the marble's own mass). Now place a bowling ball in the center of the fabric and once again roll the marble across. The path of the marble is dramatically altered by the presence of the bowling ball. Space-time similarly curves around massive objects. Brian Greene explains the effects of gravity as follows: "Right now, according to these ideas, you are anchored to the floor because your body is trying to slide down an indentation in space (really, spacetime) caused by the earth."[17]

The Block Universe and the Arrow of Time

Time can be thought of in two ways: from the perspective of its unity or its diversity. As a unity, we can think of the possibility of what scientists call "block time" or the "block universe."[18] From the

---

[15] See *Nova* Special with Brian Greene, *The Fabric of the Cosmos: The Illusion of Time* (A NOVA Production by The Film Posse in association with ARTE France and National Geographic Channel), PBS video, 53:02. WGBH Educational Foundation. PBS Airdate: November 9, 2011, http://www.pbs.org/wgbh/nova/physics/fabric-of-cosmos .html#fabric-time.

[16] Brian Greene, *The Hidden Reality: Parallel Universes and the Deep Laws of the Cosmos*, EPUB eBook ed. (New York: A. A. Knopf, 2011), loc. 22–23 of 347.

[17] Ibid., loc. 23 of 347.

[18] Note that not all scientists and theologians accept this concept of a block universe. See Chris J. Isham and John C. Polkinghorne, "The Debate over the Block Universe," in *Quantum Cosmology and the Laws of Nature*, ed. Robert J. Russell, Nancey C. Murphy, and Chris J. Isham (Vatican City: Vatican Observatory, 1993), 135–44.

perspective of diversity, we can think of the way in which we experience a direction to time moving from past to future. From Einstein's theories of relativity, some scientists have developed a theory of space-time referred to as the block universe or block time.[19] This theory is based on a mathematical or geometrical understanding of time as another dimension like space. Thus past, present, and future all exist as equally real and valid, and we can think of time in terms of its unity. Just as all space exists "out there," all time exists "out there." Every moment in time already exists.[20] Part of the reason for this belief is that, from a mathematical perspective, the laws of physics work the same forward and backward.[21] We experience time as sequential as we move through it in a similar manner to how we move through space. The main difference is that we can change direction in space at will, moving forward and backward, left and right, up and down, but we can only move one direction in time—forward. We experience time as diversity. Time moves past in a succession of moments. We remember the past and change the future, but we cannot change the past or remember the future. Why? Why do we experience time as moving only in one direction, if mathematically, it should be able to move in either direction?

One commonly held theory is that we experience the sense of time flowing due to entropy. The second law of thermodynamics tells us that entropy or disorder or information always increases. As will be discussed further in chapter 4, entropy only works one way. Things do not move from disorder to order or from more information to less information. Our experience of time's arrow, or time asymmetry, may come from the tendency of nature to evolve toward disorder. Time is the construct we use to measure that change.

Paul Davies explains that despite our experience of time as something that flows, it does not make sense to think of "time" itself as

---

[19] For a comprehensive treatment on the "arrow of time," see Carroll, *From Eternity to Here*. For a strong critique of the block universe, see George F. R. Ellis, "Physics in the Real Universe: Time and Space-Time," in *Relativity and the Dimensionality of the World*, ed. Vesselin Petkov (Dordrecht, The Netherlands: Springer, 2007), 49–79.

[20] Paul Davies, "That Mysterious Flow," *Scientific American* 15, no. 3 (February 2006): 82–88.

[21] Think in terms of the commutative property of addition 2+5 = 5+2 or multiplication 2(5) = 5(2). Note that subtraction and division are noncommutative: 2-5 ≠ 5-2 and 10/2 ≠ 2/10.

flowing.[22] Think about the fact that a river flows. A river is a sub-stance, water, experiencing motion. Time is not a substance and there-fore cannot move. Davies goes on to explain that the "arrow" of time, similar to spatial directions, does not indicate motion but rather direction:

> By convention, the arrow of time points toward the future. This does not imply, however, that the arrow is moving toward the future, any more than a compass needle pointing north indicates that the compass is traveling north. Both arrows symbolize an asymmetry, not a movement. The arrow of time denotes an asym-metry of the world in time, not an asymmetry or flux of time. The labels "past" and "future" may legitimately be applied to temporal directions, just as "up" and "down" may be applied to spatial directions, but talk of the past or the future is as meaning-less as referring to the up or the down.[23]

In other words, time doesn't move; we do. We move in a direction through time. The experience of only being able to move in one direc-tion through time is related to the experience of causality. Craig Callender notes that causality is what makes time distinct from space, as spatial relations are noncausal.[24] We experience a progression of events in our lives that are related to one another. Callender suggests that time may be an emergent property, "just as a table feels solid even though it is a swarm of particles composed mostly of empty space. Solidity is a collective, or emergent, property of the particles. Time, too, could be an emergent property of whatever the basic ingredients of the world are."[25]

Lee Smolin disagrees. As we will see in chapter 8, he suggests that time is the most fundamental aspect of reality and space is the emer-gent property. For Callender, however, time can be seen as an artificial construct that gives us a global standard for relating events to one another in a similar way to how money is used as an artificial con-

---

[22] Davies, "That Mysterious Flow," 84. Davies notes the absurdity of the question, "How fast does time pass?" and the unhelpful response of "one second per second."

[23] Ibid., 85.

[24] Craig Callender, "Is Time an Illusion?," *Scientific American* 302, no. 6 (June 2010): 61.

[25] Ibid., 60.

struct that replaces bartering.[26] He shows that we could relate events directly to one another rather than to time. Instead of measuring how many times a heart beats in a minute and how many minutes pass during one rotation of the earth, we could simply measure how many heartbeats occur in one rotation of the earth.[27] Such a system quickly proves rather unwieldy, though, as more and more variables are added, so time simplifies and unifies our measurements of change and the relationships between events that occur.

The key point we want to highlight in the understanding of time from this perspective is that time itself is about relationship. The very fabric of the cosmos is ultimately relationality. From Einstein on, we understand that our existence is governed by relativity and relationality. These two concepts can help us navigate a theological impasse between pluralism and relativism.

Theological and Pastoral Implications

God as Our Constant

Just as space-time provides the context for our very existence—although we struggle to put the reality of it into words and concepts—the God in whom "we live and move and have our being" (Acts 17:28) is our ultimate context and yet defies definition. Yet we do believe that creation itself reveals something of God to us. As was noted in the introduction, George Coyne suggests that studying the world/cosmos/reality in which we live doesn't prove that God is Creator,

[26] Ibid., 65. See graphic on p. 63.

[27] Ibid., 63, see graphic. In this graphic, Callender shows that we can measure the speed of light, the number of heart beats per minute, and the rotations of the earth according to time, but we could also correlate them directly to one another, so that we measure the number of heartbeats per rotation of the earth and how far light travels in one heartbeat, just as we can pay for coffee, shoes, and a car with money, or we can figure out how many cups of coffee would equal the cost of a car or a pair of shoes. Time, like the money we use in place of bartering, may be an artificial construct that simply makes measurement easier. Note that Callender bases this idea of a timeless reality on the theories of Carlo Rovelli and loop quantum gravity. In one of the intriguing twists and turns of developing scientific thought, when we turn to the theory of time as the fundamental reality, we will look at the work of Lee Smolin, another proponent of loop quantum gravity who concludes that space is emergent and time is primary.

but if we believe that God is Creator, then the cosmos should reveal something about the God we believe created all of reality. Likewise, John Polkinghorne states, "There is, of course, no simplistic way in which to translate science's discoveries about the character of the physical universe into implications for an understanding of the infinite reality of God. . . . Yet a cautiously expressed theology of nature might be expected to offer some insight into the manner in which the divine creation reflects, however palely, the character of its Creator."[28] Science made a shift from conceiving of space and time as a static scaffolding to understanding space-time as dynamic and relational. Similarly, notions of God that are static and monolithic give way to images that are dynamic and relational. That shift in our image of God does not imply any change in God. The change is in our perception of God. If we understand that reality is ultimately one, whole, and interconnected, that understanding should reveal something of the divine to us. When we combine this insight into the created world through science with what we believe of God in and through revelation and most primarily/primordially through the incarnation of God's Word in Jesus Christ, we understand a God for whom relationality is central. In Christian terms, we speak of this relationality as Trinity. As was mentioned in the introduction, Karl Rahner has an axiom that theology is anthropology and anthropology is theology— that what we say about God impacts our image of humanity and vice versa. So when our image of God gains new depths of dynamism and relationality, our image of what it means to be human and to be relational should also take on a new depth.

When we start to think about time and space in terms of relationality, new images arise for the triune God whose very being is relationality. Theology tells us that God is not *a being*. God is Being itself, the source of all that is. That source of all is Love. Coyne and Omizzolo suggest,

> The immense richness of the world revealed by the sciences from the microcosm to the macrocosm, the passionate, insatiable desire we have to understand it, the mysteries and the paradoxes that

[28] John C. Polkinghorne, "The Demise of Democritus," in *The Trinity and an Entangled World: Relationality in Physical Science and Theology*, ed. John C. Polkinghorne (Grand Rapids, MI: W. B. Eerdmans Publishing, 2010), 11.

continuously arise in our search, the haunting sensation that our quest may never end, all of these experiences may be leading us to a source that transcends understanding and is most fittingly approached as Love. This Love is self-revealing in all aspects of creation and is drawing us not only, or even primarily, to understand, but rather to love in turn.[29]

This love connects the events of our lives together; it weaves space and time to unify all humankind and history into an interconnected whole. Love both emerges from relationship and makes relationship possible. Like the speed of light, God as Love becomes our constant in all frames of reference.

Living Out Time

We experience that love in time as both unity and diversity. On the one hand, it is block time in that there is a wholeness to our story, and the totality of who we are is embraced by God's love. The individual moments in which we live out our lives in love cannot be understood apart from the whole. On the other hand, our experience of time, the living out of life, is also sequential. Our lives unfold as stories. The connections between the events and the relationships within which those events are embedded are what make the story. As Smolin points out, we are not objects; we are processes.[30] The story that we are unfolds in time.

That story becomes more complex as it unfolds. As was noted above, the arrow of time is connected to the concept of entropy in the sense that entropy involves an increase in information. We move through life always gaining more information, more memories in our sense of time passing from one moment to the next. There is always more to know. We can never know less (putting aside neurological conditions that involve memory loss). Life could be much easier at times if we could "unknow" something, but it is not possible to unknow something once we know it.[31] Information always increases.

---

[29] George V. Coyne and Alessandro Omizzolo, *Wayfarers in the Cosmos: The Human Quest for Meaning* (New York: Crossroad, 2002), 169.

[30] Lee Smolin, *Three Roads to Quantum Gravity* (New York: Basic Books, 2001), 50–52.

[31] Scientists actually experiment with the idea of being able to treat PTSD by erasing or reducing traumatic memories.

Therefore situations grow more complex, not less. The more we know, the more disordered and the less black and white our world becomes. The desire to cling to a world that is more black and white may be part of the reason people often stubbornly cling to false information and refuse to know something new. In Coyne and Omizzolo's words, in the increasing complexity we may find ourselves with less understanding but called to love more. We are called to let go of the comfort of certainty and surrender to the vulnerability of love.

In these risky acts of choosing love over certainty, we live out of the whole—past and future. We touch the eternity of God. As Karl Rahner puts it, "The present action of a human being embodies his whole past: his knowledge obtained through effort or through suffering, the depth of his experience, the revolutions of his life, his joys and sorrows. . . . By all these influences, the present action is given its direction, its depth and resonance."[32] In addition to bringing the depth of who we are in and through our life experiences to any act, we also bring our hopes, promises, and plans for the future. Rahner gives the example of marriage vows or ordination vows, though he recognizes that in our freedom we still must live out those hopes and promises on a day-to-day basis. Rahner suggests that by bringing to each act the "whole sum of [our] existence" and by seizing the possibilities open in our future, we realize what is eternal in us.[33] For Rahner, the very nature of being human and having freedom is to act in such a way as to become who we are and who we were created to be. In other words, we become that person who will be definitive in eternity, but we do so in and through our successive loving acts. In this sense, our very being is a unity connected to God's perspective which sees the whole of our lives, the story in its entirety, and yet we live out that story in a causal sequence.

Rahner explains that this balance between the unity and wholeness of our being and our living out our freedom moment to moment imbues the entire process of our lifetime. He explains, "Again and again, our anticipation will seize upon only a fraction of the whole, but we will not cease in our efforts to gather up past and future into

[32] Karl Rahner, *The Content of Faith: The Best of Karl Rahner's Theological Writings* [Rechenschaft des Glaubens], ed. Karl Lehmann and Albert Raffelt, trans. Harvey D. Egan (New York: Crossroad, 1993), 107.
[33] Ibid.

that one decision of freedom from which our life will receive its final and definite truth and reality."[34] In this sense, we live into our death. Death then becomes that moment when our story is complete. Rahner states, "In death the human person completes his own pattern by dying his own death. In the moment of death he is what he has made of himself, freely and finally. The actual result of his life and what he wanted to be, freely and finally become one."[35] It is in this moment of wholeness that "we can see with both horror and supreme delight the immense grandeur, depth, and density of those acts in which our whole life is involved."[36] Rahner notes that not every moment of our lives carries this kind of weight in which we sum up our entire existence in a single act of love. He maintains the hope and belief, however, that

> where an ultimate responsibility is assumed in obedience to a person's own conscience, where ultimate selfless love and fidelity are given, where an ultimate selfless obedience to truth regardless of self is lived out, and so on, at this point there is really in our life something that is infinitely precious, that of itself has the right and reality not to perish, that is able to fill out an eternity.[37]

In these moments of our lives, we touch eternity. We live out block time. In other words, we experience the wholeness, oneness, and unity of all that is, or as Rahner puts it, "Whenever life is lived in faith, hope, and love, eternity truly occurs."[38]

The very definition of who we are and who we are to be is, for Rahner, one who loves. Love of God and one another becomes the grace that holds together the patterns of our lives into a unified whole. Yet Rahner would be the first to admit that we fail regularly at this task of loving God and one another.[39] Sin is a reality in our lives. Sometimes it is a destructive force that ruins our own lives and

---

[34] Ibid., 111.

[35] Ibid., 110.

[36] Karl Rahner, "Eternity from Time," in *Theological Investigations*, vol. 19, *Faith and Ministry*, trans. Edward Quinn (London: Darton, Longman & Todd, 1984), 176.

[37] Ibid., 177.

[38] Ibid.

[39] Karl Rahner, *The Practice of Faith: A Handbook of Contemporary Spirituality* [Praxis des Glaubens], ed. Karl Lehmann and Albert Raffelt (New York: Crossroad, 1983), 107–14.

others' lives. Sometimes it is merely a mediocrity, a failure to love or take risks, choosing our own comfort over what we know is right and good. Rahner further notes that all the factors of our life and culture make us more or less culpable of these sins.

The complexity and entropy of life do not lend themselves to objective black and white judgments. Just as our frame of reference affects motion through time and space, our individual frames of reference make a difference in terms of our culpability for sin without thereby eliminating a necessary sense of responsibility and accountability. Rahner notes that some people who commit only minor or venial sins ultimately fail to live lives of love, whereas some people who commit grave sins are ultimately loving, selfless individuals. The constant against which we can measure all lives is God's love, just as the speed of light provides a constant of motion in any frame of reference.

Rahner uses the example of one of the Boxer Rebellion martyrs who was an opium addict and who had been refused absolution by his parish priest to illustrate this point. Rahner asks, "Yet, if this man longed for martyrdom, really knew and admitted before God how miserable and wretched he was and asked God to free him from his self-imposed imprisonment, may we not ask if, even before his martyrdom, his life was not really rooted and founded in the love of God—more perhaps than that of the parish priest who rightly refused absolution?"[40] Rahner notes that rather than congratulating ourselves for all of the ways in which we have not sinned (often while pointing out the sins of those around us), we should remember that we are not justified because we have not sinned but rather because God's love and grace embraces our sinfulness and empowers our goodness.

God's grace, which is God's love poured out into our hearts, is our constant for measurement. Rather than meditating on sin in a way that leads us to be more judgmental of ourselves and others, our meditation on sin should always hold in tension both our responsibility and accountability and God's gratuitous and unconditional love. Rahner maintains that in the context of such love, our meditation on sin then becomes a meditation on the source that allows us to transcend the limitations of our sinfulness, to sacrifice what we cannot

[40] Ibid., 112.

sacrifice by our own strength, and to do what we cannot do by our own resources.[41] Then Rahner concludes, "We can always act in virtue of our powerlessness, jump while absolutely dreading the leap, because God is with us, because—without our being able to observe and as it were enjoy it in advance—our impotence, our weakness, and our cowardice, are always surpassed by God's power and mercy, by his grace."[42]

Relativism vs. Relativity and Relationality

One objection frequently raised to Rahner's view of sin, grace, freedom, and fundamental option is that it leads to relativism.[43] When we talk about the interface between the church and the secular world or between faith and reason or religion and science, one word that often comes up is relativism. Relativism is most frequently a concern in two areas: interreligious dialogue and morality. Within interreligious dialogue, the fear is that if one does not hold for the supremacy of Christian belief, all revelation is denied. The unfortunate result can be a Christian triumphalism that does not lend itself to dialogue or even relationship with those of other religious traditions. Within the realm of morality, the fear is an "anything goes" mentality that lets each individual person decide right from wrong. The unfortunate result can be a Christianity that at best can seem out of touch with people's experience and at worst utterly lacking in compassion. Within both of these realms, it is often fear that drives these theological perspectives. Like the scientists with a Newtonian worldview, we cling to the idea of a stable scaffolding, whether that scaffolding be an objective and literal sense of revelation or hard definition of moral behavior. A world that is understood as a unified whole that warps and curves is frightening, and it can be very hard to find our balance. The more we fight the fabric that warps and curves, the more unbalanced we become.

In a postmodern world, our rigid scaffolding of God and revelation has collapsed to an understanding of God as mystery revealed in the

---

[41] Ibid., 113.

[42] Ibid.

[43] See Peter Joseph Fritz, *Karl Rahner's Theological Aesthetics* (Washington, DC: CUA Press, 2014), 32.

warping and curving of human lives that are shaped by our history and our context, just as our experience of space-time is shaped by the mass of nearby objects.[44] As our understanding of the very reality of space-time has changed to become dynamic and relational, so too has our understanding of the human person in a postmodern world shifted to prioritize a dynamic and relational context to human acts.

Even if one does not accept the concept of postmodernism or believes that we have moved beyond the era of postmodernism, we should reflect on the lessons learned from this era. Postmodernism's main critique is that the modern metanarrative, the universal, over-arching story at best overlooks and at worst suppresses or oppresses the stories of those on the margins of society and history. The movement critiques the concept of "Truth" with a capital "T" and the idea that there is such a thing as objectivity. The concept of religious truth or revelation has been questioned within this context. A frequent charge is made that all religious truth is both historically and culturally conditioned and represents the sociopolitical concerns of the dominant groups. The response to this critique is often a counter-charge of relativism and the concern that without any standard or universal truth, we end up with a moral collapse in which each individual gets to decide for him or herself what is true and what is right or wrong.

The science of relativity, space, and time illustrates another perspective besides the false certainty of objective truth and the false autonomy of relativism. In the new possible conceptions of space and time, we find a world of relativity (as opposed to relativism) and relationality. While relativity helps us appreciate the importance of one's frame of reference for any experience, the inherent relationality

---

[44] For example, we have moved from a historically literal reading of Scripture to one that takes into account the historical, cultural, and narrative context, but Scripture is no less revelation for that reason. It is God revealing God's self in human experience and interpretation. What we "know" about God can be real without being definitive. Our knowledge can always be deepened by God being revealed in new ways in new experiences and encounters with the other. While the canon of Scripture is considered to be closed and revelation complete in the sense that God has revealed God's self fully in the person of Jesus the Christ, our interpretation and living out of that experience of Christ is ongoing. For an extensive description of these developments, see the document published by the Pontifical Biblical Commission, *The Interpretation of the Bible in the Church* (Vatican City: Libreria Editrice Vaticana, 1993).

of time and space itself helps us understand that there is no such thing as an autonomous individual and that all persons and decisions are interconnected and interrelated. As Brian Greene notes, the reality described by Newtonian physics turned out to be false, revealing instead a reality that is relativistic.[45] Relativity indicates the interconnectedness of all things, of the very "fabric of the cosmos." It teaches us that all is interrelated—including time and space. Relativity teaches us about perspective and point of view. Relativity is what is most "real" in our world. Even space and time exist as a result of relationship.

Nevertheless, Thomas Greenlee warns us not to confuse relativity with relativism. He notes, "In relativity we say that observers in different reference frames see things differently. They see different lengths for the same objects, see different times for the same events, and if one observer sees two events as simultaneous, the other will not see them as simultaneous. There is no reference frame that is more correct than any other. When we use language like this, it is not surprising that some people will apply the language to the moral realm."[46] He argues, however, against those who would use the science of relativity to argue for a position of moral relativism: "There are frame-independent absolutes in relativity theory. In special relativity, the laws of physics, correctly expressed, are the same in all inertial frames. The speed of light is the same in all inertial frames. In general relativity, the laws of physics, correctly expressed, are the same in all reference frames, whether accelerated or in gravitational fields or inertial frames. Therefore, there are absolutes in relativity theory, and attempts to justify moral relativism by appealing to relativity theory are mistaken."[47] Frame of reference and relationality are essential to how we understand reality, and yet there are also laws of nature that we understand to be true in all frames of reference. Therefore, in relativity theory we have a both/and—both absolutes, such as the speed of light, and relativity, such as our experiences of time and motion.

[45] Greene, *Fabric of the Cosmos*, 10.

[46] Thomas Greenlee, "General Relativity, the Cosmic Microwave Background, and Moral Relativism," in *Science and Religion in Dialogue*, vol. 1 (Oxford: Wiley-Blackwell, 2010), 93–96.

[47] Ibid., 96.

Todd Salzman and Michael Lawler define relativism as the idea "that there are no universal truths, moral truth and moral terms are defined either socially or individually."[48] They go on to explain, "Both social and personal relativism deny that the good can be defined universally; they therefore assert that there is no objective basis on which to justify claims to universal truth and absolute norms or intrinsically immoral acts."[49] In his article "Truth with a Capital T," Joseph Wooddell argues that our popular culture professes a belief in moral relativism, the idea that there is no objective standard by which to judge right and wrong. At the same time, however, people live by the assumption that there are, in fact, universal norms of right and wrong.[50] He explains that people may say that there is no such thing as absolute moral truth, but when confronted by a specific example of an atrocity, they find themselves quite willing to describe the act as universally morally unacceptable.[51] In theology, the role of human experience has gained much legitimacy in recent decades, which is a vast improvement over a theology that ignored human experience. Human experience, however, does not trump all. We must recognize that human experience is subjective, and this realization should engender in us the virtue of humility, the openness to conversion, and the sure knowledge that we might be wrong. In other words, we should embrace a certain degree of uncertainty. The subjectivity of human experience and human interpretation can lead the Westboro Baptist "church" or certain terrorist organizations to use religious rhetoric in order to propagate hatred and violence in the world. While we no longer live in a modern worldview that believes an absolutely objective viewpoint is a possibility, we must neverthe-

[48] Todd A. Salzman and Michael G. Lawler, "Method and Catholic Theological Ethics in the Twenty-First Century," *Theological Studies* 74, no. 4 (December 2013): 907.

[49] Ibid., 908.

[50] Joseph D. Wooddell, "Truth with a Capital T: Does it Really Matter? Public Discussion of Social and Economic Questions in a Relativistic Age," *Criswell Theological Review* 11, no. 2 (Spring 2014): 8–9.

[51] Ibid. Wooddell uses the examples of 9/11 and a news story about a man who had abducted three young women and kept them imprisoned for a number of years, subjecting them to sexual abuse and murdering the babies they conceived as a result of that abuse. His argument holds that even when people profess a moral relativism, when given specific examples such as these, they feel that the acts described are objectively evil.

less not accept all human experience as equally valid. Somehow we must develop criterion on which we judge human acts.

Salzman and Lawler offer an alternative viewpoint of perspectivism that is congruent with the notion put forth by relativity and relationality. They suggest that Catholic theological ethics does hold for a "metaethics" or universal concept of what is "good" and "right" as being that which contributes to human dignity and flourishing.[52] Conflict arises because of disagreements over definitions of human dignity and understandings of what best lends itself to human flourishing. Consequently, Salzman and Lawler turn to Bernard Lonergan's notion of perspectivism and the idea that these different definitions arise due to different perspectives. Relativism, in this view, disavows the possibility of truth and judgment, whereas perspectivism allows for the complexity of situations and allows for judgment but notes that all judgment is based on partial truth.[53] The authors note Lonergan's three factors of perspectivism:

> First, human knowers are finite, the information available to them at any given time is incomplete, and they cannot attend to or master all the available data. Second, knowers are selective, given their different socializations, personal experiences, and ranges of data offered them. Third, knowers are individually different, so we can expect them to have different interpretations of the available data.[54]

Put in simpler terms, as finite, unique human persons, we simply cannot ever know all there is to know about a situation and will not agree on how to interpret what we do know. We all have different frames of reference.

Each one of us is limited in our perception. What we observe about the world around us is colored by our own presuppositions. Keenan Osborne describes the limits of human perception in a similar manner. Each one of us carries what Osborne refers to as a "sedimentary history," the layers of experience that have shaped who we are and

[52] Salzman and Lawler, "Method and Catholic Theological Ethics," 908.
[53] Ibid., 910.
[54] Ibid.

how we think.[55] This sedimentary history affects what we perceive and the significance we place on that which we perceive.[56] That sediment can be connected to the accumulating information of entropy as well, the information that accrues in those layers of experience as time goes by. In other words, people see and experience the world differently, and they interpret what they see and experience differently. That difference occurs both in how two people interpret the world differently and also in how we interpret the world differently at different points in our lives as we grow and change. Thus the judgments we make are always going to be limited by our perspective, and our perspective is not static.

Lee Smolin makes similar observations about the role of the observer in physics, explaining that the observer always has a partial view. He argues that the "hardest thing about science is what it demands of us in terms of our ability to make the right choice in the face of incomplete information."[57] Such a statement is true not only of science but also of life in general. As Smolin explains, we all split the world into two parts, dividing the world between ourselves as observer and that which we observe.[58] Thus each of us observes the world differently, from a different frame of reference, and each of us has blind spots in our observations. Salzman and Lawler suggest that these different perspectives are similar to viewing the world from different floors of the Empire State Building: "Each gets a different, and less partial, view of all that lies outside the window. We could expect that if they ascended to a higher story, they would get a different, and, again, still partial view."[59] They argue, however, that the "necessarily limited nature of human sensations, understandings, judgments, and knowledge" is not a source of falsity but rather a source of partial truth.[60] The fact that we see from our own frame of reference does not make our observation false; it simply makes it necessarily incomplete.

---

[55] Kenan B. Osborne, *Christian Sacraments in a Postmodern World: A Theology for the Third Millennium* (New York: Paulist Press, 1999), 148–49.

[56] Ibid.

[57] Smolin, *Three Roads to Quantum Gravity*, 146.

[58] Ibid., 47.

[59] Salzman and Lawler, "Method and Catholic Theological Ethics," 910.

[60] Ibid.

Smolin notes, "Here in the real world, we almost always reason with incomplete information" and in the face of the necessity of making decisions without all of the information suggests an ethical principle in which "different observers report what they see honestly."[61] We come to the most complete picture by combining our observations, our partial truths. We can only avoid catastrophic train wrecks through communication and cooperation. We have different frames of reference, but our shared constant is love, the Love that Christians call God. When our understanding falters, we are called to love more. Smolin goes on to explain that in this way we can come to agreement on common ground while accepting that there are questions we cannot answer. We come to that common ground by listening to one another's stories and learning from one another's experiences.

When we think of the dilemmas we face today, there are two possible approaches. The church historically has built its approach on the work of Aristotle and the idea of objective truth. There is a fear that embracing new approaches will lead to relativism, in the sense that anything goes, but what Smolin's scientific model can teach us is not relativism in the sense that any person's truth is legitimate but rather a process of shared truth through dialogue and relationship. When we look at thorny issues the church faces in the complex world today, such an approach would suggest that the first step among the faithful should be to listen. We are called to listen to those who have experiences that are different from ours. We are not called to judge. We are called to hear the observations of those whose "light cone," i.e., what they are able to see, is different from our own. Smolin argues that the most important thing about persons and cultures is history or story.[62] We gain wisdom only when we share our stories, listening and learning from one another.

The lesson of relativity with the understanding of time and space that emerges from relationship is that we cannot subtract relationship from our understanding of morality. If we look at the history of the early church, we see that in fact relationality has always been at the heart of morality, thus in the earliest Christian communities, the acts that were seen as most sinful and at times unforgivable were the ones

[61] Smolin, *Three Roads to Quantum Gravity*, 31.
[62] Ibid., 49–50.

that tore at the fabric of the community. The sacrament of reconciliation was developed to heal rifts in the community caused by heresy, apostasy, adultery, and murder, because these sins were the ones that created breaks in the bonds that formed the community. In our current culture of autonomy and individualism, we have lost this corporate meaning of sinfulness. The biblical view is much more organic than Newtonian. We are not all parts in a machine where, when the machine breaks, you find the broken piece and replace it. Rather, we are all parts of a body, and when one member suffers, the whole suffers. We seek healing and wholeness.

In a fabric of reality that warps and curves, the one constant is change. Like a person standing still in space but moving through time, even when we try to resist change, change happens. Furthermore, the fabric of my life changes due to the mass of the events I encounter. Anyone who has felt the rush of new love, for example, falling in love or becoming a parent, has experienced this disruption where suddenly one's entire life is pulled into orbit around another being. Everything changes—priorities, friends, how time is spent. Some events are so massive and cataclysmic that, like a black hole, they can draw one's entire being into their horizon so that one's light can no longer emerge.

When we are dealing with our day-to-day lives and our communities, objective standpoints give way to people's lives—real people within real relationships. We encounter the grieving man in the hospital sitting at the bedside of his dying partner of thirty years. We sit with the grieving mother of a black son killed in an encounter with the police. We sit with the grieving widow of a police officer killed in the line of duty. There are numerous examples in our lives and in the headlines of the newspaper that demonstrate the incredible moral complexity of our lives. To acknowledge that complexity is not to deny any possibility of a "metaethic," but it does recognize that there can and will be genuine disagreement about how we determine what defines human dignity and flourishing. It recognizes that we can only negotiate those disagreements when we understand life as story rather than autonomous events. In doing so, we not only encounter brokenness in the complexity of human life but also joy and hope, forgiveness and love.

We share our stories, our frames of reference, our own observations and partial truths, and in that sharing we all become more preciously and fragilely human. Even when, from our respective frames of reference, we disagree on the best course of action to protect and promote life, we hold that core value in common. We hold on to what is constant in all our frames of reference—the love of God and the preciousness of life.

Chapter Two

Particle Wave Complementarity[1]

Scientific Developments—
Particle Wave Complementarity

Many of us, I would guess, learned about atoms in science in a way that described them as miniature solar systems with a solid nucleus of protons and neutrons that was being orbited by a certain number of electrons.[2] In this classical understanding of the atomic world, everything was composed of tiny particles, and elements of the world were understood by breaking them down into their tiniest parts or particles and understanding how those particles interacted and related to one another.

Quantum physics has engendered a huge paradigm shift in how we conceive reality. Everything we thought we knew and understood about the so-called material world gets turned on its head, starting with the fact that what we think of as matter, often imaged as particles or tiny little balls, is actually the manifestation of energy, what physicists call quanta or little packets of energy manifesting themselves out of a field.[3] John Polkinghorne explains: "Today all theories of elementary particles (such as the quark theory of matter) are quantum

---

[1] This chapter is a revision of the author's article, "Quantum Anthropology: Re-imaging the Human Person as Body/Spirit," *Theological Studies* 74 (December 2013): 934–59.

[2] The solar system model was developed by Ernest Rutherford in 1911. John C. Polkinghorne, *Quantum Theory*, vol. 69 (Oxford: Oxford University Press, 2002), 10–11.

[3] Ibid., 73–75.

field theories. Particles are thought of as energetic excitations of the underlying field."[4] The road that brought scientists to this realization actually began with the debate about whether light is particle or wave and their realization that light exhibits both wave-like and particle-like qualities. As Richard Feynman notes, "Things on a very small scale behave like nothing that you have any direct experience about. They do not behave like waves, they do not behave like particles, they do not behave like clouds, or billiard balls, or weights on springs, or like anything that you have ever seen."[5] The realization that light, which had been primarily understood to be waves, actually exhibited properties of little quanta or packets or lumps of energy we call photons, led other physicists to ask, if light can behave like particles, is it possible that particles can behave like waves? This question led to the famous double-slit experiment with electrons.[6]

[4] Ibid., 73, 75. According to Polkinghorne, "A field is an entity spread out in space and time" that has "an infinite number of degrees of freedom," whereas a particle "has only a finite number of degrees of freedom." An example of a field that we experience in everyday life is an electromagnetic field. Brian Greene explains: "A magnetic field provides a magnet what an army provides a dictator and what auditors provide the IRS: influence beyond their physical boundaries, which allows force to be exerted out into a field," in Brian Greene, *The Fabric of the Cosmos: Space, Time, and the Texture of Reality* (New York: A. A. Knopf, 2004), 40. He goes on to explain that there are force fields (electromagnetic, gravitational, strong nuclear, weak nuclear) and matter fields (electron, up-quark), in which particles are excitations of their respective fields. Greene, *Fabric of the Cosmos*, 256, 518n4. Quantum field theory has led to many important developments in physics, and in combination with string theory, holds out hope for a grand unified theory that is able to unite the electromagnetic, strong nuclear, weak nuclear, and gravitational forces. QFT teaches us that there is no such thing as empty space, that even what we have called a vacuum is teeming with activity, albeit motion "in its lowest energy state." Polkinghorne, *Quantum Theory*, 74. QFT enables quantum mechanics to deal with systems with many particles. For an excellent description of QFT and its relation to both quantum mechanics and the theory of special relativity, as well as some of its philosophical implications for ontology, see Meinard Kuhlmann, "Quantum Field Theory," *The Stanford Encyclopedia of Philosophy* (Winter 2012 Edition), http://plato.stanford.edu/entries/quantum-field -theory/.
[5] Richard P. Feynman, Robert B. Leighton, and Matthew L. Sands, *The Feynman Lectures on Physics*, vol. 3 (Reading, MA: Addison-Wesley, 1963), 1.1.
[6] For accounts of these experiments as well as pictures of the images the patterns described below and the mathematical equations involved, see Ibid., 1.1-1.11; John Gribbin, *In Search of Schrödinger's Cat* (New York: Bantam Books, 1984), 163–76; Polkinghorne, *Quantum Theory*, 22–38.

Imagine shooting a pellet gun at a wall but placing a barrier between the gun and the wall with a slit in it. Clearly some pellets will go through the slit while others will be stopped by the barrier. The result on the wall behind the barrier is a band of hits roughly equivalent to the slit, heaviest in the exact center and tapering off on either side. Now imagine that we put two slits in the barrier. Again, not surprisingly, you end up with two bands on the wall, roughly corresponding to the place of the two slits, heaviest in the center and tapering off on either side (see figure 2.1).[7]

Figure 2.1

Two Slit Experiment Particles[8]

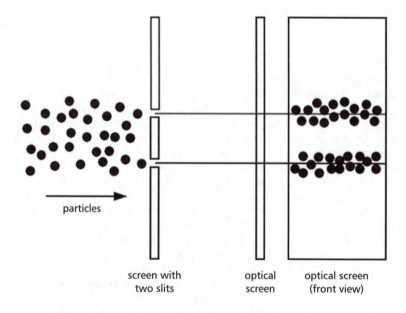

particles

| screen with | optical | optical screen |
| two slits | screen | (front view) |

Now imagine that we repeat this experiment with water waves. Send a wave of water through one slit, and it will hit the wall with the most intensity at the point corresponding to the slit in the barrier and taper off on either side. If, however, you put two slits in the barrier,

---

[7] Feynman explains, "The probabilities just add together. The effect with both holes open is the sum of the effects with each hole open alone. We shall call this result an observation of 'no interference.'" Feynman, *The Feynman Lectures*, 1.3.

[8] Inductiveload, "Two-Slit Experiment Particles," *Wikimedia Commons*, http://commons.wikimedia.org/wiki/File:Two-Slit_Experiment_Particles.svg.

the wave going through both slits will form two new wave patterns that will interfere with one another. Brian Greene explains that when the peaks of the two waves coincide, their heights are added together, increasing the height of the wave; when the troughs coincide, the depths are added together, increasing the depth of the wave; and when a peak and a trough coincide, the two will cancel each other out, negating both the height and the depth.[9] When done with light waves, the pattern on the detector wall shows bands of light where the peaks coincide and where the troughs coincide, alternating with bands of darkness where they cancel each other out, resulting in a striped pattern on the detector wall (see figure 2.2).

Figure 2.2

Wave Interference Pattern [10]

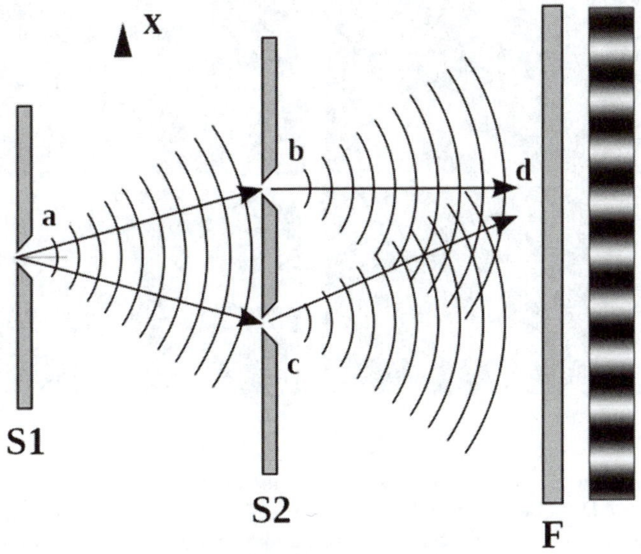

⁹ Greene, *Fabric of the Cosmos*, 85. Feynman describes the waves as interfering constructively and destructively. Feynman, *The Feynman Lectures*, 1.3-1.4. In mathematical terms, the difference is that with the pellets or particles, the end result is simply the sum of the two intensities of pellets being shot through one slit. For waves, the equation is different to account for the interference and mathematically is the square of the sum of the two intensities found when done with the single slit. Ibid., 1.3.

¹⁰ Stannered, "Ebohr1 IP," *Wikimedia Commons*, http://commons.wikimedia.org/wiki/File%3AEbohr1_IP.svg.

This experiment was done by shooting electrons against a detection wall with a barrier in between. The expectation was that electrons, as particles, would behave as the pellets would; but when the experiment was performed, the pattern on the detection screen was one of interference (alternating bands of hits and nonhits), like waves. Scientists thought that perhaps the electrons were bouncing off of one another to create the interference pattern, but when they shot the electrons out of the gun one at a time, they still found that over time, when enough electrons had been shot out of the gun, the pattern was still one of interference (see figure 2.3).[11]

Figure 2.3

Slit Experiment Results[12]

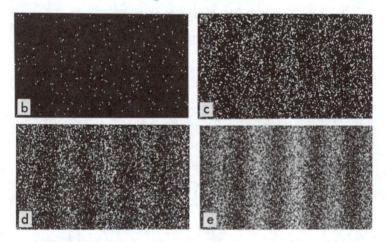

[11] See Brian Cox and Jeff Forshaw, *The Quantum Universe: And Why Anything That Can Happen, Does* (Boston, MA: Da Capo Press, 2012), 25. Cox and Forshaw note that the electron "doesn't seem to behave *exactly* like a regular wave either because the pattern is not built up as a result of some smooth deposition of energy; rather it is built out of many tiny dots. We always detect Thomson senior's [J. J. Thomson's] single, point like electrons." In other words, the experiment cannot be done with one single electron. The pattern occurs with the accumulation of many electrons. Each single electron is still one single point on the detection screen, but the pattern over time with the accumulation of many electrons becomes one of interference (alternating bands across the entire screen), like waves, rather than the pattern of particles (two bands directly behind the slits).

[12] Tonomura and Belsazar, "Slit Experiment Results," *Wikimedia Commons*, http://commons.wikimedia.org/wiki/File%3ADouble-slit_experiment_results_Tanamura_four.jpg.

To figure out what was really happening, the scientists modified the experiment by putting a measuring device at the barrier so that they would be able to tell exactly which slit each electron went through; however, when they did the experiment in this manner, the interference pattern disappeared, and the result over time was two bands of hits, roughly corresponding to the two slits in the barrier, exactly as if the electrons were indeed tiny pellets or particles.[13]

To understand how uncanny the results of this experiment are, John Gribbin explains:

> When we try to look at the spread-out electron wave, it collapses into a definite particle, but when we are not looking it keeps its options open. In terms of Born's probabilities, the electron is being forced by our measurement to choose one course of action out of an array of possibilities. There is a certain probability that it could go through one hole, and an equivalent probability that it may go through the other; probability interference produces the diffraction pattern at our detector. When we detect the electron, though, it can only be in one place, and that changes the probability pattern for its future behavior—for that electron, it is now certain which hole it went through. But unless someone looks, nature herself does not know which hole the electron is going through.[14]

Physicists understand the wave aspect or wave function of electrons to be a wave of probability that the electron will be found in a particular place.[15] In theory, the electron could be found anywhere,

---

[13] For a more detailed account of this experiment, including a description of the use of light to detect which slit the electron passed through, see Feynman, *The Feynman Lectures*, 1.6-1.9. Feynman concludes: "If one looks at the holes or, more accurately, if one has a piece of apparatus which is capable of determining whether the electrons go through hole 1 or hole 2, then one *can* say that it goes either through hole 1 or hole 2. *But*, when one does *not* try to tell which way the electron goes, when there is nothing in the experiment to disturb the electrons, then one may *not* say that an electron goes either through hole 1 or hole 2. If one does say that, and starts to make any deductions from the statement, he will make errors in the analysis. This is the logical tightrope on which we must walk if we wish to describe nature successfully." *Feynman Lectures*, 1.9.

[14] Gribbin, *In Search of Schrödinger's Cat*, 171.

[15] Note that there is some disagreement on what is meant by the "wave," whether it is a wave of probability or a physical wave of some type. This disagreement will be further addressed below, but for our purposes, we are primarily following the Copenhagen interpretation, which understands the wave as a wave of probability.

including on the other side of the universe, but there is a higher probability that the electron will be found in certain places, and in the world of statistics, the most extreme possibilities tend to cancel one another out, while the most likely possibilities reinforce one another. Nevertheless, it is still impossible to know exactly where the electron will end up without looking, and once we look, we have collapsed the wave function so that the electron is now only in one possible place.[16]

Niels Bohr called this particle/wave aspect of reality complementarity. If the notion of particle/wave complementarity is difficult to grasp, we are in good company. Richard Feynman is famously quoted as having said, "I think I can safely say that no one understands quantum mechanics."[17] John Gribbin explains that in Niels Bohr's theory:

> particle physics and wave physics, are equally valid, complementary descriptions of the same reality. Neither description is complete in itself, but there are circumstances when it is more appropriate to use the particle concept and circumstances where

[16] See Feynman, *The Feynman Lectures*, 2.2ff and Polkinghorne, *Quantum Theory*, 25–26, 36–38, 44–46. Cox and Foreshaw describe this dilemma as follows: "The crucial point is that it makes no sense to say that 'the electron could have ventured along each of these routes, but really it went along only one of them.' To say that the electron really ventured along one particular path would be to give ourselves no more of a chance of explaining the interference pattern than if we had blocked up one of the slits in the water wave experiment. We need to allow the wave to go through both slits in order to get an interference pattern, and this means that we must allow all the possible paths for the electron to travel from source to screen. . . . We need to describe a spread-out wave that is also a point-like electron, and one possible way to achieve this is to say that the electron sweeps from source to screen following all possible paths at once. . . . This is what it means to be a quantum particle." Cox and Forshaw, *The Quantum Universe*, 30–31. See p. 40 on the concept of probability.

[17] Cited in Polkinghorne, *Quantum Theory*, vii. A more extensive version of the quote reads, "There was a time when the newspapers said that only twelve men understood the theory of relativity. I do not believe there ever was such a time. . . . On the other hand, I think I can safely say that nobody understands quantum mechanics. . . . Do not keep saying to yourself, if you can possibly avoid it, 'But how can it be like that?' because you will get 'down the drain,' into a blind alley from which nobody has yet escaped. Nobody knows how it can be like that." Richard P. Feynman, *The Character of Physical Law* (Cambridge, MA: MIT Press, 1965), 129. Cited in Jeffrey Bub, "The Entangled World: How Can It Be Like That?," in *The Trinity and an Entangled World: Relationality in Physical Science and Theology*, ed. John C. Polkinghorne (Grand Rapids, MI: W. B. Eerdmans Publishing, 2010), 15–16.

it is better to use the wave concept. A fundamental entity such as an electron is neither a particle nor a wave, but under some circumstances it behaves as if it were a wave, and under other circumstances it behaves as if it were a particle. . . . But under no circumstances can you invent an experiment that will show the electron behaving in both fashions at once. The idea of wave and particle being two complementary facets of the electron's complex personality is called complementarity.[18]

The idea that we can know either the position or the momentum of an object on a quantum level, but not both, is called Heisenberg's uncertainty principle.[19] If we measure the position, we are looking for a particle like property; if we measure the momentum, we are looking for a wave-like property. Quantum physics has traditionally held that you cannot know both at once, although even this concept is being challenged today in certain experiments.[20] The importance of these new experiments is the question of whether the position and momentum of a microphysical object are by nature unknowable (epistemologically exclusive in Polkinghorne's terms), or if science has simply not advanced enough yet to discover the way of knowing both position and momentum. For this reason, it is important to apply these concepts analogically and not literally in theology, or we run the risk of developing a God-of-the-Gaps theology, a theology in

---

[18] Gribbin, *In Search of Schrödinger's Cat*, 118.

[19] "It is impossible to design an apparatus to determine which hole the electron passes through, that will not at the same time disturb the electrons enough to destroy the interference pattern." Feynman, *The Feynman Lectures*, 1.9. C. N. Villars explains that the properties being measured are not properties of the microphysical object itself but rather properties of the microphysical object interacting with the instrument of measurement. See C. N. Villars, "Observables, States and Measurements in Quantum Physics," *European Journal of Physics* 5, no. 3 (July 1984): 177–83. In terms of the impossibility of knowing both position and momentum, he explains that "position-defining and momentum-defining interactions are mutually exclusive because they require mutually exclusive apparatuses" (178). Polkinghorne states: "One can know where an electron is, but not what it is doing; or one can know what it is doing, but not where it is." Polkinghorne, *Quantum Theory*, 33. Polkinghorne concludes, "Observables come in pairs that epistemologically exclude each other." For an explanation of the mathematics, see pp. 106–7.

[20] John Gribbin, *Schrödinger's Kittens and the Search for Reality: Solving the Quantum Mysteries* (Boston: Little, Brown, 1995), 18. For a more recent example, see Lee A. Rozema et al., "Violation of Heisenberg's Measurement-Disturbance Relationship by Weak Measurements," *Physical Review Letters* 109, no. 10 (2012): 100404–08.

which we insert God into the gaps in our scientific knowledge. The problem with such a theology is that when science discovers the knowledge to fill these gaps, the place for God disappears.

Brian Greene offers another image for thinking about position and momentum:

> as a rough analogy, think about photographing that impish fly. If your shutter speed is high, you'll get a sharp image that records the fly's location at the moment you snapped the picture. But because the photo is crisp, the fly appears motionless; the image gives no information about the fly's speed. If you set your shutter speed low, the resulting blurry image will convey something of the fly's motion, but because of that blurriness it also provides an imprecise measurement of the fly's location. You can't take a photo that gives sharp information about position and speed simultaneously.[21]

Physicists explain that this complementary nature of reality is not just applicable to light or electrons but to everything that exists.[22] Robert John Russell notes that some challenge the usefulness of theologians addressing issues in quantum physics since the laws of quantum mechanics technically only apply to the subatomic world, but he responds as follows:

> I find this view curious. Certainly the minute value of Planck's constant limits the effects of many quantum phenomena. Yet, though the domain of quantum physics may be the realm of the atom, the repercussions of quantum physics are felt throughout the levels of nature from the atom to the cosmos. For example, quantum physics underlies human vision and the sensation of

[21] Brian Greene, *The Hidden Reality: Parallel Universes and the Deep Laws of the Cosmos*, EPUB eBook ed. (New York: A. A. Knopf, 2011), loc. 40 of 347. Note the analogy is problematic, as all analogies are, by its limitations. The fly does have both a position and momentum simultaneously, and given that information, one could predict a trajectory for the fly. According to the Copenhagen interpretation, in quantum theory, one cannot know both position and momentum of a quantum particle.

[22] In terms of the nature of reality, the way we experience the world, the wave aspect of matter is negligible if the object is larger than Planck's constant, which is 6.63×10^{-34} joule-seconds, so we do not experience or "see" these quantum realities in our day to day lives. For Planck's constant, see Feynman, *The Feynman Lectures*, 1.11, and Polkinghorne, *Quantum Theory*, 48–50, 100.

taste, the expansion of water as it freezes, the color of the sky, the light from our Sun and the glow of embers in a cooling fire. It underlies all of astrophysics, chemistry, and molecular biology. Without quantum physics we would not have such technologies as electrical lighting and power, computers, nuclear fission, solar power or communication satellites. On a cosmic scale, without quantum physics we would not have life in this universe, or possibly even the universe itself if one believes in the Anthropic Principle at all![23]

Interpretation in Quantum Mechanics

The earliest and most widely accepted school of interpretation of quantum mechanics is known as the Copenhagen interpretation. The Copenhagen interpretation focuses on the role of the observer. As Gribbin explains, "It is the act of observing the wave that made it 'collapse' to become a particle."[24] He goes on to explain that the wave is not a material wave at all but rather a wave of probability.[25] In other words, the wave function describes the probability of finding the so-called particle at a particular place. To use Gribbin's own words:

> An electron that is not being observed literally does not exist in the form of a particle at all. There is a certain probability that you might find the electron here, and another probability that you might find it there, but in principle, it could turn up literally anywhere in the Universe. Some locations are very probable . . . and some are extremely unlikely. . . . Once the electron is observed, however, the odds change. The wave function collapses

[23] Robert J. Russell, "Quantum Physics in Philosophical and Theological Perspective," in *Physics, Philosophy, and Theology: A Common Quest for Understanding* (Vatican City: Vatican Observatory, 1988), 369n2.

[24] Gribbin, *Schrödinger's Kittens*, 10.

[25] The "reality" of the wave aspect as material, potential, virtual, etc., is one of the things that is debated among the different schools of interpretation. No definitive answer has yet been experimentally demonstrated, and multiple theories work out mathematically to explain the experimental results. For an explanation of wave as an aspect of reality rather than a mathematical probability, see C. N. Villars, "Microphysical Objects as 'Potentiality Waves,'" *European Journal of Physics* 8, no. 2 (April 1987): 148–49.

. . . and at that moment it is 100 percent certain where the electron is. But once you stop looking, the probability starts leaking out from that location. The probability of finding the electron in the same place that you last looked decreases, and the probability of finding it somewhere else increases as the probability wave spreads out through the universe.[26]

Even within the Copenhagen interpretation, there are different understandings about what qualifies as an observer. Is the observer simply the apparatus of measurement, or must the observer be conscious? Some will argue that reality only exists when there is a conscious mind observing it. Much to the dismay of many physicists, the Copenhagen interpretation has led to a certain degree of theological speculation about God as the conscious observer that ultimately is collapsing the wave function.

Today there are multiple interpretations of quantum mechanics competing with the Copenhagen interpretation, including the Many Worlds Theory (MWT), the Bohmian interpretation, and the consistent histories interpretation. This chapter focuses primarily on the Copenhagen interpretation. While it is beyond the scope of this chapter to explore these other interpretations, it is important to note that the MWT is gaining prominence among physicists precisely because it avoids the necessity of collapsing the wave function.[27] Ultimately there is no way to prove which of these interpretations is correct. In regard to the popularity of the MWT and its implication of a multiverse, Ellis, Kirchner, and Stoeger note: "There is no evidence that the postulated physics is true in this universe, much less in some pre-existing metaspace that might generate a multiverse. Thus belief in the validity of the claimed physics that could lead to such consequences is just that, a belief—it is based on unproved extrapolation

---

[26] Gribbin, *Schrödinger's Kittens*, 12.

[27] For an in-depth discussion of the Copenhagen interpretation versus Many Worlds Theory, see Max Tegmark, "The Interpretation of Quantum Mechanics: Many Worlds or Many Words?," *Fortschritte Der Physik* 46, nos. 6–8 (November 1998): 855–62, here 855. Tegmark notes that "when environment-induced decoherence is taken into account, the experimental predictions of the MWI [Many Worlds Interpretation] are identical to those of the Copenhagen interpretation except for an experiment involving a Byzantine form of 'quantum suicide.' This makes the choice between them purely a matter of taste, roughly equivalent to whether one believes mathematical language or human language to be more fundamental."

of established physics to vastly beyond where it has been tested."[28] In other words, one cannot prove the existence of a multiverse any more than one can prove the existence of God, though we will discuss implications of a possible multiverse in a later chapter. Furthermore, as Robert John Russell notes, when engaging in philosophical and theological conversations with quantum mechanics, one must make a decision about what he calls the "multiple interpretability and historical relativity" of quantum mechanics.[29] That is to say, when using an analogy from the Copenhagen interpretation of quantum mechanics, one must recognize that there are competing interpretations and that in time, this interpretation may be proved false, but one must pick an interpretation with which to dialogue nonetheless.

Theological and Pastoral Implications

The Human Person as Body/Spirit

Just as the scientists for many years thought of particles and waves as two separate realities, Christians have tended to think of the body and the spirit as two separate realities. In modern times, largely due to the influence of Descartes's substance dualism, there has been a popular tendency to think of the spirit as something that inhabits the body at conception and leaves the body at death. This spirit is considered to be the core essence of who I am.

---

[28] G. F. R. Ellis, U. Kirchner, and William R. Stoeger, "Multiverses and Physical Cosmology," *Monthly Notices of the Royal Astronomical Society* 347, no. 3 (2004): 934. See also William R. Stoeger, "Epistemological and Ontological Issues Arising from Quantum Theory," in *Quantum Mechanics: Scientific Perspectives on Divine Action*, ed. Robert John Russell et al. (Vatican: Vatican Observatory, 2001), 91–93. Stoeger comments on the hidden variables interpretation and the Many Worlds Interpretation, noting that "And, though we cannot rule out these approaches, I consider them less adequate than others, either because of the difficulties in meshing them with special relativity, their lack of fruitfulness (e.g., in quantum field theory), or the somewhat extreme and counterintuitive philosophical positions to which some seem to lead." Stoeger, "Epistemological and Ontological Issues," 82.

[29] Robert J. Russell, "Divine Action and Quantum Mechanics: A Fresh Assessment," in *Philosophy, Science, and Divine Action*, ed. F. Leron Shults, Nancey C. Murphy, and Robert J. Russell (Leiden: Brill Academic Publishing, 2009), 363n28.

This dualistic conception of body and spirit leads to many problems and in many ways has returned us to an early heresy in Christianity called Gnosticism. Gnosticism was a philosophical system that focused on the salvific power of *gnosis*, or knowledge. Gnosticism was a dualistic system that saw the spiritual world as good and the material world as at best an obstacle to the spiritual life and at worst as evil. One's spirits had become trapped within this material world, and with the proper knowledge or *gnosis*, one could escape the material world and return to the spiritual realm that is one's true home. In Christian Gnosticism, Jesus was the savior who came from the spiritual realm to impart this knowledge and help us to return to the spiritual realm. Christian Gnostics tended to deny the humanity of Jesus, taking a position called *docetism*, the belief that Jesus seemed to be human, but that his humanity was really an illusion.

The problem with both Gnosticism and substance dualism is that these positions tend to lead to a denigration of the material world and of our bodies in particular. I would suggest that the image given to us by quantum mechanics of a particle/wave complementarity can give us an analogy through which to think about body/spirit so that the two are understood to be one reality. Such a perspective also helps us to understand the Christian doctrine of the resurrection of the body, a doctrine that doesn't make much sense in a framework of either substance dualism or Gnosticism. In the former, if the spirit is the essence of who I am and separate from my body, what need have I of a body in the resurrection? In the latter, the body was considered a hindrance to resurrection or return to the spiritual realm.

To begin to reimagine our concept of body/spirit, we need to start by redefining these terms. If by spirit I do not mean this other substance within me that leaves my body at the time of death, what do I mean? To redefine these concepts, I am going to draw on the theology of the Jesuit theologian Karl Rahner. Rahner defined the human spirit as a potential for the infinite and, ultimately, as our capacity for God. He pointed to the experience of human dynamism, our sense of movement, or as Augustine might say, our restless heart. Humans, he argues, are never satisfied by anything finite. Every answer leads us to a new question. Every experience leaves us eager for more, for the next experience in life. As one of my professors used to say, the human condition is that we want it all! There is a dynamism to the way we live and experience our lives, always moving beyond each moment in life, ready and eager (for the most part, recognizing that at times this very openness can engender fear rather than eagerness) for the next thing that will happen. Even when we want to stay in a moment and savor it for as long as possible, we cannot. We cannot hold on to our experiences other than in our memories. Because we are not only spatial creatures but also temporal creatures—caught up in our human existence of space-time—even when we try to stand still, we are moving. We move through time. We are constantly in motion. Hence our lives are dynamic.

Rahner also calls this movement, or dynamism, human transcendence. To transcend something means to move beyond it. We transcend or move beyond every finite experience. Why? Rahner would say that we do so because we are built for the infinite; we are created for God. We are created with this dynamism or transcendence, which means that no single human experience can ever leave us completely fulfilled and satisfied, because only the infinite mystery of Love that we call God can satisfy that longing and that transcendence within us. Which is not to say that we do not try to satisfy the longing; we constantly try to fill that openness for the infinite with all sorts of finite things and experiences and people. We look to the finite to fill that infinite, God-sized hole in our hearts.

Rahner explains that this human transcendence, this dynamism that drives our lives and is our openness to God, is what in theology we call spirit. Rahner explains the human spirit as reaching beyond one's finiteness, which includes one's spatial-temporal existence, toward an infinite horizon, which is to say, one experiences oneself as infinite possibility.[30] Spirit is this human capacity for the incomprehensible and infinite mystery we call God, but this capacity manifests itself in our everyday lives as we actualize this potential in the here and now. This very movement and openness for the infinite is what enables us to become the persons we are in this finite world. Spirit as infinite potentiality is the dynamism that makes us *living* creatures, not static. In this potentiality is the freedom that makes us able to be individualized, albeit always interconnected, beings as we enact those potentialities in time and space. Such is what it means to be human, which is to say, an embodied spirit.

[30] Karl Rahner, *Foundations of Christian Faith: An Introduction to the Idea of Christianity* [Grundkurs des Glaubens], trans. William Dych (New York: Crossroad, 1978), 32.

The absolute fulfillment of this open potential is ultimately God. In theological terms, this fulfillment is found in union with God, which in this life we would call grace and after death we would call glory (or beatific vision, to use Thomas Aquinas's term). Nonetheless, Rahner maintains that the potential of human spirit is meaningful not only in terms of its ultimate fulfillment in God but also in the becoming of the human person in time and space through freedom and self-actualization.[31] The potential is for the infinite, but that potential is actualized in and through the finite.

So what is our embodiment in this body/spirit reality that we call human existence? Rahner talks about matter as limited and frozen spirit, but that which is created for the sake of spirit and the potential to be spirit's own reality.[32] He defines matter as "the openness and the bringing itself-to-appear of the personal spirit in the finite world . . . it is a moment in the spirit."[33] In other words, Rahner flips our normal conception of reality on its head, in which we usually start with our material existence and then try to figure out what it means to talk about a spiritual existence. Rahner starts with our spiritual reality and then understands our material reality as the manifestation of that spiritual reality in space-time.

Rahner also describes the body as the symbol of the human person, in that our embodiment is how we express ourselves, how we communicate ourselves in this world. He explains that human persons express the unity of their being, i.e., their spirit, in a plurality, in a succession of moments in time and space, in other words, through history and embodiment.[34] Embodiment is the expression of who we are as persons in space and time. We cannot express or manifest our infinite potential in one given moment, as we are finite beings. We must do so, as Rahner notes, in a succession of moments that is the

---

[31] Karl Rahner, "Nature and Grace," in *Theological Investigations*, vol. 4, *More Recent Writings*, trans. Kevin Smyth (Baltimore: Helicon Press, 1961), 186.

[32] Karl Rahner, "The Unity of Spirit and Matter in the Christian Understanding of Faith," in *Theological Investigations*, vol. 6, *Concerning Vatican Council II*, trans. Boniface Kruger and Karl-H. Kruger (Baltimore: Helicon Press, 1969), 170. Note that Barbara Brown Taylor calls matter "frozen energy." See Barbara Brown Taylor, *The Luminous Web: Essays on Science and Religion* (Cambridge, MA: Cowley Publications, 2000), 67.

[33] Rahner, "The Unity of Spirit and Matter," 170.

[34] Karl Rahner, "The Theology of the Symbol," in *Theological Investigations*, vol. 4, *More Recent Writings*, trans. Kevin Smyth (Baltimore: Helicon Press, 1961), 227–28.

history of our lives and our becoming as persons. That manifestation and expression of who we are in our infinite potential, i.e., our embodiment, is what others experience of us; it is that aspect of our being that interacts with others. Those interactions then influence both our potential and others' potential because of the ways in which we are interrelated, interconnected, and interdependent as spirit.

With this concept of spirit as potential for the infinite and body as the manifestation and actualization of that potential in time and space, we can turn to the analogy of particle/wave to elaborate what it means to be body/spirit, using the concept of wave function as potential and probability and particle as the actualization of one of those probabilities. When employing such a theological analogy, it is important to note that all analogies are limited and eventually do break down. Joseph Bracken notes:

> First of all, given contemporary postmodern sensibilities, most of us are aware of the conceptual dangers in claiming that a single theoretical scheme provides all the answers for any given problem-situation. Metaphysical systems are models or symbolic representations of reality that are never fully adequate to their task. As Ian Barbour shrewdly commented several years ago, models in theology as well as in the natural sciences should be taken seriously but not literally; something is always missing in the description of reality.[35]

These cautions hold even truer when we use an analogy from science as an analogy in theology, in the sense that we are using an analogy for an analogy. In other words, the terms "particle" and "wave" are already analogies for mathematical formulas in science, and we are now using these terms as further analogies for body and spirit in theology.

Furthermore, as was noted above, the formulas are not describing the behavior of a single particle/wave in isolation but describe the way the system operates as a whole; the parts cannot be separated from the whole. William Stoeger explains that particle and wave, as

---

[35] Joseph A. Bracken, "The Body of Christ: An Intersubjective Interpretation," *Horizons* 31, no. 1 (Spring 2004): 7–8. Cited by Ian G. Barbour, *Religion and Science: Historical and Contemporary Issues* (San Francisco: HarperOne, 1997), 119.

manifestations of different types of measurement, "are not simultaneously real, according to the standard interpretation, and are not properties that the underlying quantum reality possesses independently of the measurements."[36] These images are inexact ways of trying to put into language what science can only accurately describe in terms of mathematical formulas. Barbara Brown Taylor quotes Niels Bohr as saying, "we must be clear, when it comes to atoms, language can be used only as in poetry."[37] Paul Davies puts it another way: "By employing mathematics as a language, science can describe situations which are completely beyond the power of human beings to describe."[38] Ian Barbour explains that both science and theology end up employing language and images to describe realities that are beyond words.[39] Thus when employing these scientific analogies as theological analogies, one operates in the realm of image and poetry, which allows for certain facets of the mystery to be glimpsed but will never provide an exact correspondence to reality.

As Niels Bohr has pointed out, wave as potential/probability and particle as actualization are complementary descriptions of the same quantum reality. In an analogous manner, spirit and body are complementary descriptions of the same reality, the human person, who is body/spirit. To use Karl Rahner's terminology, spirit and matter "though essentially different, are everywhere correlative constitutive moments of one reality."[40] These aspects are complementary facets of the human person, and if we explain spirit as potentiality or probability and embodiment as actuality, the analogy is helpful in the sense that we cannot "look" at both. In other words, once probability has been actualized or embodied in space and time, the "spirit" function has been "collapsed." Note that while the human person has agency—the ability to make a conscious choice and take conscious action—an electron or another particle does not, and the position of

---

[36] Stoeger, "Epistemological and Ontological Issues," 89.

[37] Taylor, *The Luminous Web*, 34, quoting George Johnson, *Fire in the Mind: Science, Faith, and the Search for Order* (New York: A. A. Knopf, 1995), 146.

[38] Paul C. W. Davies, *God and the New Physics* (New York: Simon and Schuster, 1983), 18.

[39] Ian G. Barbour, *When Science Meets Religion: Enemies, Strangers, or Partners?* (New York: HarperCollins, 2000), 2–3.

[40] Rahner, "The Unity of Spirit and Matter," 166. See also Karl Rahner, *Hominisation: The Evolutionary Origin of Man as a Theological Problem* (New York: Herder and Herder, 1965).

the particle when measured is random. The electron does not choose its position; the system is nondeterministic. Once measured, the position of the electron is known in the moment it is observed, but there is also a wave of probability in terms of where it will appear next. Analogously, when we actualize a possibility in life (not randomly like the electron, but through the agency of self-determination), all of the other paths we could have taken, that infinite potential of possibilities, collapses into the one concrete, embodied act we chose in the process of becoming, but a new wave of potential possibilities now emerges and spreads out from the new point in the becoming that we have actualized. New potentiality exists but has shifted. The process is dynamic, so that if we look at a snapshot, we only catch the single embodied moment; if we look at the potential, there is no way to know which possibility will be actualized. We can know our history and that history creates us to be who we are and shapes the probability of our future potential, but we cannot know our future.

As our analogous particle behavior, embodiment is our actualization in space-time; it is our particle property of definitively being located in a particular place as opposed to all possible places or making a choice which inevitably means not choosing other paths or courses of action. Human beings are finite but have a capacity for the infinite. Spirit is what we call this openness to the infinite/God and, as wave function, is our infinite potentiality. Embodiment is the finite fact that we cannot live all of our infinite potentiality simultaneously.

Ian Barbour notes that for Heisenberg, "tendencies in nature include *a range of possibilities.* The future is not simply unknown; it is 'not decided.' More than one alternative is open, and there is some opportunity for unpredictable novelty."[41] In theology, we would call this "opportunity for unpredictable novelty" freedom. Rahner explains that "when freedom is really understood, it is not the power to be able to do this or that, but the power to decide about oneself and to actualize oneself."[42] In other words, freedom is ultimately my ability to decide for myself the person I want to be and the ability to actually become that person. Freedom is integral to God's creation, both in nature and in the human person. We must collapse the wave of potentiality into concrete particle, that is, choice, history, and act.

---

[41] Barbour, *When Science Meets Religion*, 69.
[42] Rahner, *Foundations of Christian Faith*, 38.

Rahner explains that this self-actualization happens in and through individual choices and acts. He states, "We do not everlastingly do this or that, we do not constantly react to ever-new objects and situations, but by doing what we do we make ourselves, once and for all, despite the temporal sequence. Freedom is not the capacity for indefinite revision, for always doing something different, but the one capacity to create something final, something irrevocable and eternal, the capacity of what by itself is everlasting. Freedom alone creates that which is final."[43]

No one act or choice determines who we are as persons, but we only become who we are as persons in and through the choices and acts of our everyday lives, through enacting our potentiality. Freedom is self-actualization, but that self-actualization happens through our individual choices in space-time.[44] Freedom always ensures that our future is open possibility. In that potentiality, freedom makes us able to be individualized, albeit always interconnected, beings as we enact those potentialities in time and space. Doing so in turn opens up another infinite wave of potentiality.

Thus we can talk about spirit as not only potentiality but also probability. Every human person as body/spirit has infinite potential, and yet not all possibilities in our lives have an equal probability of coming to be. Spirit as our analogous wave function is our infinite potential to actualize ourselves, albeit a potential that is limited by the finite world and our finite embodiment, and therefore one that involves different probabilities of how likely we are to make a certain choice or succeed in a certain course of action. Similarly, recall that an electron could be anywhere, but there will be a higher probability of finding it in certain places than others, and the most extreme probabilities cancel one another out. Villars explains, "Though each electron has a wide range of possible interactions open to it, it has a different tendency, or inclination, towards each possibility. These tendencies are described by a weight, assigned to each possibility,

---

[43] Karl Rahner, *Grace in Freedom* [Gnade als Freiheit], trans. Hilda C. Graef (New York: Herder and Herder, 1969), 228.

[44] Rahner uses the terms transcendental freedom and categorical freedom to describe this relationship between self-actualization and individual choices. He notes, "In this active freedom man decides his own destiny. Of course, the one free act of man in which he realizes himself once and for all is dispersed in space and time as many free actions, in which the one fundamental decision of the one man is enacted."

corresponding to the probability that the electron will take up that possibility."[45] Analogously, each of our choices and opportunities can be described as having a certain "weight," a certain probability that we will or will not take up that possibility. That is to say, not all of our choices, options, and capacities have equal probability of being enacted. We tell children that any US citizen can grow up to be president of the United States, and that statement is true, but there is a higher probability that children from specific families, educational backgrounds, socioeconomic statuses, etc., will actually become president. In addition, most of the time, only one US citizen becomes president every four years, so the statistical probability of any person becoming president would be quite low.

So spirit is the unlimiting of matter, and matter is the particularizing of spirit, the collapsing of the analogous wave function, the collapsing of potentiality and probability into actuality. Part of our embodiment is being limited by historicity and interrelatedness. In other words, my past actions and decisions, that is, the ways in which I have collapsed my spirit/wave function, shape and limit the probability of future courses of action. Thus historicity limits my infinite potential, making certain courses of action highly probable, whereas other courses of action become extremely improbable. In this sense, we can also correlate body/particle with the past, that which has already been actualized, and spirit/wave with the future, the openness and unknowability of the future. We know our past but cannot know our future with certainty. The present is the interaction of the two—how our past impacts the probability of current actions, how our freedom plays a role in determining which future probability gets actualized, and how that actualization impacts future probabilities.

Freedom can be limited by external circumstances as well. Our potentiality is not limited by our own past choices alone. Probability has to do with this concept of interdependence and interconnectedness. Quantum physics is teaching us that everything that exists is interconnected and affects everything else that exists. Reality, by its very nature, is interconnectedness. In quantum mechanics, the idea of entanglement[46] gave physicists insight into the interconnected

---

[45] Villars, *Observables, States and Measurements in Quantum Physics*, 179–80.

[46] This concept, also known as nonlocality, will be explored further in chapter 3.

nature of microphysical reality. Particles only exist as part of a system; they are never isolated, individual particles. As was noted above, when physicists speak of particle/wave complementarity, they are speaking of particles within a system, not individual particle/waves. The interference pattern only appears after a number of electrons have been shot at the detector screen over a prolonged period of time. Similarly, while the analogy is being used here to speak of individual human persons as body/spirit, our potentiality as human persons never exists in isolation. Human beings exist within a system or ensemble of relationships as well. We are always part of a larger system—that of society, culture, history, and humanity itself, and being part of that larger system effects and shapes our potentialities into probabilities.

Analogously, we are not autonomous, individual beings, but we are interconnected. The actions and decisions of others, both in the present and past, also shape and limit the probability of my future course of action. I do not exist in isolation. Thus the choices and actions of others can impact my sphere of freedom and potential and make certain paths more or less probable for me. Rahner notes, "Every free act of one person changes the objective possibilities of the free act of his neighbor, it enlarges, changes or limits the sphere of the other's freedom before this latter can freely intervene."[47] Those interactions then influence both our own potential and others' potential because of the ways in which we are interrelated, interconnected, and interdependent as spirit. Our spirit as a wave of potential becomes probability because all of our possibilities are impacted in their likelihood by our situatedness in a particular context (sociopolitical, historical, economic, racial, ethnic, gendered, etc.) and by our interrelationships with other human persons. Thus we can only understand the individual human person as part of a larger system while at the same time recognizing that the system does not ultimately define the individual. Rahner notes, "Despite its original subjectivity freedom is realized in a common sphere of the unity of historical subjects. By realizing my own freedom I also partly determine the sphere of the freedom of others. True, I do not change their freedom, but the sphere in which their freedom is realized, hence this affects the possibilities of their subjective freedom."[48] While all op-

---

[47] Rahner, *Grace in Freedom*, 233.
[48] Ibid., 232–33.

tions might be possible, not all options are equally probable. In other words, my choices and actions influence the system in which others are making their choices and actions and vice versa. The other is no more or less inherently free due to my actions, but the probability of that other to take a certain course of action may be impacted.

Sin, Grace, Freedom, and Choice

Probability can be understood as the freedom within humanity as well as freedom within creation. We have freedom, but our options are limited by probabilities. Not all possibilities have an equal probability. You cannot accurately predict the behavior of humans; human choices are impacted by relationship and context and the circumstances around them. Choice involves both the freedom of the individual and the freedom of others connected to them, both directly and indirectly.

Understanding the way our freedom is formed, conditioned, and limited by the world around us and the choices of those who have gone before us gives us a concrete way of understanding the concept of original sin. Many people still struggle with the concept of original sin as God punishing us for something we didn't do and the fear that if you don't baptize a baby, this capricious God might send that baby to hell.

Original sin, however, is not a doctrine about damnation. Rather, it is most basically a doctrine about salvation which teaches that all people are in need of the absolutely free gratuitous gift of salvation given to us in Christ. We are born needing salvation. We never exist in a state where we don't need salvation, not even as infants, which is not the same thing as saying that a nonbaptized infant is damned. Rather, this doctrine says that even an infant needs to be in relationship with Christ, regardless of whether or not the infant is conscious of that relationship. The good news is that the infant does not need to do anything to be in relationship with Christ. She or he is in relationship to Christ by the very fact of being created in and through Christ.

We can, however, go beyond this basic theological understanding of original sin to address the pastoral situation of original sin, which is that we are born into a sinful world, and that world has a definitive impact on who we are as persons. We are personally affected by this sin from the first moment of our existence, and there is nothing we can do to escape or avoid being impacted by this sin. Here again we return to the fact that our freedom is not absolute. Our freedom operates within a system that is limited and conditioned. We are born into a world of socioeconomic, political, racial, and cultural factors, to name just a few, that will impact our opportunities in life. We are born into a family that is fallible and sinful, and the sinful choices and actions of our family impact us both physically, psychologically, and emotionally. We literally know that babies in utero are affected by choices their mothers make from things as drastic as drug use to everyday levels of stress hormones. When mom and dad get into a fight, it impacts that baby. Likewise we know much more about infant brain development so that we understand that in the first year of life, a baby's external circumstances and relationships literally form their neural pathways in ways that will enable them to engage in healthy relationships as they mature or will stymie that ability to form relationships. That child's own ability to parent will be dramatically affected by the bonds that baby does or does not form within the first months of life, as well as by how often that baby is exposed to trauma and how that trauma is handled.[49]

In pastoral ministry, we encounter people struggling with the limits and conditions on their freedom. When dealing with people's guilt and anguish over bad choices they have made, there can be great comfort in understanding a sense of lessened culpability through understanding how their choices might have been limited by historical or societal circumstances and/or the choices and behavior of others around them. The social sciences, such as psychology, sociology, economics, and political science can help us understand these external limits and forces both in our own lives and in the lives of those around us.

One can look at a situation, analyze the impact of issues like race, culture, socioeconomic status, education, etc., and respond to the call for reflective praxis. Such reflective praxis can be the action of the community that embraces and supports individuals who struggle against these limits and conditions to their freedom which skew their probability for better opportunities in life. The community of faith is

---

[49] Daniel A. Hughes and Jonathan Baylin, *Brain-Based Parenting: The Neuroscience of Caregiving for Healthy Attachment* (New York: W. W. Norton, 2012), 252.

not simply called to forgiveness and charity but rather to systemic social change that works toward more equality in those probabilities for having opportunity and for being able to take advantage of opportunity. Such reflective praxis is also necessary on an individual level and may help people find a path out of a crippling stagnancy that could engender feelings of helplessness and powerlessness.

Such an understanding of freedom and probability can provide a sense of hope and a real possibility of conversion. One of the extraordinary things about human beings is that we see people overcome unbelievable odds every day. While the probabilities might limit the choices that individual has available, it also allows space for the improbable. Understanding freedom in conjunction with probability means that we can acknowledge the struggle and the inequality inherent in the system of which we are all a part while still empowering people to make very difficult choices for real change in their lives. As noted above, to do so with any authenticity also requires an active engagement in the struggle to change the systemic issues that create a culture of oppression in the lives of marginalized individuals.

Nonempirical Reality and the Choices We Did Not Make

Scientist Lothar Schäfer argues that through quantum physics, we have learned that reality is not limited to the physical, material world.[50] Rather, reality has both empirical and nonempirical aspects, with the empirical being the material, visible, and actual elements and the nonempirical being the hidden, nonmaterial, and potential elements.[51] He describes these domains as the realm of actuality and

---

[50] Note that once a physicist moves from mathematical equations and experimental results to interpretation, there is much more room for debate due to the speculative nature of such interpretations.

[51] Lothar Schäfer, "Nonempirical Reality: Transcending the Physical and Spiritual in the Order of the One," *Zygon* 43, no. 2 (May 2008): 329. Schäfer seems to want to leave the door open to dialogue with both followers of the Copenhagen interpretation, as indicated by his use of the words "nonmaterial" and "potential," while depending more on the hidden variables interpretation from his own perspective. Note, however, that Schäfer is drawing on the work of C. N. Villars who clearly explains, "Potentiality waves differ from *probability waves* in that the latter are usually conceived

the realm of potentiality. Another way to think about these concepts is the realm of what has happened and the realm of what might happen. For Schäfer, the nonempirical realm of potentiality makes up the transcendent cosmic order, and virtual states are the way in which that order expresses itself in the material world.[52] Schäfer makes a very important point that empty or virtual states of an electron are part of quantum reality. So when we speak of the wave aspect, the probability that the electron could be anywhere, Schäfer is arguing that all of those possible places the electron could be are part of the electron's reality and, in fact, part of reality itself. Schäfer calls possible or potential places virtual states. Schäfer explains that virtual states are more than mere mathematical formulas and uses Aristotle's

---

as abstract, mathematical devices which represent, in a statistical way, the behaviour of *particles*. By contrast, potentiality waves, as their more concrete name suggests, are conceived as physically real waves which exist in their own right, not merely as representations of the behaviour of particles. Microphysical objects are not particles 'guided' in some mysterious way by 'waves of probability,' but rather, microphysical objects *are* waves of potential observation interactions." Villars, *Microphysical Objects as 'Potentiality Waves,'* 148. Similarly, theology has struggled to define spirit as reality in a worldview that has typically defined reality in terms of physicality or substance, leading into the historical quagmire of substance dualism.

[52] Lothar Schäfer, "Quantum Reality and the Consciousness of the Universe: Quantum Reality, the Emergence of Complex Order from Virtual States, and the Importance of Consciousness in the Universe," *Zygon* 41, no. 3 (September 2006): 512, 523. Note that in the series of articles in this volume of *Zygon* that address Schäfer's theory of empty or virtual states, Ervin Lazlo suggests the wording of potential states rather than virtual states and asks what is meant by the term real or reality, whereas Carl Helrich argues that wave functions have no physical reality and that wave/particle complementarity is an epistemological clarification, not an ontological clarification. See Ervin Laszlo, "Quantum and Consciousness: In Search of a New Paradigm," *Zygon* 41, no. 3 (September 2006): 562; and Carl S. Helrich, "On the Limitations and Promise of Quantum Theory for Comprehension of Human Knowledge and Consciousness," *Zygon* 41, no. 3 (September 2006): 562. Both men charge that Schäfer's interpretation sets up a dualistic system of mind and matter, whereas they would propose a single system that has both physical and mental aspects, but Schäfer disputes the accuracy of this accusation. See Schäfer, "Nonempirical Reality," 342. In his response, Schäfer amusingly notes that "Helrich takes me to task for giving virtual states too much reality . . . while I am reprimanded by Ervin Laszlo for not granting virtual states enough of that precious commodity, reality." Lothar Schäfer, "A Response to Carl Helrich: The Limitations and Promise of Quantum Theory," *Zygon* 41, no. 3 (September 2006): 587. This idea of a cosmic transcendent order is also controversial because it follows David Bohm's hidden variables interpretation rather than the Copenhagen interpretation, an interpretation that is less accepted by many physicists.

concept of *potentia* to explain that these virtual states "are part of the realm of potentiality in physical reality because they contain the future empirical possibilities of the universe."[53] In other words, some of these virtual states will be actualized; therefore all of the possibilities are part of reality. All of the states in which the electron can possibly exist are an essential part of the overall system and continue to exist as empty or virtual after the wave function is collapsed. The "occupied states" (those that are actualized) form the visible part of reality, but the empty states (those that are not actualized) are also a part of reality, a reality that is nonactualized potentiality.

Schäfer draws on the work of C. N. Villars to emphasize the fact that the virtual states are part of reality. Villars explains that reality in quantum physics is not simply actuality as was thought in the classical system; reality is both actuality and potentiality.[54] Similarly, we can think of our spirit as our Aristotelian *potentia* that is actualized in and through our embodiment. Our reality is one of potentiality

[53] Schäfer, "Nonempirical Reality," 334. See Schäfer, "Quantum Reality," 510–11. See also Ernan McMullin, who states, "Aristotle saw matter as, among other things, the reservoir of potentiality. That role has now become the dominant one. The fields postulated by relativity theory at the scale of the large and of quantum theory at the level of the small are designators of potentiality, of dispositions, of 'what-would-happen-if.' Energy itself is in a real sense an expression of potentiality. It almost seems that it is to the potential, rather than the actual, that reality should be attributed at the most fundamental level. Yet can there be potentialities without the actual? The potentialities here are not indefinite: they are quantified in various ways depending on the kind of field in question. Going from Aristotelian matter to the materialism of the early modern period involved a move from an indefinite potential, constrained eventually only in terms of quantity, to spatially extended, and indisputably actual, hard massy particles. From these particles to the 'matter' of present-day physics could be described as a move back again to potentiality, although no longer indefinite." Ernan McMullin, "From Matter to Materialism . . . and (almost) Back," in *Information and the Nature of Reality: From Physics to Metaphysics*, ed. Paul Davies and Niels Henrik Gregersen (New York: Cambridge University Press, 2010), 33.

[54] Villars, *Observables, States and Measurements in Quantum Physics*, 181. Villars explains, "Probability waves evolve in a complex, infinite-dimensional vector space, called Hilbert space. Hilbert space is real. It is not merely an abstract, mathematical construction existing solely in the human mind, but rather, is an aspect of physical reality itself. Classical physics identified reality with actuality. In quantum physics, this concept is extended to include two aspects; actuality and potentiality. Hilbert space is the space of potentialities, i.e. the weighted possibilities alternative to what actually occurs, which encompasses and goes beyond the ordinary three-dimensional space of actualities."

and actuality. Likewise, the actualization of our potential occupies one possibility of our infinite potential. The probabilities of our future choices thus shift and change in response to the potentialities we actualize. As Schäfer explains:

> After each transition from "the possible to the factual," as Heisenberg called it, the evolution of new "tendencies or possibilities" for future actual events starts anew, but now from a different starting point than before. There is a continuous flux from the evolution of tendencies to their actualizations—empirical events—and from empirical events to new tendencies. Each new state of potentiality carries in it, like a stamp, the memory of the last event.[55]

To translate this concept into my own analogy, all of the possible choices or paths we could take, the infinite potential of being spirit, are part of what makes up our reality; and once we have actualized a certain choice or path, all of the options we did not choose continue to exist as part of our being, part of what makes us who we are. Within the theological question of freedom versus determinism, this model allows us to take a perspective that all of our potentiality exists in God, that whatever choices we make or paths we actualize, all of our possibilities are always held within God as part of God's creation. The choices we did not make and the paths we did not take also continue to have a reality and make us who we are in our ability to look back on them, reflect on them, and grow. The ability to understand those choices in new ways in retrospect deeply influences the person we become. The very process of reflecting on those "virtual" paths helps shape the probabilities regarding which paths we will take in the future. Recall that drawing on Karl Rahner's definition, freedom is the ability to decide about oneself rather than the ability to do this or do that.[56] For Schäfer, virtual states are part of a predetermined cosmic transcendent order. Thus nothing we do or choose puts us outside of God, even when our choice is against God. Rahner would explain this concept as the fact that our very freedom to choose

[55] Schäfer, "Nonempirical Reality," 343. Cites Werner Heisenberg, *Physik Und Philosophie* (Stuttgart: S. Hirzel, 2000), 80, 262.

[56] Rahner, *Foundations of Christian Faith*, 38.

against God is grounded in and borne by God.[57] All of our potential or possible choices are part of a larger reality that is encompassed by God in the same way that all of the virtual states of microphysical objects are part of a quantum reality that encompasses both potentiality and actuality.

Such an analogy can help us understand the relationship between freedom and providence. God holds all of our choices simultaneously; in our freedom, we actualize some of that potentiality, but what we do not actualize continues to exist virtually in God. The choices we did not make shape us as much as the choices we do. To ask, does God know what choice we are going to make before we make it places a false temporality on God. God contains the whole. Our temporal decisions play out within that whole. Some would take this line of thought one step further to say that all of our choices are actualized in different worlds of the multiverse, but I would be hesitant to go that far. I do not affirm or deny the possibility of the multiverse, but if another "me" in another world makes a different choice, that person is no longer me. For who am I if I am not the being who has become, who has actualized myself through my freedom and the choices I have made?

The human person is body/spirit, the continuous interplay between potentiality and actualization. Every actualization or collapse of the spirit/wave function creates new potentiality. That interplay between actualization and potentiality is what it means for us to have an openness to the infinite while being limited by the finite, by time and space. We actualize this freedom and potential, analogously collapsing these continuous wave functions, throughout the course of our lives as we become the person we will eventually be in all eternity in and through the limits of time, space, and embodiment. Rahner explains this relationship of freedom to the temporal and the eternal as follows: "Freedom is the event of something eternal. But since we

---

[57] Note that I am using this concept of a cosmic transcendent order differently than Schäfer in that he is applying this idea literally whereas I am applying it analogously. Applying the concept literally puts much more weight on the side of determinism, in that Schäfer is proposing that God's cosmic order is the hidden variable in the universe which then manifests itself through the actualization of virtual states. Schäfer, "Nonempirical Reality," 342. I am using the idea analogously which puts much more weight on the side of freedom. I am not suggesting there is a hidden predetermined order that manifests itself in the choices we make.

ourselves are still coming to be in freedom, we do not exist with and behold this eternity, but in our passage through the multiplicity of the temporal we are performing this event of freedom, we are forming the eternity which we ourselves are becoming."[58] Salvation then is the eternal validity of this person we have become.[59] The process of self-actualization culminates in the definitive collapse of the wave function that Christian theology calls the resurrection of the body, but we will come back to that concept in a moment.

The analogy of body/spirit as particle/wave also allows us to understand that all of our potentiality is always held in God, so that no matter what choices we make, we never put ourselves "outside" of God. There is no "outside" of God. Our traditional theology of "mortal" sin has given people the false impression that they can irreparably damage their relationship with God in the sense that they can commit sins that will make God cease to love them, and that in those situations God is no longer present to them. Note that this concept does not necessarily deny the possibility of eternal damnation; it simply reimages that possibility. Rahner notes that comprehending the reality of who we did not become, the potential that we did not actualize, in the light of God's unconditional love, may cause that love to burn like fire.[60] One image of this relationship is that moment we might experience when we have done something we know is wrong but, rather than punishing us, the one who loves us embraces us and forgives us instead. That response of love to our failings can make us realize our own guilt far more deeply than retribution or punishment.

In an image that draws on Schafer's concept of nonempirical reality, we can understand that all of our "quantum" states are held within the reality of God. Nothing we can do, choose, or decide can

---

[58] Rahner, *Foundations of Christian Faith*, 96.

[59] Ibid.

[60] In the context of talking about a human being having a potency for the Love which is God himself, Rahner states: "And he must have it always: for even one of the damned, who has turned away from this Love and made himself incapable of receiving this Love, must still be really able to experience this Love (which being scorned now burns like fire) as that to which he is ordained in the ground of his concrete being." Karl Rahner, "Concerning the Relationship between Nature and Grace," in *Theological Investigations*, vol. 1, *God, Christ, Mary and Grace* (Baltimore: Helicon Press, 1961), 311–12.

put us outside of God. All of our potential held within our creation is part of God, and even when we don't actualize that potential, when we don't become the person we could have been, the person we did become is still God's creation. Our shortcomings, our failures, and our sinfulness are always held within the realm of God's unconditional love. That love always calls, beckons us to be more, to fulfill our potential, but not doing so cannot put us outside of God. There is no outside of God. All that is created is held within God's reality.

Resurrection of the Body

The final theological concept I want to address is this idea of the resurrection of the body. First of all, on a literal, rather than analogous level, quantum physics has huge implications for our understanding the body and thus the resurrection of the body. If the so-called particles out of which we are made are in fact not particles but manifestations of fields of energy, quanta or little packets of energy, if you will, then this thing we call a body is not a thing at all! There is a falsity to the concept of object, matter, or body. There is really no such thing as particles or objects or matter but rather only space and energy. What we call the material world is not matter at all but rather occasions or processes. Matter is vibratory, so there can be no such thing as materialism. The term particle simply denotes the collapse of the wave function and tells us position in time and space creating a sense of history and individuality. Body is the collection of previous occasions, processes, and events that shape the probability waves of the future. This new understanding of body, however, should in no way denigrate the importance of our embodiment. Our bodies are who we are as persons. They are the way, *the only way*, that we actualize ourselves, our spirit, our potential. When we talk about the resurrection body, we must remember that matter as we experience it in this world is something of an illusion, not in that it is not real, but in that it is not what we experience it to be, i.e., a world of solid, individual objects in which each of us is one separate individual object among others. People get stuck in the question of whether or not this body, understanding body to be this thing that I can touch, will exist in a "place" called heaven. If matter is not material, we need not conceive of the body as a thing so much as the actualization of who we are, and that history, that actualization and individuation, continues to have eternal significance after death in a way that is no longer limited by time and space.

Within the analogy of body/spirit as particle/wave, we can talk about this resurrection of the body as our definitive collapse of the wave function, the point when we have actualized our embodied potential. Rahner defines death as "the supreme act of man in which his whole previous life is gathered up in the final decision of his freedom and mastered, so that he ripens for his eternity."[61] For Rahner, death is not one act among others but rather the totality of one's life, "the definitive act of [one's] freedom, the complete integration of [one's] time on earth with [one's] human eternity."[62] If we think of embodiment as the actualization of our infinite potential, albeit limited by probabilities, then this moment of death is the definitive actualization of our potential, culminating in union with the infinite God and thus the definitive collapse of the wave function. For Rahner, death is necessary because without death we can never achieve our definitive actualization, and an endless existence of becoming would be absurdity. It would, ultimately, be damnation.[63] Furthermore, Rahner explains that our entire lives are lived in this process of dying. He states, "In reality we *are* dying all our lives through right up to this, the final point in the process of dying. Every moment of life is a stage on the way to this final goal, a stage which already carries this end within itself and derives its significance from it. . . . Dying takes place throughout life itself and death when it comes is only the ultimate and definitive completion of the process."[64] Each time we collapse our spirit/wave function of potentiality into act, we die to all of the potentialities we do not enact. Rahner adds

---

[61] Karl Rahner, "Dogmatic Questions on Easter," in *Theological Investigations*, vol. 4, *More Recent Writings* (Baltimore: Helicon Press, 1961), 129.

[62] Ibid.

[63] Karl Rahner, "On Christian Dying," in *Theological Investigations*, vol. 7, *Further Theology of the Spiritual Life* (Baltimore: Helicon Press, 1961), 288.

[64] Ibid., 290. On this concept that death is the summation of our existence and that this death takes place throughout our entire lives, see also Karl Rahner, "Ideas for a Theology of Death," in *Theological Investigations*, vol. 13, *Theology, Anthropology, Christology*, trans. David Bourke (New York: Seabury, 1975), 169–86; and Karl Rahner, "Christian Dying," in *Theological Investigations*, vol. 18, *God and Revelation*, trans. Edward Quinn (New York: Crossroad, 1983), 226–56.

that each of these acts of dying is an act of faith or despair, culminating in the ultimate act of faith or despair that is death. Ultimately, do I believe that my existence has eternal and irrevocable validity in the eyes of God? That definitive collapse of the wave function of potentiality in which I am no longer becoming in time and space but now am who I am in union with God is the resurrection of the body. In this "collapse," spirit is not eliminated but rather actualized. The resurrection of the body is not the elimination of spirit but rather the concretization of spirit. As beings that are embodied spirit, our existence after death cannot be purely spiritual or pure potentiality. Rather, it is actualized potentiality. When we return to the original understanding of spirit as potential for God, in death that potential is actualized in union with God. In death, who we have become in our life, lived in the temporal moments of day to day becoming, is now taken up into the oneness and wholeness of God without in any way losing the uniqueness and individuality of that person we have become. This enduring existence and uniqueness of our actualization is what we mean by resurrection of the body.

In addressing the resurrection of the body, we must address the concept not only on a personal or individual level but also on a communal level. In tradition and Scripture, we find the idea that the resurrection of the body is something that happens simultaneously to everyone at the end of the age when the dead shall be raised. Rahner would explain this concept as nothing more or less than the absolute interconnectedness of the individual with all humanity and the fate of creation itself. Thus Rahner argues that union with God and belonging to the material world are not concepts that can be thought of as being in inverse proportion.[65] Nearness to God does not mean remoteness from the world.[66] So for Rahner, in a sense, our final definitive actualization is bound up with the final definitive actualization of the entire world. Again, I would point to Schäfer's theory that "reality is a homogenous wholeness in which potentiality is entwined with actuality and matter is nothing but 'coagulated potentiality' or 'coagulated form' (Dürr and Oesterreicher-Mollwo, 2004). . . . It is only in relation to this, the limited human receptor,

---

[65] Karl Rahner, "The Resurrection of the Body," in *Theological Investigations*, vol. 2, *Man in the Church*, trans. Karl-H. Kruger (Baltimore: Helicon Press, 1963), 211.

[66] Ibid.

that the terms empirical and nonempirical, spiritual and physical, material and formal, are perceived like the characters of a dualistic reality."[67] In other words, there is a wholeness, interrelatedness, and interconnectedness to reality that supersedes both our individuality and the distinctions we make between part/whole, matter/spirit, and individual/communal. In this sense, our embodiment as our actualized potential shapes not only our own wave function probabilities but also the probabilities of the potential of those who are interconnected with us and as a result, the probabilities of those interconnected to them, on to infinity. Rahner states this sentiment more simply: "The history—which has remained within the framework of the world—of those who by their lives have already effected their personal finality, reaches its real completion and explicit expression together with the consummation of the world."[68] Each individual is connected to every other person who exists, has existed, and will exist. The Roman Catholic tradition calls this connection the communion of saints. Therefore my personal finality that is achieved in my death continues to be intertwined with the lives of those who come after me, and thus my personal finality must ultimately come to a conclusion in a communal finality that we call the resurrection of the dead. Thus our ultimate realization, the playing out of our self-actualization, becomes definitive when the whole of creation has been actualized, and God is all in all.

Death is part of the reality we deal with in pastoral ministry and in our lives as Christians. As Christians, we believe that life triumphs over death in the resurrection. A loved one does not disappear or cease to exist in death but, rather like the famous story of the Velveteen Rabbit, becomes real in death because he or she is loved by God. The experiences of our lives and the choices we have made acquire a definitive validity in death.

---

[67] Schäfer, "Nonempirical Reality," 342. Cites Hans-Peter Dürr and Marianne Oesterreicher-Mollwo, *Auch Die Wissenschaft Spricht Nur in Gleichnissen: Die Neue Beziehung Zwischen Religion Und Naturwissenschaften* (Freiburg im Breisgau: Herder, 2004), 33. It is important to note here that Schäfer is following David Bohm's hidden variables interpretation rather than the Copenhagen interpretation of Niels Bohr, et al. He also moves beyond the scientific to the philosophical and theological in developing his concept of Cosmic Consciousness. For our analogous purpose in this article, what is important is the understanding that nonempirical reality can be interpreted as the interconnectedness of empirical reality.

[68] Rahner, "The Resurrection of the Body," 213–14.

As Rahner pointed out above, dying is a part of the process of living. How I live my life, the choice I make to actualize one potential or occupy one state is to die to others. There is a certain grieving that takes place throughout our lives over our "virtual states," the choices we did not make and the paths we did not choose. At the same time, there is a celebration of who I am as a person and the fact that all of those choices, good and bad, made me the person I am today, and it is this concrete actualization of who I am that is loved unconditionally by God and in death given eternal validity.

This prospect for becoming in death can influence the choices I do make and give me an added sense of personal responsibility. Rather than focusing on what I will physically look like in heaven—will I be this age or younger, will I be this weight or twenty pounds lighter—the resurrection of the body should help me focus on who I will be in the resurrection. As I make decisions in my life, I ask myself is this really who I want to be for all eternity? Is this the person I want to bring into ultimate union with God? Likewise, there is an element of communal responsibility in my personal becoming. Is this person I am becoming the legacy I want to leave to the world? Recognizing that our interrelatedness means my decisions, choices, and paths will impact the sphere of freedom in which others actualize their freedom even after my death, how can I live in a way that expands rather than contracts that sphere of freedom for others? Understanding body/spirit as particle/wave or actuality/potentiality helps us see how we are one reality with two aspects that allow us to be cocreators of our own reality along with the God in whom all that we are and all that we might be is held in unconditional love.

Chapter Three

Entanglement

Scientific Developments—Entanglement

Quantum mechanics led to a disagreement in the world of physics between those who wanted to maintain the classical, Newtonian view of the world and those who accepted the Copenhagen interpretation that reality was built on probability, indeterminacy, and uncertainty. Albert Einstein was one of the physicists who believed that our lack of understanding in the quantum world was epistemological, that is, having to do with our knowledge. In other words, he believed the issue was that we simply did not know enough yet. He believed that discoveries would eventually be made that would clear up the quantum mysteries and restore a sense of Newtonian certainty. As Brian Greene explains, Einstein believed that if we measured a particle at a specific place, then the moment before we measured it, it must have been very close to that space. It had a position; we just did not know what that position was until we measured it.[1] Niels Bohr and the Copenhagen interpretation disagree. They argue that such a reality would not give us the interference pattern in the double slit experiment. The electron is truly not anywhere, that is, it does not have a position until we measure it. All that it has is a wave of probabilities of the likelihood of it being in one place or another.[2] Those following the Copenhagen interpretation believe that the lack of understanding

---

[1] Brian Greene, *The Fabric of the Cosmos: Space, Time, and the Texture of Reality* (New York: A. A. Knopf, 2004), 94.

[2] Ibid.

is ontological, which is to say part of the being (onto) or reality of things. In other words, it is not simply that we *don't* know; it is that we *cannot* know. Reality does not allow us to know both position and momentum of a particle simultaneously. Before we measure a particle, we simply cannot know where it is located. To sum up this debate, we can use Einstein's oft-quoted line, "God does not play dice," by which he meant that God would not create a world that is inherently uncertain and unpredictable. Niels Bohr's response to Einstein's famous comment was, "stop telling God what to do."[3] At stake in this debate is our entire picture of reality. For believers, the debate also influences how we view the God we believe created that reality.

In 1935, Einstein published a paper along with Boris Podolsky and Nathan Rosen that proposed a thought experiment from which we get the idea of "entanglement" (what is also called the EPR paradox after the three men trying to disprove the very effect named after them) or what Einstein called "spooky action at a distance." According to Greene, "They wanted to show that every particle does possess a definite position and a definite velocity at any given instant of time, and thus they wanted to conclude that the uncertainty principle reveals a fundamental limitation of the quantum mechanical approach."[4] Einstein, Podolsky, and Rosen argued that if two particles are entangled and you measure the position of one, you know the position of the other, without measuring/observing it, and likewise if you measure the velocity.[5] Therefore, the particles must have a definite position and velocity before measurement.

Greene goes on to explain that for Einstein, measuring the one particle could not have had an effect on the other particle "because they are separate and distant entities."[6] Our understanding of local causality is that for one thing to have an effect on another, there must be a physical connection between the two. Now this connection might be direct, in the sense that if I push a ball, it starts to roll. The connection can also be indirect in the sense of fields, in that I can move

---

[3] "The Center for the History of Physics," American Institute of Physics, http://www.aip.org/history/einstein/ae63.htm.

[4] Greene, *Fabric of the Cosmos*, 99.

[5] Ibid., 101.

[6] Ibid.

a metal object with a magnet, even if the magnet is not touching the object, because the object is in the magnet's magnetic field or field of influence. The magnet is not touching the object, but the field is touching the object. Likewise, we can hear a message broadcast on the radio only as fast as the radio waves move through space (which to us seems instantaneous). No message or wave, however, can move faster than the speed of light. Einstein argued that since knowing the position or velocity of one entangled particle allowed us to know the position or velocity of the other entangled particle, and since this point would hold true no matter how far apart the particles might be, they must not be communicating with one another nor operating under some quantum "spooky action at a distance," but rather the particles must have a definite position and velocity prior to being measured. Greene uses the concrete illustration of two gloves.[7] If I drop one of my gloves outside and, once inside, realize that I only have my left-hand glove, I immediately know that my right-hand glove is outside. The glove outside, Einstein would argue, did not become right-handed when I looked at my left-hand glove. It was always a right-hand glove.

In 1964, John Bell came up with a possible experiment, albeit without the equipment to carry it out, that could conceivably test this theory. The experiment involved adding a third element that could not be determined prior to measurement into the equation, the spin of the particle. Work on carrying out this experiment continued throughout the 1970s and 1980s until Alain Aspect successfully conducted an experiment demonstrating that Einstein's, Podolsky's, and Rosen's assumptions were incorrect.

Robert John Russell explains that in this experiment, "an atom in an excited state decays, emitting two electrons in opposite directions."[8] The spins of the respective electrons are measured in two different labs, and while the results in both look to be entirely random, it turns out that when the spins of both electrons are measured along the same axis, "the data were 100% anti-correlated,"[9] that is, if one was up, the other was down. Russell concludes,

[7] Ibid., 502n14.

[8] Robert J. Russell, "Quantum Physics in Philosophical and Theological Perspective," in *Physics, Philosophy, and Theology: A Common Quest for Understanding* (Vatican City: Vatican Observatory, 1988), 343–74.

[9] Ibid., 346.

If we compare the data from the two labs afterwards, the individual data taken simultaneously along the same axis do match (e.g., for electrons the spins are always opposite)! In this sense, the *correlations* in the data are *non-local*. So while we should not say that the measurement process at A influences the measurement process at B, we must admit that the results of the measurements of A and B indicate that the processes producing A and B are to a certain extent inseparable.[10]

Russell does not use the word "influence," because influence suggests local causality (like when I push the ball, and it rolls). This experiment demonstrates a causality that is nonlocal, and in that sense it is outside of anything we experience in our everyday world, but what we gain from this knowledge is an understanding that at the most fundamental level of nature, things are interconnected. Creation is holistic. Russell explains that "this element of wholeness gives to nature a 'social' character even at the atomic level."[11] He goes on to note:

> We may need to abandon the assumption that the electrons in one lab are totally separate phenomena from the electrons in the other lab. Instead, the correlations suggest a unitive or nonseparable feature about matter at the subatomic level which is strikingly contrary to the way matter behaves at the ordinary, macroscopic level. These strong correlations lead to the notion that the electrons still form a single system, though they are being measured in labs which are arbitrarily distant from each other. The result is that local measurements suggest a non-local character to nature.[12]

Einstein, Podolsky, and Rosen had made the assumption that any causality must be local. Bell's experiment, finally carried out by Aspect, demonstrated that the assumption behind their theory was incorrect. In fact, what occurs in the experiment is what Einstein might call "spooky action at a distance." Greene explains that the assumption is mistaken:

> The universe is not local. The outcome of what you do at one place can be linked with what happens at another place, even if nothing

[10] Ibid., 347.
[11] Ibid., 351.
[12] Ibid., 352.

travels between the two locations—even if there isn't enough time for anything to complete the journey between the two locations. Einstein's, Podolsky's, and Rosen's intuitively pleasing suggestion that such long-range correlations arise merely because particles have definite, pre-existing, correlated properties is ruled out by the data.[13]

In other words, the entangled particles did not correspond because they had preexisting programs for their spin (the right-hand glove, left-hand glove analogy), nor did they correspond because they somehow communicated with each other across vast distances or through some sort of "quantum telepathy" faster than the speed of light. They corresponded not because they act as two separate entities but rather, even with vast distances separating them, they act as one entity, as one system. Thus, a measurement of one of the particles along a particular axis will mean that the other particle will have the opposite spin along the same axis. This phenomenon is called nonlocality because the causation cannot be local causation. The particles are not touching, communicating, and do not share a field of influence.[14]

Just to give a few other illustrations of this experiment, John Polkinghorne uses the images of balls in an urn.[15] According to Einstein's assumptions, if an urn contains a black ball and a white ball and we each pull one out, when you discover that your ball is black, you know that mine is white.[16] In looking to see which ball you have, you become aware of the color of my ball. The balls did not change; your knowledge changed, and thus the issue is epistemological, meaning it is about what we do or do not *know* about reality rather than being about reality itself. Entanglement (also called the EPR paradox or nonlocality) is not an epistemological issue (one about our knowledge of the situation). It is an ontological issue, which means that the effect has to do with the reality of the situation or the very "being" (*ontos*)

---

[13] Greene, *Fabric of the Cosmos*, 114–15.

[14] Note that some physicists, such as David Bohm, would suggest that they do share a field of influence, a hypothetical quantum field, that causes the correlations, but no evidence currently exists to support the idea of a quantum field. Of course, no evidence exists to disprove it either.

[15] John C. Polkinghorne, *Quantum Theory*, vol. 69 (Oxford: Oxford University Press, 2002), 80. See also, John C. Polkinghorne, "The Demise of Democritus," in *The Trinity and an Entangled World: Relationality in Physical Science and Theology*, ed. John C. Polkinghorne (Grand Rapids, MI: W. B. Eerdmans Publishing, 2010), 6–7.

[16] Polkinghorne, *Quantum Theory*, 80.

of the particles involved. Polkinghorne goes on to explain, "In the EPR effect, by contrast, what happens at 1 *changes* what is the case at 2. It is as if, were you to find that you had a red ball in your hand, I would have to have a blue ball in mine, but if you found a green ball, I would have to have a yellow ball and, previous to your looking, neither of us had balls of determinate colours."[17] Again, Polkinghorne points out that entanglement is not about communication between the two particles. No communication can take place that is faster than the speed of light. Rather he explains that "quantum entanglement is a subtle form of interrelationality."[18]

To give you one more illustration to understand this effect, Anton Zeilinger uses the picture of a pretend pair of quantum dice. These quantum dice are not normal dice. Zeilinger explains, "These quantum dice, which might become a favorite Christmas present for children at some time far in the future, behave as follows: if we throw the two dice, they will always show the same number. Unpack the next pair of dice, throw them—again they will each show the same number. This number might vary from one pair of dice to the next, but for each pair, the first throw always specifies what that number will be."[19] So in this example, you and your friend each take one die and throw it, and no matter what, both dice will land on the same number. There is no way to predict which number they will land on, but they will always end up being the same number. Zeilinger explains Einstein's perspective as the idea that the dice are loaded but notes that this possibility can be ruled out by throwing the dice more than once in that the number would only be the same on the first throw.[20] After the first throw, each die would produce a random sequence of numbers. Likewise, it is not possible that the dice are communicating with one another because the dice are thrown at the same time. So what is the explanation? The answer is actually that the individual throw of each die is random, but that together they show the same result. Zeilinger notes, "Both dice, however, show the same result, which

---

[17] Ibid. See also Polkinghorne, "The Demise of Democritus," 6–7.

[18] Polkinghorne, "The Demise of Democritus," 6–7; Polkinghorne, *Quantum Theory*, 113.

[19] Anton Zeilinger, "Quantum Physics: Ontology or Epistemology?," in *The Trinity and an Entangled World: Relationality in Physical Science and Theology*, ed. John C. Polkinghorne (Grand Rapids, MI: W. B. Eerdmans Publishing, 2010), 35–36.

[20] Ibid., 36.

begs the question, 'How can two random events give the same result without there being any connection between them?' This mystery is the reason why Erwin Schrödinger called entanglement *the* essential feature of quantum mechanics, the issue that forces us to abandon all our cherished views about how the world works."[21]

Entanglement demonstrates that two seemingly random events can be interconnected to one another. Anton Zeilinger explains how this discovery changes our worldview:

> While the properties of the individual system (for example, the number that a die will show) are completely undefined, and the observed result is random in an absolute way, the relation between the two sides is fully defined. They both have to show the same result. *Therefore, it is impossible to build an ontology of the individuals, but it is possible to build an ontology of relations.* The relation between two objects is well defined and can be predicted with certainty. That is, we can predict with certainty that the two dice will show the same number, even though the properties of the individuals are completely undefined. We therefore conclude that one consequence of entanglement is that relations are more important than individuals.[22]

To make such a shift in our ontology from focusing on the individual to focusing on the relationship between individuals has profound implications for our understanding of the created world, our relationships with one another, and our God. Analogously, we cannot have certainty about who we are or who another is or even/especially who God is, but we can have certainty that we are in relationship with one another, that we impact one another, and who each of us is/becomes depends on our relationship to one another.

Zeilinger connects this ontology to epistemology, arguing that

> a separation between reality and information, between existing and being known, and in other words between ontology and epistemology, should be abandoned. What are the practical implications of this view? It is important to bear in mind that, when considering what existence might mean, we are simply reflecting

---

[21] Ibid.
[22] Ibid.

on the information we have gathered so far about what exists. Our knowledge that we have acquired of the experimental results is what we are really talking about. Being, therefore, without also being known, makes no sense at all.[23]

One might say, in the tradition of Jean-Luc Marion, that being, without also being loved, makes no sense at all.[24] For theologically, what does it mean to be known if not to be loved? Polkinghorne concludes:

Thus the separability of entities from each other that seems to be so apparent a part of our everyday experience, and which is needed by science for the possibility of successfully contained experimentation (since otherwise one would have to take every-thing into account before being able to investigate anything), is far from being unproblematic. The older style of scientific think-ing started with isolated systems and then asked how they might be conceived to interact with each other. We now see that this is too simplified an account, which needs supplementation by an adequate recognition that holistic effects are also active in the physical world.[25]

Theological and Pastoral Implications

Body of Christ as Christian Community

In the Christian tradition, we have a concept that addresses reality in an intrinsically relational form. That image is the image of the Body of Christ. The use of this image to refer to the whole, to the Christian community itself, is first found in the Pauline and then the deutero-Pauline letters.[26] Paul's key theological insight is that the Christian community is the Body of Christ. At a later date, the author of the

---

[23] Ibid., 38–39.

[24] See Jean-Luc Marion, *God without Being: Hors-Texte* [Dieu sans l'être.], trans. Thomas A. Carlson, 2nd ed. (Chicago: The University of Chicago Press, 2012).

[25] Polkinghorne, "The Demise of Democritus," 7.

[26] Arland Hultgren notes that "the word 'body' was used to refer to corporate entities in philosophical and political writings of Paul's time, but there is not a general consensus that Paul was drawing on those writings in his usage of the term." "The

Acts of the Apostles gives a narrative form to this insight in the famous story of Paul on the road to Damascus: "On his journey, as he was nearing Damascus, a light from the sky suddenly flashed around him. He fell to the ground and heard a voice saying to him, 'Saul, Saul, why are you persecuting me?' He said, 'Who are you, sir?' The reply came, 'I am Jesus, whom you are persecuting. Now get up and go into the city and you will be told what you must do'" (Acts 9:3-6). The insight illustrated by this story is the idea that if we persecute the community, we persecute Jesus. Thus the community is the Body of Christ. The earlier Pauline letters use this image to emphasize the wholeness of the community, a wholeness like entanglement that is more than just the sum of its parts.

Paul connects the concept of the Body of Christ as a corporate entity to the Eucharistic celebration: "Because there is one bread, we who are many are one body" (1 Cor 10:17).[27] In Corinth, the community is experiencing divisions between rival factions, between those who eat food sacrificed to idols and those who do not, as well as between the wealthy and the poor. In addressing the inequalities between the wealthy and the poor, Paul warns the community that "anyone who eats and drinks without discerning the body, eats and drinks judgment on himself" (1 Cor 11:29). He refers here to recognizing the Body of Christ in the oneness of the community of believers. Paul elaborates on this image of the body, noting both its unity and its diversity. We are all baptized into the one body. That one body has many different parts, but no one part is any less essential than another (1 Cor 12:12-26). Each part is necessary to the body as a whole. No part can exist without the others. Paul concludes that "God has so constructed the body as to give greater honor to a part that is without it, so that there may be no division in the body, but that the parts may have the same concern for one another. If [one] part suffers, all the parts suffer with it; if one part is honored, all the parts share its joy" (1 Cor 12:24-26).

Paul in Romans 12 goes on to use this image to talk about the different gifts that different members of the community may possess. Ultimately, a gift is only valued if it builds up the body, which is to

Church as the Body of Christ: Engaging an Image in the New Testament," *Word & World* 22, no. 2 (March 2002): 125.

[27] Ibid.

say, if it serves the good of the whole community (1 Cor 14:3-5, 12, 17). Gifts should foster the oneness and unity of the community, not create divisions and hierarchy in the community. The priority is not given to the individual but to the whole. Paul admonishes,

> For by the grace given to me I tell everyone among you not to think of himself more highly than one ought to think, but to think soberly, each according to the measure of faith that God has apportioned. For as in one body we have many parts, and all the parts do not have the same function, so we, though many, are one body in Christ and individually parts of one another. (Rom 12:3-5)

For Paul, being part of the body means more than being part of a community; it means that the others in the body are actually part of me as I am part of them. They are my reality now. As in entanglement, the system along with the relationships among its component parts is the greater reality.

This image of the body, with priority given to relationship and emphasis placed on the whole, informs Paul's ethical exhortations as well and is the foundation of his teaching on the law. In the end, the ethical standard for Paul is the unity of the body. If an action, be it following the law or not following the law, causes division within the body, then one should not do it. The law becomes secondary to the wholeness of the community. Thus Paul will chastise those who follow the Jewish purity laws for not eating with the Gentiles, but he will also chastise the Gentile Christians who eat meat sacrificed to idols and thus scandalize the Jewish members of the body. The main concern is always maintaining the unity of the body.

Anthony Kelly notes that this image of the body is picked up in the letter to the Ephesians, where the oneness of the members is also highlighted. Kelly states, "The members of this Christ-Body are drawn into the vitality of self-giving love. For they are, in Christ, 'members, one of another' (Eph 4:25)."[28] Like the entangled particles in the EPR experiments, the members are interconnected in such a way that they create an undivided whole. Rather than understanding

---

[28] Anthony J. Kelly, " 'The Body of Christ: Amen!': The Expanding Incarnation," *Theological Studies* 71, no. 4 (December 2010): 808.

them as separate entities, there is a way in which we must consider the Body of Christ as a single entity. Doing so changes the way we understand our relationships with one another. Like the particles, the members seem to be discrete individuals, but in reality, they act as one system. Kelly, therefore, concludes, "In this renewed embodied existence, believers are offered a new sense of corporate coexistence: 'In that renewal there is no longer Greek and Jew, circumcised and uncircumcised, barbarian, Scythian, slave and free, but Christ is all and in all' (Col 3:11)."[29]

The scriptural image of the Body of Christ has become a foundational image in our sacramental and ecclesiological theology. The celebration of the sacrament of Eucharist is not simply about communion with Christ; it celebrates and effects our communion with one another in Christ.[30] The Body of Christ, which includes the members in union with Christ the head, is the ongoing incarnation, the sacramental presence of God in the world.[31]

Anthony Kelly points out that when we use the image of "body," we are already inherently talking about a reality that is relational in its very being. Kelly explains a body as "a field of relationships shaping human consciousness."[32] He goes on to specify that "the flesh, our incarnate consciousness, is a field of mutual indwelling, of being with and for the other."[33] When we then apply this concept of body to the Body of Christ, Kelly concludes, "For a theological phenomenology, Christ's Body is the organic field of his relationship to the world. It affects and is affected by the manifold reality of our embodied coexistence in him. Though Christ is the form, goal, and agent of a transformed existence, his risen body continues in its 'natal bond' with the world."[34] When we are incorporated into that body, we are incorporated into that relationship with the world. Such a relationship has very practical implications.

---

[29] Ibid.

[30] Susan K. Wood, "Body of Christ: Our Unity with Him," *Word & World* 22, no. 2 (March 2002): 187.

[31] Note that this view of the Body of Christ as the ongoing incarnation is controversial. See Wood, "Body of Christ," 188, and Hultgren, "The Church as the Body of Christ," 131.

[32] Kelly, "The Body of Christ," 804.

[33] Ibid.

[34] Ibid., 807.

Lois Malcolm explains that in the Pauline worldview, this inter-relationship means that at the most basic level, we share in one another's experiences, rejoicing with those who rejoice and weeping with those who weep.[35] Malcolm points out that union in Christ's body necessarily does away with division. She celebrates with Paul the "havoc proclamation of Jesus' crucified and raised body unleashes when it overturns conventional notions of power. This proclamation does create—within the very messy complexity of our lives—a new humanity out of men and women, and out of people of different ethnic groups, religious backgrounds, races, and social classes. Jesus' broken and raised body will—and should —continue to threaten anyone concerned with securing turf."[36] Likewise, within the church itself, concern must be given to the importance of all of the members. Understanding our interconnectedness and the unitive nature of the whole should lead us to listen anew to the voices of those that are often excluded. For example, this concern for the whole could mean rethinking the role of women in the church. Likewise the whole must recognize the value of the LGBTQ community and be open to how the relationship with that community has an impact on the whole body. When we experience fractures within the body, our first response should not be amputation.

Pope Francis tells the story of being asked if he approved of homosexuality:

> I replied with another question: "Tell me: when God looks at a gay person, does he endorse the existence of this person with love, or reject and condemn this person?" We must always consider the person. Here we enter into the mystery of the human being. In life, God accompanies persons, and we must accompany them, starting from their situation. It is necessary to accompany them with mercy. When that happens, the Holy Spirit inspires the priest to say the right thing.[37]

---

[35] Lois Malcolm, "Body of Christ: Our Diversity in Him," *Word & World* 22, no. 2 (March 2002): 187.

[36] Ibid., 189.

[37] Antonio Spadaro, "A Big Heart Open to God: The Exclusive Interview with Pope Francis," *America* 209, no. 8 (September 2013): 26.

As the Body of Christ, we are part of one whole, one system, and the parts are interrelated and interconnected in such a way that what happens to one part happens to the entire system in an analogous manner to what we see happening in quantum entanglement. The particles are able to have a nonlocal connection because they are part of the same system.

Mark Taylor notes the challenge of living out this interconnectedness in our contemporary culture, stating:

> Precisely this understanding of belongingness to Christ, being a social experience, is often difficult to hold in the US cultural milieu. Here the reigning discourses of the churches fixes on "a personal relationship with Jesus," which usually means the primary experience of grace comes as an individual experience of God that is only secondarily social.[38]

Flora Winfield would agree, arguing that the reality of relationship is primary in the Body of Christ, more real than individuality. She states:

> We need one another in order to function and be whole. We belong together, and cannot come to healing and freedom without the other parts of the body: "There is no life that is not in community." That we are joined together, in koinonia and mutual need, is essential to the continuing life and function of every part, every participant in the life that makes up the body. The recognition of this koinonia in mutual need is humbling, and helps us to locate ourselves and our own experience of the body in the frame of the question. This is therefore an intensely personal question about belonging, not one to be considered in the abstract, as if about a group of people separate from ourselves; it is about us and those with whom we live in the daily community of neighbours and friends.[39]

Similarly, a change in perspective is needed in terms of how we understand human affairs. Just as it makes no sense to look at indi-

---

[38] Mark Lewis Taylor, "Torture and the Body of Christ," *Touchstone* 24, no. 3 (September 2006): 16.

[39] Flora Winfield, " 'For Nothing Can Separate Us from the Love of Christ': Who Does Belong to the Body of Christ?," *Ecumenical Review* 47, no. 3 (July 1995): 364–65.

vidual electrons apart from the system to which they belong, beginning with the individuals affected by societal ills and then looking at their interactions with society is no longer an adequate way to address the deepest problems faced by our societies. Rather, it makes more sense to begin with the relationships themselves and the systems that govern interactions, thus recognizing the holistic effects of interrelationship. Herein lies the heart of the debate around race in this country today.

While some want to focus on the individuals and the specific circumstances leading to their very tragic deaths, the black community challenges us to look at the entire system and the pattern that emerges when one starts from the perspective of the whole. The inability to deal with social issues in isolation is demonstrated in the interlocking nature of "-isms." One cannot look at the effects of racism, for example, without also considering the effects of classism, sexism, and all of the other "-isms," as well as systems of education, culture, family of origin, etc. Trying to understand the impact of the interlocking relationships of the whole so as to begin to address the societal issues that arise as a result is not an easy task. Polkinghorne notes a similar challenge faced in physics: "What all of this implies for physics and metaphysics is far from being well worked out, but it is clear that atomism has to give way to some intrinsically more relational form of the structure of physical reality."[40] Similarly, we must work out the implications for human society, but it is clear that individualism must give way to some intrinsically more relational form of human reality.

When we talk about the idea of social sin or systemic sin, we might think of it in terms of nonlocal causality. Of course, we can also describe it in terms of local causality. For example, when I buy in an American store a piece of clothing that was made in a sweatshop in Southeast Asia, the workers in that factory are within my field of influence in that my choice directly affects them. One can, however, also use the analogy of nonlocal causality in the sense that we can think of the global world, including all humanity and all of creation, as one system. Things that happen in one part of the world or even the individual choices that one person makes do impact the whole,

---

[40] Polkinghorne, "The Demise of Democritus," 7.

and the whole in turn impacts all of the individual parts. If we start to think of the world as an interconnected whole, it should start to impact the way in which we make decisions, both individually and corporally. My concern for my neighbors, both near and far, should be as great as my concern for myself, the tradition tells me.

As the lessons about reality in entangled quantum reality teach us, the fact that the parts are interrelated and part of one system means that the system as a whole is affected by each of the parts and the parts are impacted by the whole. This impact is not always or only the result of local causality, but there is an integrated "non-locality" involved. What happens to one part can and must impact the rest. Such an image gives new and much-needed weight to the idea of a global church. Those who are Christians in industrial and postindustrial countries cannot live large on the backs of those who live in nonindustrialized countries. Globalization becomes a huge concern when the wealthy live off of the poor and when the members of the richest nations consume the resources that are so desperately needed by those in the poorest of nations. What we do in developed countries has a direct impact on the nondeveloped and underdeveloped countries.

The uncertainty and random nature of entanglement also provides a good analogy as we undertake the work of social justice. I cannot predict all of the effects of my actions. I can make an educated guess based on probability about the effect I think my action will have, but I cannot know for certain until the action is performed. Thus, there are always unexpected consequences to my actions, both positive and negative. Karl Rahner talks about this unintentional negative consequence as part of the concept of original sin. Even when I am working for justice and attempting to do the "right" act and make the "right" choice, there can be negative consequences that I did not foresee. My actions and choices hurt others. Such is part of the frailty of the human condition, a human condition we have traditionally called original sin. We seek the mercy and forgiveness of God and neighbor for this unintentional sin, as well as for those sins for which we are culpable. These unintended consequences are why the role of reflection is so important in our Christian theology and discernment. That reflection cannot be solipsistic. We must engage the other in our reflection before we take action and after we take action if we are to truly understand the impact and the consequences of our actions.

Hence, we no longer simply live in the era of paternalistic, charitable works. It is not enough to simply feed the hungry and clothe the naked. While we are clearly called to give to those in vulnerable situations and meet their immediate needs, we are also called to a deeper reflection about the root causes of their vulnerable situations, an awareness of how we as society contribute to the vulnerability of their situations, and an engagement of the other whom we are trying to serve so that the other is not a passive recipient of our "charity" but rather an active participant in her own liberation and the one who proclaims God's liberating Word.

The Body beyond the Church

Through the incarnation, Christ is united not only to baptized Christians but also to all humankind; so is the Body of Christ limited to Christians? Can the Body of Christ metaphor be extended beyond the church?[41] Humanity, in Karl Rahner's words, is the grammar of God; humanity is potential for incarnation, albeit not a potential any individual can fulfill.[42] Incarnation is something that God does in and through Christ. In the incarnation, God and creation are irrevocably united. So how is humanity related to the Body of Christ, if we understand wholeness and relationship to be a greater reality than individual parts? The church functions as the sacrament of this unity and is the symbol of creation's unity with God, but the reality being symbolized is much deeper than the limits of the Christian church. Flora Winfield notes:

> In the incarnation God, in Christ, breaks down everything that separates us from one another and from God. This is the context in which we ask, who belongs to the body of Christ? By his saving grace, Christ has overcome sin and death and opened the possibility of healing and liberation in new relationship with

[41] For an argument that the Body of Christ does not include all humanity but rather is limited to Christians who have accepted the call and the faith, see Daniel Payne, "Radical Atonement and the Cosmic Body of Christ," *Journal of Ecumenical Studies* 47, no. 2 (2012): 290ff. Payne does allow a cosmic body from God's perspective.

[42] Karl Rahner, *Foundations of Christian Faith: An Introduction to the Idea of Christianity* [Grundkurs des Glaubens], trans. William Dych (New York: Crossroad, 1978), 223.

God and between human beings. At the heart of the gospel are the words you are forgiven, and these are spoken to the whole human community, ourselves and our neighbours. God's self-offering generosity calls us, in turn, to respond to the need of the world, in our neighbour, for healing and freedom.[43]

Stephan Edmondson is a theologian and pastor of an Anglican congregation that practices completely open communion, not even requiring that a person be baptized in order to receive communion. He notes, "We invite all to the table, discerning in them not their baptismal status or lack thereof, but their status as the beloved of God to whom God has extended Godself in Christ, inviting them to come and eat. To withhold this invitation would be to call into question the welcome at the table of us all, since our worthiness to come to the table is grounded solely in the 'manifold and great mercy' of God."[44] While Edmondson's open approach may be disconcerting to many Christians, there is a key theological insight eloquently summarized by one of his parishioners: "We need to recognize that some cannot be 'more children of God' than others."[45] As is illustrated so beautifully in the story of the prodigal love of the father, the father does not love his sons because of what they have done or not done; he loves them because they are his sons. God does not love us because we are Christians; we are Christians in response to God's love.

The idea of this unity of all that exists is not unique to the Christian tradition. Nonlocality gives us a new way to think about interconnectedness that is congruent with the great Eastern religious traditions of Hinduism and Buddhism, and using science as a metaphor can give us a common language in interreligious dialogue. In Hinduism, there is an understanding of this unity of all that exists grounded in an understanding that everything that exists is a manifestation of the divine. Thus Hinduism teaches that another's well-being should be as important to me as my own because we are one. For Christians, the idea that all of reality is ultimately interconnected must have implications for how we think about the God that we believe created that reality and the way in which we relate to one another and crea-

---

[43] Winfield, "For Nothing Can Separate Us," 367.

[44] Stephen Edmondson, "Opening the Table: The Body of Christ and God's Prodigal Grace," *Anglican Theological Review* 91, no. 2 (March 2009): 219.

[45] Ibid., 222.

tion. The Buddhist notion of Indra's net illustrates not only the inter-connected nature of reality but also the way in which the whole is contained in each of the parts. At each interstice in Indra's net, there is said to be a jewel that reflects back all of the other connections. We are not individual beings, but rather we are in our very nature related and connected. The Buddhist doctrine of *anatman* or "no self" also expresses this interconnected nature of reality. The "no self" doctrine does not say that I don't exist as a person, an oft-mistaken interpreta-tion, but rather that I do not exist as an *independent* self. We have a different image of this "no self" doctrine in the Christian tradition, and it is the cross, the idea that the only way to save one's life is to lay it down for another. To take up one's cross and deny oneself is not self-denigrating any more than the Buddhist "no self" doctrine is self-denigrating; it simply acknowledges that the whole is greater than the parts, and the parts only have an existence as part of the whole. The reality behind this statement is that I have no life that is not interconnected with others. I only exist in and through my rela-tionships with others and with all of creation. Reality is one; reality is whole.

Christianity teaches this same principle in terms of loving one's neighbor as oneself. All three traditions can resonate with this new image of reality given by entanglement in which we are all one be-cause we are all part of one integrated, interconnected system. My well-being depends on the well-being of the whole, and vice versa. Thus I am compelled to work for social justice, for the well-being of the whole on a systemic level. This moral compulsion now goes beyond my individual, personal choices and my individual sin. There is a need for an awareness that my individual decisions impact the whole. There is an accountability not only for my personal decisions but also for the whole itself.

I am called, like the prophets of old, to look at the social, political, and economic structures of society and call for change when they are systems of oppression rather than liberation. The liberation of my brothers and sisters both in my own neighborhood and on the other side of the globe are my concern. I am my brothers' and sisters' keeper because they are part of me, and I am part of them. With a guiding image of reality based on the idea of entanglement and nonlocality, I can take a new perspective—one in which my fate is tied up with theirs and vice versa. This perspective, however, must not stay at the level of compassion but rather must translate into concrete action. To return to Paul's image of the body, if I were to have a gaping wound in my leg, my reaction would not be just to look at it and feel bad about it. I would seek medical attention because when my leg is in pain and not functioning properly, *I* am in pain. The *I* is more than just a collection of interchangeable and disposable parts.

Incarnation is the Christian doctrine at the heart of this unity of the divine with all humanity, but the incarnation refers not only to God being united to humankind but also, ultimately, to creation, to matter itself. God takes the created, material world and unites it to God's own reality. From Karl Rahner's perspective, the entire point of creation is for the sake of this union with God. God creates in order to unite what is other than God to God's self.[46] Paul asserts in Romans 8:22 that, in and through humanity, creation itself is groaning for the salvation we find in Christ. In the ancient hymn of Colossians 1:15-20, we read that Christ is the firstborn of all creation and that everything that exists was created in and through Christ.

What might change in our view of the world, if we start to think of creation as one system, one whole, rather than a collection of individual parts? Might we start to recognize that humans are not necessarily privileged over everything else that exists but rather are part of a system? When we don't value all parts of the system, we can damage the whole. When the whole is damaged, we destroy the very system that enables our own existence. This perspective has great consonance with Catholic social teaching on stewardship and care for all of God's creation. Our tradition teaches us to think of creation as a whole and to understand that God gives us the vocation of serving creation. We read in Genesis 2:15, "The LORD God then took the man and settled him in the garden of Eden, to cultivate and care for it." God asked Adam to cultivate the Garden of Eden, and in its most inaccurate interpretation, this passage can be falsely read as God giving humanity "dominion" over creation in the sense that we have the right to do with it as we please or whatever best serves our interest. Calvin DeWitt points out that the word that is used in this passage is *'abad*, which most often means to serve.[47] The same

---

[46] Rahner, *Foundations of Christian Faith*, 196–97.

[47] Calvin B. DeWitt, "Contemporary Missiology and the Biosphere," in *The Antioch Agenda: Essays on the Restorative Church in Honor of Orlando E. Costas*, ed. D. Jeyaraj, R. Pazmi, and R. Peterson (Delhi: ISPCK, 2007), 319–20.

word is used in Joshua 24:15, "choose today whom you will serve. . . . As for me and my household, we will serve the LORD." In expressing our service and care for creation, we are serving God. Likewise *shamar*, which is translated as "care" for the garden or the charge for Adam to "keep" the garden is the same word that is used in the blessing from Numbers 6:24, "The LORD bless you and keep you."[48] In other words, we are to care for creation in the same manner that God cares for us. The care and service we are supposed to give to creation is parallel to the service we are to give God, which again speaks to the unity and the wholeness of the "system."

Rarely in our congregations do we see the same emphasis on care for creation that we see on doing Bible studies, joining prayer groups, or taking our kids to Sunday School. Congregations do not over-whelmingly seem to associate a concern for the entirety of creation with the heart of Gospel values and what it means to be Christian. Particularly in a consumer culture, there is a sense that the earth exists to serve us rather than we exist to serve creation. Environmental concerns are secondary to economic concerns. The well-being of humanity, not only in the sense of survival but also in the sense of prosperity and wealth, is put before the concerns about the system as a whole. Understanding that reality itself is an interconnected whole can help us to look at creation differently. We can start to encourage congregations to get involved in urban gardening, recycling, and political lobbying efforts that highlight care for creation.

When we speak of the Body of Christ, we are talking about the reality that we are one whole and exist in relationship with one another. Like the particles in the EPR paradox, we are one entity, one system. We are entangled. Each part depends on the other parts and the actions of one affect the whole. Likewise, the actions of the whole impact the parts. The parts only have an identity in and through their relationships which make up the whole. In the Christian tradition, the Body of Christ image is usually used to describe the Christian family. The Second Vatican Council also used the image of the people of God to go beyond the Christian family to include all people of good will and, ultimately, all humankind. The people of God are the

[48] Calvin B. DeWitt, "Three Biblical Principles for Environmental Stewardship," Au Sable Institute of Environmental Studies, http://www.leaderu.com/theology/environment.html; DeWitt, *Contemporary Missiology and the Biosphere*, 315–16.

people that God has created and with whom God has chosen to be in relationship. We relate to God as a people. This relationship does not preclude our individual relationship with God, but rather it enables our individual relationship to God. Another way of stating this sentiment is the duality of loving God and loving one's neighbor, or to use the words from the letter of John, "For whoever does not love a brother whom he has seen cannot love God whom he has not seen" (1 John 4:20).

The worldview that sees reality as an interconnected whole has a perfect resonance with Paul's understanding of the community as the Body of Christ. As Barbara Brown Taylor points out, most often our congregational model is that of a corporation rather than a luminous web.[49] We need to use these more organic images such as web and entanglement to reinforce our sense of being part of something that is bigger than ourselves. Pope Francis likewise says, "Belonging to a people has a strong theological value. In the history of salvation, God has saved a people. There is no full identity without belonging to a people. No one is saved alone, as an isolated individual, but God attracts us looking at the complex web of relationships that take place in the human community. God enters into this dynamic, this participation in the web of human relationships."[50] Paul gives us the organic image of a body: one with different parts, but one in which all of the parts work together and are necessary for the greater whole. No part can be considered less important than another part. Likewise, one cannot be the Body of Christ by oneself. I am only a member of the Body of Christ in and through my relationship with others. I can only be the ongoing, sacramental presence of God's Love as part of the whole.

---

[49] Barbara Brown Taylor, *The Luminous Web: Essays on Science and Religion* (Cambridge, MA: Cowley Publications, 2000), 29.

[50] Spadaro, "A Big Heart Open to God," 20, 22.

Chapter Four

Chaos and Complexity

Scientific Developments— Chaos Theory and Complexity

The second law of thermodynamics tells us that we are in a universe that is evolving toward entropy or disorder.[1] Words like "randomness" and "chaos" often have negative connotations in our everyday usage. In chaos theory, however, we see that the complexity that leads to life only exists on the edge of chaos. Some basic concepts in chaos theory and the development of nonlinear complex systems in creation can help us come to a greater appreciation of complexity in our human interactions by recognizing that complexity is an inherent part of the created order. Rather than seeing chaos and complexity as a threat to our ability to control and predict our environment, complexity can be seen as an inherent part of creation. Thus one can appreciate the beauty and intricacy that exists when things are not simple, enabling us to enter hopefully into a more civil and compassionate discourse that embraces diversity in a context of unity and wholeness.

At the outset, we need to make some distinctions between the terms "chaos" and "complexity."[2] In science, a complex system is one

---

[1] The first law of thermodynamics is the conservation of energy; the second is the increase of entropy.

[2] Dean Rickles, Penelope Hawe, and Alan Shiell, "A Simple Guide to Chaos and Complexity," *Journal of Epidemiology and Community Health* 61 (2007): 933–37.

that has a very large number of parts that interact with one another which allows the system to self-organize.[3] John Haught notes that complex systems refer to "all emergent, adaptive, self-organizing, informationally rich systems in both non-human nature and human culture as well" with "the concept of 'complexity' as the broader of the two notions, inclusive of the physics of chaos."[4] A chaotic system may have many parts or very few parts, but as will be explained in more detail below, the system is extremely sensitive to its initial conditions and creates very intricate patterns of interaction.[5] In his book, *Deep Simplicity: Bringing Order to Chaos and Complexity*, John Gribbin notes that when science uses the word "chaos," it does not mean the same thing the word means in our colloquial language.[6] Gribbin explains that the scientific understanding of chaos is that it "is completely orderly and deterministic, with one step following from another in an unbroken chain of cause and effect that is completely predictable at every stage—in principle. It is just that in practice it is impossible to predict in detail what is going to happen more quickly

---

[3] Ibid., 933. The authors also make the distinction between a complex system and a complicated system. In a complex system, if one part is removed, the remaining parts can adapt. In a complicated system, such as a complicated machine, if one part is removed, the system will cease functioning.

[4] John Haught, "Chaos, Complexity, and Theology," in *Teilhard in the 21st Century: The Emerging Spirit of Earth*, ed. Arthur Fabel and Donald P. St. John (Maryknoll, NY: Orbis Books, 2003), 185. Note that Rickles, et al., emphasize that chaos and complexity have similarities, but that they are not the same thing: "*Chaos* is the generation of complicated, aperiodic, seemingly random behaviour from the *iteration* of a simple rule. This complicatedness is not complex in the sense of complex systems science, but rather it is chaotic in a very precise mathematical sense. *Complexity* is the generation of rich, collective dynamical behaviour from simple *interactions* between large numbers of subunits. Chaotic systems are not necessarily complex, and complex systems are not necessarily chaotic." Rickles, Hawe, and Shiell, "A Simple Guide to Chaos and Complexity," 934. Both chaotic systems and complex systems are nonlinear and therefore extremely sensitive to initial conditions, concepts that will be described in more detail in what follows. Chaos and complexity are related to one another at a point that is referred to as a critical point, also referred to as the edge of chaos: "A system that is at a critical point has an extremely high degree of connectivity between its subunits: everything depends on everything else! Complex systems are said to be poised at such a position, between order and chaos." Rickles, Hawe, and Shiell, "A Simple Guide to Chaos and Complexity," 935.

[5] Ibid., 933.

[6] John Gribbin, *Deep Simplicity: Bringing Order to Chaos and Complexity* (New York: Random House, 2004), xvii.

than events unfold in real time."[7] What makes a system chaotic, according to John Gribbin, are two basic features: extreme sensitivity to initial conditions and feedback.[8]

A chaotic system is nonlinear, and so it is extremely sensitive to its initial conditions. Gribbin uses a good image to illustrate this point in his book *Deep Simplicity*. He notes that we walk in a linear way—if you take two steps down the road, you are twice as far as if you take one step. If you could walk in a nonlinear fashion, however, each step would take you twice as far as the one before, so let's say your first step is about a foot, your second would be two feet, so you have now gone three feet in two steps. Your third step would be four feet and your fourth would be eight feet, moving you a total of fifteen feet in four steps. Now it starts to get really interesting as your fifth step moves you sixteen feet, your sixth thirty-two feet, and your seventh sixty-four, etc. In ten steps, you will have moved one thousand twenty-three feet. To take Gribbin's example a step further, imagine you are following a treasure map that tells you to take ten steps in a certain direction, but your first step is angled about fifteen degrees in the wrong direction. When you start digging for your treasure, you will end up pretty close to where you were meant to be when you started—perhaps even close enough to find the treasure; certainly close enough to easily correct your mistake once you realize that you made it. Now imagine you moved ten nonlinear steps in the wrong direction. You have a much bigger error in your path now. You certainly will not find the treasure where you are digging, and you will need to make a much bigger correction to put yourself on the "X" that marks the spot. Another way of stating this point is that a linear system is basically the sum of its parts—ten steps is equal to ten feet—but a nonlinear system is either much greater or much less than the sum of its parts, as we see when ten steps equals 1023 feet. This nonlinear feature of chaotic systems means that they are often unsolvable as well as unpredictable. Steven Strogatz explains that nonlinear problems are unsolvable because complex problems are generally solved by breaking them down into simpler components,

---

[7] Ibid., 74.
[8] Ibid., xx.

solving the components and then adding them back together.[9] Non-linear systems cannot be solved by adding together their component parts.[10] Strogatz goes on to point out that nonlinear systems are more common than linear systems in nature, explaining, "Whenever parts of a system interfere, cooperate, or compete, there are non-linear interactions going on."[11]

Nonlinear systems are not only unsolvable but also unpredictable. One of the hallmarks of a chaotic system explained above is its extreme sensitivity to initial conditions. The slightest change in initial conditions has results that are completely unpredictable. Unlike quantum mechanics, where the unpredictability may be part of reality itself, in chaotic systems the unpredictability has to do with what we are capable of knowing about the system (epistemology—what we can know), not how the system is in itself (ontology—what really exists). The system itself is completely deterministic. In theory, if we could get all of the information about the system, we could completely predict what it would do. Take the example of weather. If we could know everything there is to know about a weather system, we could, in theory, precisely predict the weather. The problem is that it is completely impossible for us to know all of the conditions of a weather system, and the smallest amount of missing information leads to exponentially large miscalculations, hence we can predict the weather in the next hour or even the next day or maybe two, but the further out we try to predict, the more inaccurate our calculations become. The issue is that we can never know the initial conditions precisely enough to do the calculations. Consider the fact that between an interval, say 1 and 0, there are an infinite number of points, some of which can be described by fractions, but most of which cannot be described by fractions because they are what we call irrational numbers. An irrational number is a decimal with an infinite number of decimal places that display an erratic sequence such that no sequence ever repeats itself; thus one has to round it off at some point

[9] Steven H. Strogatz, *Nonlinear Dynamics and Chaos: With Applications to Physics, Biology, Chemistry, and Engineering* (Reading, MA: Addison-Wesley, 1994), 8–9.

[10] Ibid., 9.

[11] Ibid.

in order to use it in a calculation or a computer algorithm.[12] A familiar example of an irrational number is *pi*. As soon as we round off an irrational number, for example *pi*, in our calculations, our calculation is now inaccurate, and the magnitude of that error increases exponentially throughout the system so that our initial calculations are entirely off base. As Gribbin points out, "In a system that is sufficiently sensitive to initial conditions, it is always possible that, no matter how many digits we choose to work with, the entire future of the system may, as Lorenz discovered, depend significantly on the value of the next digit, the one we have in effect thrown away."[13] Likewise, Davies points out that because the systems grow exponentially, "more and more information must be processed to maintain the same level of accuracy, and the calculation can barely keep pace with the actual events."[14] He concludes, "In other words, we are not predicting anything, merely describing the system to a certain limited level of accuracy as it evolves in real time."[15] While *pi* actually can be specified by a finite computer algorithm, it turns out that most numbers cannot; they "require infinite computer programming information for their generation, and can therefore be considered infinitely complex." As such, they are "completely incalculable."[16] Many might be vaguely familiar with the title of Edward Lorenz's 1972 talk, "Predictability: Does the Flap of a Butterfly's Wing in Brazil Set Off a Tornado in Texas?" or what came to be known as the Butterfly Effect. Unfortunately, what we learn from Lorenz is that even with the fastest supercomputer conceivable, it would take longer to do the calculations to predict the weather than it would take for the weather to happen, so that by the time we finished our calculations, the day for which we were trying to predict the weather would have long since come and gone.

---

[12] Paul Davies, *The Cosmic Blueprint: New Discoveries in Nature's Creative Ability to Order the Universe* (Philadelphia, PA: Templeton Foundation Press, 2004), 32. An algorithm is a description of a number that can be used for the purpose of computing. John Gribbin gives the example of "the decimal 0.6754867548675486" written as an algorithm, which would be "take the digits 675486 and keep repeating them forever." Gribbin, *Deep Simplicity*, 71.

[13] Ibid., 72

[14] Davies, *The Cosmic Blueprint*, 54.

[15] Ibid.

[16] Ibid., 34.

We cannot keep up with chaotic systems; the systems grow faster than we can calculate. Davies illustrates this point with an example of trying to compute a chaotic orbit of some particle one minute ahead. For a certain computer it might take one hour (note, the computation time is already significantly longer than the time of the orbit we are trying to compute) to compute that one minute. To compute two minutes would take ten times the amount of data and ten hours; three minutes, one hundred times the data and one hundred hours; four minutes would take one thousand hours, and so on.[17] Paul Davies highlights the work of Joseph Ford making the argument that the difference between epistemology and ontology gets very fuzzy at this point—what we do not know is in fact unknowable, and these scientists argue that any determinism is a myth. He cites Ford's conclusion:

> Unfortunately, non-chaotic systems are very nearly as scarce as hen's teeth, despite the fact that our physical understanding of nature is largely based upon their study [45]. . . . For centuries, randomness has been deemed a useful, but subservient citizen in a deterministic universe. Algorithmic complexity theory and nonlinear dynamics together establish the fact that determinism actually reigns only over a quiet finite domain; outside this small haven of order lies a largely uncharted, vast wasteland of chaos where determinism has faded into an ephemeral memory of existence theorems and only randomness survives [44].[18]

In other words, much of what exists in our world is chaos and indeterminacy; we live in a world of uncertainty and unpredictability, despite the fact that our human nature tends to long for the opposite.

Another hallmark of chaotic systems, as was seen in the earlier example of nonlinear footsteps that went one, two, four, eight feet, etc., is repeated bifurcations. Repeated bifurcations, also known as period doubling, lead to "patterns within patterns that are said to be self-similar."[19] In other words, with period doubling, one sees a pattern that is repeated on different scales. A nautilus shell is an image that illustrates a self-similar pattern (see figure 4.1).

---

[17] Ibid., 54.

[18] Joseph Ford, "How Random Is a Coin Toss?," *Scientific American* 36, no. 4 (April 1983): 44, 45. Cited in Davies, *The Cosmic Blueprint*, 55.

[19] Gribbin, *Deep Simplicity*, 80.

Figure 4.1 [20]

Nautilus shell with a self-repeating pattern

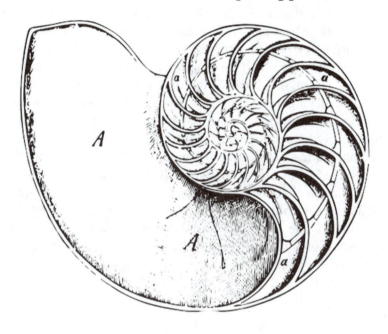

One of the fascinating points about this process of bifurcation is that the ratio of one step relative to the next is constant; in any system it is (to three decimal places) 4.669:1.[21] In chaos theory, there are what are called "strange attractors." To quote Gribbin, a strange attractor is one in which "the trajectory through phase space of the point describing the system would correspond to an infinitely long line wrapped in a complex way, without ever crossing itself, around a finite surface."[22] These strange attractors are called fractals. A fractal

---

[20] J. Sterling Kingsley, "Popular Natural History: A Description of Animal Life, from the Lowest Forms Up to Man, vol. 1," *Wikimedia Commons*, http://commons .wikimedia.org/wiki/File%3ANautilus-pompilius.svg.

[21] Gribbin, *Deep Simplicity*, 84. This ratio is referred to as Feigenbaum constant after the mathematician Mitchell Feigenbaum who discovered this ratio. Gribbin gives examples of several types of systems in nature that follow this ratio, such as earthquakes, mass extinctions, and the way rocks (or potatoes, for that matter) break.

[22] Ibid., 87. Rickles, et al., explain phase space as the representation of a system and the values of its variables at an instant in time where "a state [of the system] is represented by a point in geometrical space (phase space), with axes corresponding

involves the combination of the infinite and the finite in that it falls between spatial dimensions or more accurately has a dimension that is a fraction, hence why it was named a "fractal." Gribbin describes this aspect of a fractal as a line that is trying to be a point, or a line that is trying to be a plane. He gives the example of a Peano curve (see figure 4.2), a line that can "be made to twist and turn inside a plane in such a way that it passe[s] through every point in the plane, without ever crossing itself."[23] In other words, "a line that is more than a line, 'trying' to be a plane."[24] Another example is a Cantor set (see figure 4.3), which is "a line that is less than a line, 'trying' to be a point."[25] Other examples that are fascinating to ponder are the Sierpinski triangle[26] (see figure 4.4) and the Koch curve[27] or snowflake (see figure 4.5). Fractals often involve stretching and folding so two points on a line that are very far away from each other may end up right next to each other as the line is stretched and folded. This intricate pattern is the result of a fractal not fitting neatly into our preconceived ideas of dimensions. To only see in two or three dimensions is to miss the wonder and the beauty of the between.

---

to the variables. The coordinates then correspond to particular assignments of values to each variable. The number of variables defines the dimension of both the space and the system. Each point in the phase space represents a way in which the system could be at a time, corresponding to an assignment of particular values to the variables at an instant. . . . A path through the phase space corresponds to a trajectory of the system, or a way in which the system could evolve over time." Rickles, Hawe, and Shiell, "A Simple Guide to Chaos and Complexity," 933.

[23] Gribbin, *Deep Simplicity*, 88.

[24] Ibid., 90.

[25] Ibid.

[26] The Sierpinski gasket can be drawn as a game. See the description in Gribbin, *Deep Simplicity*, 93–94; to see a great animation of this chaos game online, see Zoharby, "Sierpinski Chaos Animated," *Wikimedia Commons*, http://commons.wikimedia.org/wiki/File%3ASierpinski_chaos_animated.gif.

[27] For a description of how to draw a Koch Curve, see Gribbin, *Deep Simplicity*, 97–98. This same concept can be applied to measuring a coastline because a coastline is not straight—it has an irregular border. The smaller the scale you use to measure the coastline (e.g., a ruler versus a yardstick), the more irregularities are accounted for and the longer the coastline. The measurement can approach infinity as you use smaller and smaller scales.

Figure 4.2

Peano Curve[28]

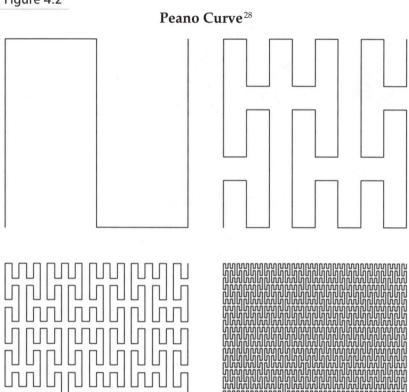

Figure 4.3

Cantor Set[29]

[28] Gunther, "Peano Curve," *Wikimedia Commons*, http://commons.wikimedia.org/wiki/File:Peano_curve.png.

[29] "Cantor Set in Seven Iterations." *Wikimedia Commons*, http://commons.wikimedia.org/wiki/File%3ACantor_set_in_seven_iterations.svg.

Figure 4.4

Sierpinski Triangle[30]

Figure 4.5

Koch Curve or Snowflake[31]

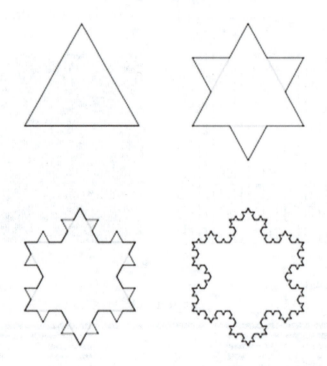

[30] "Sierpinski Triangle Evolution." *Wikimedia Commons*, http://commons.wikimedia.org/wiki/File:Sierpinski_triangle_evolution.svg.

[31] W. Xavier Snelgrave, "Koch Flake," *Wikimedia Commons*, http://commons.wikimedia.org/wiki/File:KochFlake.svg.

The final concept of chaos theory that needs to be considered is entropy. Entropy is the measure of order/disorder in a system. While the laws of physics do not specify a direction to time, which is to say that the laws (or equations) of physics work equally well in either direction,[32] many speculate that the increase of entropy over time is what gives time its arrow of direction. As Gribbin points out, over time things wear out and break down.[33] Gribbin notes that the universe works in this way. He explains that you cannot put the universe back the way it used to be.[34] Paul Davies describes the second law of thermodynamics as the

> natural tendency for order to give way to chaos. It is not hard to find examples in the world around us: people grow old, snowmen melt, houses fall down, cars rust, and stars burn out. Although islands of order may appear in restricted regions (e.g., the birth of a baby, crystals emerging from a solute), the disorder of the environment will always rise by an amount sufficient to compensate. This one-way slide into disorder is measured by a quantity called entropy.[35]

Other common examples of our experience of entropy are an egg breaking or a glass of wine spilling, or more viscerally, our bodies aging. We do not experience a broken egg reassembling or a spilled liquid coalescing. It is important to note that in theory it could, it is just highly improbable. One common example used to explain entropy is a deck of cards. Consider a deck of cards in order by number and

---

[32] Recall from chapter 1 that in its simplest form, this statement refers to the commutative property of mathematics, e.g., $A+B=B+A$, in which changing the order of the terms does not change the results. The laws or equations of physics demonstrate this property, so that mathematically, past and future do not make a difference in the results of the equations—the terms are reversible.

[33] Gribbin, *Deep Simplicity*, 26.

[34] Ibid., 27.

[35] Paul Davies, "Complexity and the Arrow of Time," in *From Complexity to Life: On the Emergence of Life and Meaning*, ed. Niels Henrik Gregersen (New York: Oxford University Press, 2003), 72. Note that the example of snow or ice melting presumes a temperature above freezing. Water freezing does not violate the second law of thermodynamics. Heat always moves from the warmer body to the colder body. We experience this phenomenon when someone touches us with cold hands. The heat from our body moves to the other person's body, so we experience the sensation of cold at the point of contact.

suit. If you randomly shuffle the cards, it is highly unlikely that they will return to the same order, no matter how many times you shuffle them.[36] The reason is that there are many, many ways in which the cards can be out of order but only one way they can be in order, so it is much more probable that randomly shuffling them will result in their being disordered rather than ordered. Again, I would note, however, that it is not impossible, just highly, highly improbable.[37] Of course, Paul Davies notes that in this example, we have designated one state of the cards as ordered and every other state of the cards as disordered.[38] Thus the arrow of time "clearly does not come from the shuffling as such; rather, it owes its origin to the special, orderly nature of the initial state."[39] The sequential order we designate is no more or less likely to emerge than any other specified order. The difference is that we specify one sequence as ordered on the one hand, and every other possible sequence as disordered on the other, so in terms of statistics and probability, the shuffled deck is most likely to have a sequence that we have designated as disordered.

Ultimately, maximum entropy of an isolated system is a state called thermodynamic equilibrium, which is a state of maximum entropy (or disorder) and minimum energy. The term "equilibrium" in a scientific sense is a bit counterintuitive to our everyday experience, as we tend to think of chaos or disorder and equilibrium as opposite terms. Here equilibrium is equivalent to the maximum state of disorder or high entropy.[40] The state of equilibrium is an attractor, meaning exactly what it sounds like, that systems are attracted or drawn toward that state.[41] Brian Greene suggests that the big bang created

---

[36] If you were to do a perfect shuffle, in which the deck is cut exactly in half and the cards are shuffled every other one, instead of a random shuffle, you would return to your original sequence in eight shuffles. See Francis Edward Su, "Perfect Shuffles," Harvey Mudd College Math Department, https://www.math.hmc.edu/funfacts /ffiles/20001.1-6.shtml.

[37] Gribbin, *Deep Simplicity*, 26–27; Davies, *The Cosmic Blueprint*, 16–17.

[38] Ibid., 16.

[39] Ibid., 17.

[40] Consider a gas in an enclosed space in thermodynamic equilibrium. The molecules will be spread out evenly within the space, and while intuitively one might think of this arrangement as very ordered, in scientific terms it is considered "disordered." Order would indicate a lack of uniformity, because to create order, molecules would be joined together or moving in various arrangements instead of evenly distributed.

[41] Gribbin, *Deep Simplicity*, 29.

a situation of incredibly low entropy and that all of the order we experience today is still a result of that initial order, but it continues to evolve toward disorder, which is to say that entropy continues to increase, hence the egg cracks and the wine spills.[42]

While not denying that entropy in the universe increases, John Haught argues that order and complexity are also increasing in the universe: "The universe seemed to be heading down the slopes of entropy to an abyss of absolute disorder. But a growing number of scientists now acknowledge that there is nothing in the notion of entropy itself that helps us understand why the cosmos, from its very beginning, has also moved toward increasingly diverse and more complex forms of order."[43] Furthermore, while thermodynamic equilibrium is inevitable in an isolated system, John Gribbin points out that in nature "there is no such thing as an isolated system (except for the entire universe),[44] and no system is ever in perfect equilibrium. It may get very close to equilibrium—close as you like, if you wait long enough—but the equilibrium is never literally perfect."[45]

Why is this idea that systems may be close to equilibrium, but not perfect, so important? Because it turns out that very interesting things happen in systems that are not in equilibrium. Our very existence depends on disequilibrium.[46] Disordered systems can in fact create order spontaneously.[47] Gribbin explains, "The pieces of the system interact with one another to produce something that is greater than

---

[42] Brian Greene, *The Fabric of the Cosmos: Space, Time, and the Texture of Reality* (New York: A. A. Knopf, 2004), 173–74.

[43] Haught, "Chaos, Complexity, and Theology," 181–94. Cites Ilya Prigogine and Isabelle Stengers, *Order Out of Chaos: Man's New Dialogue with Nature* (Toronto: Bantam Books, 1984) and Louise B. Young, *The Unfinished Universe* (New York: Simon and Schuster, 1986).

[44] While many cosmologists take it for granted that our observable universe is an isolated system, there are theories today that suggest that it could be an open system that is a part of a larger whole referred to as a multiverse. John Polkinghorne notes that "there are some perplexities and disputed points about the application of thermodynamics to the whole universe. They arise from consideration of the exact sense in which it might be said to be an isolated system and from some subtleties in the thermodynamic properties of large-scale gravitating systems." *Science and Theology: An Introduction* (Minneapolis, MN: Fortress Press, 1998), 45.

[45] Gribbin, *Deep Simplicity*, 29.

[46] Davies, *Complexity and the Arrow of Time*, 73.

[47] Gribbin, *Deep Simplicity*, 29.

the sum of its parts. And that's complexity founded upon deep sim-plicity."[48] Patterns form spontaneously through interacting parts of a system in a process of self-organization. This emergence of patterns happens at the edge of chaos. The beauty of chaos is that what looks very disordered and random from one perspective, for example, examining individual points in a system, displays an extremely com-plex and intricate pattern from another perspective, for example, looking at the fractal pattern that emerges as the points move through phase space. This creation of order out of disorder and complexity out of simplicity is often referred to as symmetry-breaking. Symmetry-breaking may contribute to the arrow of time, in addition to the increase in entropy discussed above, resulting in an increase of dis-equilibrium and complexity in the universe.[49] Furthermore, extremely complex and intricate patterns often emerge from very simple laws. Haught explains that "chaotic activity is apparently guided in some largely unknown way by 'strange attractors' that hold the chaos within bounds and bestow on it a surprisingly rich pattern."[50] To put it another way, John Polkinghorne talks about structured randomness where the future options are contained within the limits of the strange attractors.[51] Haught describes these attractors as influencing the present from the future, invoking Wolfhart Pannenberg's idea of "the arrival of the future in the present."[52] Paul Davies argues for something like a "principle of increasing complexity," elaborating that "the rich and complex state of the universe as observed today did not exist at the outset. Instead it emerged in a long and compli-cated sequence of self-organizing and self-complexifying processes, involving symmetry breaking, gravitational clustering, and the dif-ferentiation of matter."[53] Haught suggests, "If natural order were

---

[48] Ibid., 147.

[49] Haught, "Chaos, Complexity, and Theology," 188, quoting Davies, *The Cosmic Blueprint*, 112–15.

[50] Haught, "Chaos, Complexity, and Theology," 182.

[51] John C. Polkinghorne, *The Faith of a Physicist: Reflections of a Bottom-Up Thinker* (Minneapolis, MN: Fortress, 1996), 25.

[52] Haught, "Chaos, Complexity, and Theology," 189. Haught cites Wolfhart Pannen-berg and Ted Peters, *Toward a Theology of Nature: Essays on Science and Faith* (Louisville, KY: Westminster/J. Knox Press, 1993), 83–85.

[53] Davies, *Complexity and the Arrow of Time*, 85. Note that Davies is clear that such a principle would in no way contradict the second law of thermodynamics. He ex-plains that the complexification of the universe received energy from the rapid expan-sion of the universe which created an "entropy gap." That gap is closing. Thus, the

absolutely inflexible and resistant to processes like 'symmetry break-ing,' there could be no emergent novelty, no growth, no life, no evo-lutionary adaption, no new patterning. From this point of view, entropy is the occasion less for cosmic pessimism than for hope that the universe is always open to new creation."[54]

Complexity

As was noted in our initial definitions, a complex system is one that contains a large number of parts, and it involves an emergent process of self-organization.[55] Complex systems often exist or emerge at that critical point between order and chaos. As John Haught points out, "Many physical processes that start out with a simple kind of orderliness suddenly move toward turbulence, but end up producing surprisingly richer forms of order out of the chaos, an order often so intricate and complex that it can be mapped only with the help of computers."[56]

John Gribbin explains that complexity is what happens in an open system, and as was noted above, most systems are open. He argues that in an open system, one finds nonequilibrium and the dissipation of energy, which lead to irreversibility and an arrow of time.[57] A state that is open is open to its environment.[58] Complexity only happens

---

total entropy of the cosmos is increasing, but it will do so over a vast amount of time. He also holds out the possibility that unknown factors could increase the entropy gap in the future, thus slowing or possibly even reversing the slide of the universe into heat death. Davies, *Complexity and the Arrow of Time*, 83–86.

[54] Haught, "Chaos, Complexity, and Theology," 191.

[55] Niels Henrik Gregersen explains that chaos and complexity both "deal with non-linear processes in which small and simple inputs can lead to large and complex outputs," but the two are different in that complex systems "are more robust" with the ability to adjust to a "variety of initial conditions." Niels Henrik Gregersen, ed., *From Complexity to Life: On the Emergence of Life and Meaning* (New York: Oxford University Press, 2003), 207.

[56] Haught, "Chaos, Complexity, and Theology," 182.

[57] Gribbin, *Deep Simplicity*, 110.

[58] Rickles, Hawe, and Shiell explain the concept as follows: "Complex systems often exhibit *self-organisation*, which happens when systems spontaneously order them-selves (generally in an optimal or more stable way) without 'external' tuning of a control parameter (see below). This feature is not found in chaotic systems and is often called *anti-chaos* [cites Donald S. Coffey, "Self-Organization, Complexity and Chaos: The New Biology for Medicine," *Nature Medicine* 4, no. 8 (1998): 882–85]. Such

with openness. With a closed or isolated system, one that is closed to or isolated from its environment, one gets equilibrium and entropy. Robert John Russell explains that open, nonlinear systems "can undergo spontaneous and rapid transitions into new and more complex states. This principle means that in these open systems, new levels of order and complexity, and thus lower entropy, spontaneously occur as entropy is exchanged with the environment containing them."[59] Systems that develop a stable pattern of complexity on the edge of chaos exist in a state called self-organized criticality.[60] What makes a system complex and allows it to self-regulate in this way are the networks and interactions between its component parts.[61] In the study of living chaotic and complex systems, equilibrium is equivalent to death, whether one looks at the scope of the universe in its increasing entropy or the human person in death. Life occurs at this critical complex point on the edge of chaos.

Creation of the Universe

In the beginning, there was (perhaps) a quantum fluctuation, and some form of energy pushed out the fabric of space. Creation evolves from order and simplicity, a universe that was dense, hot, and smooth in its beginning, bursting into a uniform existence of particles out of which developed primarily just hydrogen and helium toward entropy, disorder, and chaos.[62] Ultimately the second law of thermodynamics,

---

systems also tend to be *out of equilibrium*, which means that the system never settles in to a steady state of behavior. This is related to the concept of openness: a system is *open* if it is not or cannot be screened off from its environment. In *closed systems*, outside influences (exogenous variables) can be ignored. For open systems, this is not the case. Most real-world systems are open, thus this presents problems both for modeling and experimenting on such systems, because the effect of exogenous influences must be taken into account. Such influences can be magnified over time by sensitivity to initial conditions." Rickles, Hawe, and Shiell, "A Simple Guide to Chaos and Complexity," 935.

[59] Robert J. Russell, *Time in Eternity: Pannenberg, Physics, and Eschatology in Creative Mutual Interaction* (Notre Dame, IN: University of Notre Dame Press, 2012), 329.

[60] Gribbin, *Deep Simplicity*, 169.

[61] Ibid., 174.

[62] Note again Davies's explanation that while the universe was in a very high entropy state, hence its smoothness (remember that for a gas, the maximum state of entropy is thermodynamic equilibrium, in which the molecules are spread out evenly),

which tells us that entropy or disorder always increases, predicts a rather gloomy future for the universe in which the energy of the universe is eventually all used up (e.g., all of the stars burn up all of their fuel, expending all of their heat), leaving a dark, cold place in which life no longer exists. Greene argues, "Incredible order at the beginning is what started it all off, and we have been living through the gradual unfolding of higher disorder ever since."[63] All current cosmological observations to date seem to confirm that the universe is expanding at an ever increasing rate, and eventually the stars will be too far from one another to even be seen, leading to a cold, dark universe in which the stars go out one by one and eventually matter

the rapid expansion of the universe created an "entropy gap" and the gravitational field provided the energy (think of the clumpiness rather than smoothness that comes from gravity pulling together those molecules of gas) thus creating the conditions for complexity. Davies, *Complexity and the Arrow of Time*, 76–83.

[63] Greene, *Fabric of the Cosmos*, 172. Greene maintains that the uniform gas we see at the beginning of the universe might seem to indicate high entropy, but in fact, when gravity is added to the equation, a high entropy state would be one of massive black holes, so the uniform gas is actually a state of low entropy. Gravity has the effect of making the universe very "clumpy," as matter is drawn together. In Greene's words, "atoms and molecules evolve from a smooth, evenly spread configuration, into one involving larger and denser clumps." While it might seem that such arrangements indicate an increase in order (and thus a decrease in entropy), in fact the heat and light that are generated by the formation of stars actually totals an increase in entropy (172–73). He goes on to note that "in the formation of order there is generally a more-than-compensating generation of disorder" (173). As was noted above, Paul Davies explains that in the beginning state of the universe, matter and radiation were in a high entropy state, thus it was smooth or uniform, a fact that we see in the uniform state of the cosmic microwave radiation background today. Davies, *Complexity and the Arrow of Time*, 79. The gravitational field, however, was in a low entropy state (80). Davies continues, "As the universe expanded, there was a transfer of energy from the gravitational field to the matter. . . . Because the rate of expansion was very rapid relative to the physical processes involved, a lag opened up between the maximum possible entropy and the actual entropy, both of which were rising. In this way, the universe was pulled away from thermodynamic equilibrium by the expansion" (82). Davies concludes, "The history of the universe, then, is one of entropy rising but chasing a moving target, because the expanding universe is raising the maximum possible entropy at the same time" (82). Davies notes that "the effect of starlight emission is to slightly close the entropy gap, but all the while the expanding universe serves to widen it" (83). While Davies speculates that the gap may be starting to close, he also notes that given the current observation of the acceleration of the expansion of the universe, the gap could open up again. Thus the fate of the universe is unknown. The expanding universe could "continue to provide free energy for life and other processes," or it could "fail to keep pace with the dissipation of energy by entropy generating processes such as starlight emission" (83).

itself disintegrates. But before we arrive at that final state of entropy or on our journey there, we find that out of this movement toward entropy, disorder, and chaos, but prior to reaching a state of thermodynamic equilibrium, what emerges are astonishing points of complexity. In these places, order spontaneously evolves out of disorder, even while the total disorder or entropy continues to increase.

John Polkinghorne, in his work *Science and Theology*, introduces the idea of the evolution of complexity. He states, "The whole history of the universe, and particularly the history of biological life on Earth, has been characterized by the steady emergence of complexity. The story moves from an initial cosmos that was just a ball of expanding energy to a universe of stars and galaxies; then, on at least one planet, to replicating molecules, to cellular organisms, to multicellular life, to conscious life, and to humankind."[64] He calls this process "the spontaneous generation of order out of chaos" and following Stuart Kauffman suggests that there may be "a natural propensity for matter to organize in particular, complex ways."[65] Paul Davies explains that "the primeval universe was probably in a state of extreme—perhaps maximal—simplicity. At the present epoch, by contrast, complexity abounds on all scales of size from molecules to galactic superclusters. So there exists something like a law of increasing complexity."[66] Complex systems, according to Davies, generally have four features: complexity appears abruptly, the systems have a very large number of components, they are open, not closed systems, and they are nonlinear.

Gribbin notes that "a system can only be held in an interesting state away from equilibrium if it is dissipative and open to the environment, so there has to be an outside source of energy."[67] He explains that for the earth, that source of energy is the sun, and for the universe, the source of energy is gravity. Gravitational fields "swallow up entropy," to use Gribbin's phrase, and explain why the universe is not in thermodynamic equilibrium.[68] Gravity pulls together dust and gases that become stars. Stars heat up through nuclear fusion,

[64] Polkinghorne, *Science and Theology: An Introduction*, 44.
[65] Ibid.
[66] Davies, *Complexity and the Arrow of Time*, 21.
[67] Gribbin, *Deep Simplicity*, 115.
[68] Ibid., 120.

and thus they are also not in a state of thermodynamic equilibrium, and they produce energy. As previous generations of stars die, they explode into clouds of gases and elements, which again due to gravity pull together to give birth to new stars. Our star is a third-generation star, which created the heavier elements that enabled carbon-based life to emerge.[69]

Complexity is not just the law of the cosmos—it is the law of life itself. Gribbin explains that the earth itself is an open, dissipative system dependent on the energy from the sun to "maintain itself far from equilibrium, on the edge of chaos."[70] Most of us are probably familiar with the chain of life that sustains our system on earth. Plants get their energy from photosynthesis, animals eat plants, carnivores eat those animals, etc.[71] Life on earth itself is an open, complex system on the edge of chaos. One sobering way in which we see that the earth's ecosystem has self-organized and regulated is through the pattern of mass extinctions. There is every reason in terms of statistics to assume that humanity will eventually be the victim of one such mass extinction long before the sun burns up the earth and long, long before the possible entropic death of the universe. Such an extinction could be set off by a collision with an asteroid, but it need not be; the study of extinctions in terms of a complex system tells us that an extinction of any size might be set off by a trigger of any size. A large extinction does not necessarily need a large trigger.[72] Because our entire ecosystem functions as a complex system, what seems to be inconsequential, say the extinction of an obscure species of bug, could prove to be catastrophic for human life. The system is more than the sum of its parts, and small triggers can have exponentially large effects. The image Gribbin uses to explain this system response is a pile of sand. Add one grain of sand at a time to the pile, and most of the time nothing happens or what happens is a very insignificant shift of grains in the immediate area, until at one point a single grain of sand is added, and the entire side of the pile collapses.[73] Furthermore,

---

[69] George V. Coyne and Alessandro Omizzolo, *Wayfarers in the Cosmos: The Human Quest for Meaning* (New York: Crossroad, 2002), 112.

[70] Gribbin, *Deep Simplicity*, 120.

[71] Ibid., 121.

[72] Ibid., 165.

[73] Ibid., 169–70.

a variety of types of events follow the same exact power law—mass extinctions, earthquakes, the light from quasars, traffic jams, grains of sand, the way that asteroids break as they collide in space, and the way that frozen potatoes break when fired against a wall, to name a few examples.[74] These simple laws that generate complex systems also govern human existence in the very way our DNA interacts with our cells.

When we look at the cosmos, people are one of its most complex features, as John Gribbin points out.[75] Gribbin explains that on very small scales, such as the atom, interactions tend to be one-to-one, whereas when many atoms are together, such as in a person, interactions get very complex. Continuing to add more and more atoms, however, adds to the total mass so that structure is crushed by gravity. As Gribbin summarizes, "An atom, or even a simple molecule like water, is simpler than a human being because it has little internal structure; a star, or the interior of the planet, is simpler than a human being because gravity crushes any structure out of existence. And that is why science can tell us more about the behavior of atoms and the internal workings of the stars than it can about the way people behave."[76]

Systems that have to be maintained in a state far from equilibrium are self-regulating or self-organizing. Our ecosystem exists in such a state as does our earth in terms of the way it maintained its atmosphere in the shifting conditions of the development of the sun. The earth as such a living system is often referred to as Gaia (a reference coined by James Lovelock). As such, life itself on earth, both plant and animal, is a part of that self-regulating system. One can think of the earth as a living system, just as one thinks of the solar system, and the galaxy, as self-organizing systems.[77] Gribbin concludes that "chaos and complexity combine to make the Universe a very orderly place, just right for life-forms like us. . . . But it isn't that the Universe has been designed for our benefit. Rather, we are made in the image of the Universe itself."[78]

---

[74] Ibid., 145–86.
[75] Ibid., xix.
[76] Ibid.
[77] Ibid., 247.
[78] Ibid.

Theological and Pastoral Implications

God and Creation

John Haught asks, "What kind of Maker would create a universe in which novelty and creativity emerge mostly 'at the edge of chaos,' and in which the order and complexity emergent out of chaos cannot be specified in advance of its arrival? Does the surprising fact that randomness is bounded by strange and intricate forms of order (attractors) tell us anything significant about the relationship of the cosmos to its Creator?"[79] He argues that this complexity which emerges from and exists on the edge of chaos upholds the idea of novelty in creation. Thus for Haught, God is the source of both order and the novelty that enables chaos.[80] For Haught, "a biblically based theology is not surprised to find divine creativity hovering very close to turbulence."[81] In the Christian creation narrative, God overcomes chaos, both in Genesis and the Psalms. God orders the world. Haught goes on to explain that novelty is part of the creation process, but in order for there to be novelty in creation, there must be at least transitional periods of chaos, while still not allowing disorder to have the last word.[82] Haught maintains that there is an openness in creation and that the creative process is not coercive but alluring. God as Creator does not compel but rather entices creation into new and complex states. Haught argues, "It is almost as though the specific pattern toward which a system is attracted quietly 'influences' it out of some misty region of futurity, enticing it away from sheer determination by the past and inviting it to experiment with a wide range of possibilities before it settles into a specific morphological pathway."[83] Can we understand the law of complexity that bounds the chaos as an analogy of God's breath/spirit/wind moving over the waters of chaos? God orders the chaos of our world and brings meaning out of complexity, unity out of diversity, even when we cannot make it make sense. Reading this creation narrative of ordering, can everything from the cosmos to our everyday lives be understood within a framework of meaningful complexity rather than absurd chaos?

---

[79] Haught, "Chaos, Complexity, and Theology," 185.
[80] Ibid., 190.
[81] Ibid., 191.
[82] Ibid., 190.
[83] Ibid., 189.

"In the beginning, when God created the heavens and the earth—and the earth was without form or shape, with darkness over the abyss and a mighty wind sweeping over the waters . . . " (Gen 1:1-2). Scripture opens with this image of creation as God ordering chaos, the wind sweeping over the waters. The word we translate as wind is *rûaḥ* and is translated as God's wind, breath, or spirit. The images of darkness and the abyss or the deep (*tĕhôm*) are images of chaos.[84] The waters and the abyss are images of chaos taken from neighboring Near Eastern myths and cosmogonies. In the Hebrew account, these chaotic elements of darkness and water, however, are included in creation as part of creation. Noting the elements of chaos in the creation narrative of Genesis is not meant to imply in any way that this story should be taken literally, nor that there is a direct correspondence to the way in which creation happens in the story and the way it happens in nature. Such correlations do not work given the order of creation in Genesis—the vegetation of the earth cannot appear before the sun. The order in the narrative is symbolic, not literal. The point of Genesis is to tell of God's creative activity; part of that activity includes bringing order out of chaos and sustaining that order on the edge of chaos. The Hebrew cosmology pictures a dome in the heavens that God creates to literally hold back the waters of chaos. These are the waters that are subsequently released in the story of the great flood.[85] Their release indicates that without maintaining our relationship with God, our lives once again become flooded with chaos. At the end of the flood, in chapter 8 of Genesis, God's *rûaḥ* once again sweeps over the waters, closes floodgates and holds the chaos at bay, renewing the covenantal relationship with humankind.[86]

---

[84] See Richard Clifford and Roland Murphy, "Genesis," in *The New Jerome Biblical Commentary*, ed. Raymond Brown, Joseph Fitzmyer, and Roland Murphy (Englewood Cliffs, NJ: Prentice Hall, 1990), 10. See also Terence Fretheim, "The Book of Genesis," in *The New Interpreter's Bible: A Commentary in Twelve Volumes*, ed. Leander Keck, David Petersen, et al., vol. 1 (Nashville, TN: Abingdon Press, 1994), 321–674.

[85] Genesis 7:11, "All the fountains of the great abyss burst forth, and the floodgates of the sky were opened."

[86] Genesis 8:1, "God remembered Noah and all the animals, wild and tame, that were with him in the ark. So God made a wind sweep over the earth, and the waters began to subside. The fountains of the abyss and the floodgates of the sky were closed, and the downpour from the sky was held back."

The creation stories of Genesis are not the earliest references to creation in Scripture.[87] Some of the ancient psalms are dated much earlier than Genesis 1. In these ancient psalms, the act of creation is understood as "a victory over the powers of chaos" and "the ordering of the cosmos."[88] In these psalms, as well as in references in Job and Isaiah, chaos is personified as Leviathan or Rahab, the great water monster.[89] The act of creation is the taming of chaos, and Psalm 104:26 has a wonderful image of Leviathan whom God "formed to play with," thus taking the monster of chaos and making it into a playful pet. The footnote to this verse in the *New American Bible Revised Edition* states, "God does not destroy chaos but makes it part of the created order."[90]

As an interesting side note to the use of these ancient images of water and wind that we find in the Scripture narratives, water and wind are themselves the fount of chaos theory. In studying the weather patterns and turbulence in water, scientists came to new discoveries about the links between chaos and complexity, recognizing that in that moment, right before a system becomes chaotic, there often exists quite stable and breath-taking complexity. The complexity of our created world often exists right at that place where chaos is just barely being held back by the forces of nature, and yet that "holding back" endures in a remarkably stable system.

Creatio ex Nihilo *and* Creatio Continua

From 2 Maccabees 7:28, we get the only biblical reference to creation out of nothing, "I beg you, child, to look at the heavens and the earth and see all that is in them; then you will know that God did not

---

[87] Ernan McMullin notes that the story of Genesis 2 is from the time of David and Solomon in the tenth century BC, whereas Genesis 1 is much later. It is from the time of the Babylonian exile in the sixth century BC. See Ernan McMullin, "Creation *Ex Nihilo*: Early History," in *Creation and the God of Abraham*, ed. David B. Burrell, et al. (New York: Cambridge University Press, 2010), 11–13.

[88] John Kselman and Michael Barré, "Psalms," in *The New Jerome Biblical Commentary*, ed. Raymond Brown, Joseph Fitzmyer, and Roland Murphy (Englewood Cliffs, NJ: Prentice Hall, 1990), 526. See Psalms 74, 89, 104, and 136. Also see Job 9 and 26, as well as Isaiah 51.

[89] See Psalms 74, 89, 104, and 136. See also Job 9 and 26; Isaiah 51.

[90] United States Conference of Catholic Bishops, *New American Bible Revised Edition*, "Psalms, Chapter 104," http://www.usccb.org/bible/ps/104:13#23104026-1.

make them out of existing things. In the same way humankind came into existence."[91] John Haught points out that " 'no order' means 'no thing'—that is, 'nothing.' "[92] Following that understanding, one can understand creation from nothing to be order emerging out of chaos and, in the process, the complex cosmos we inhabit today, including space-time, coming into existence. Robert John Russell explains the doctrine of *creatio ex nihilo* as simply maintaining that God is the source of all that exists and that God's creation is a free and unconditioned act of God.[93]

Russell also highlights the concept of *creatio continua* in which the dynamics, indeterminacy, and novelty of creation demonstrate an openness to God's ongoing participation in creation. In the theological tradition, *creatio ex nihilo* refers to God bringing into existence everything that is. In other words, God did not create using preexisting eternal matter. Anything that has existence is God's creation. *Creatio continua* is used to refer to God's act of sustaining creation, understanding God to have an ongoing, active role in creation. The two are sometimes put at odds against one another, as in a deist who may accept the idea of *creatio ex nihilo* but reject the idea of *creatio continua*, believing in a God who sets everything in motion but then has nothing to do with creation after that act. While not conflating the two, Russell notes that the two can be complementary rather than opposed, so that on the one hand, *creatio ex nihilo* emphasizes God's transcendence and the contingency of existence as the finitude of creation, thus addressing the question of why there is something instead of nothing.[94] To say existence is contingent means nothing has to exist. To say that we are finite and that God is transcendent means God is totally other, the very ground of anything existing at

---

[91] As will be discussed further in chapter 5, this biblical verse is somewhat artificially attached to the doctrine of *creatio ex nihilo*, as the biblical author would not have intended this meaning and the doctrine develops much later.

[92] Haught, "Chaos, Complexity, and Theology," 185. Haught makes this argument based on the idea from Alfred North Whitehead that existence is connected to internal organization and that for a thing to be actual, it must be ordered in a specific way. Haught cites Alfred North Whitehead, *Science and the Modern World* (New York: Free Press, 1967), 94.

[93] Robert J. Russell, *Cosmology: From Alpha to Omega; The Creative Mutual Interaction of Theology and Science* (Minneapolis, MN: Fortress Press, 2008), 34.

[94] Ibid., 36.

all. *Creatio continua*, on the other hand, emphasizes God's immanence to creation and the contingency of existence as openness to novelty, God's ability to do something new.[95] Likewise, John Haught notes the importance of God's sustaining role in the creative process as invitational rather than coercive. He concludes: "The ongoing creation of the universe through the self-organizing processes disclosed by the sciences of chaos and complexity, therefore, can be thought of as ultimately made possible by the nonintrusive persuasive love of God, by a calling-into-being that arrives faithfully out of the realm of an inexhaustible future. It is this promising, yet paradoxically self-restraining and self-outpouring, divine love that invites the world into being and continually challenges it to raise itself every day, as Teilhard would put it, 'a little farther above nothingness.' "[96]

Niels Henrik Gregersen asserts that the act of creation itself implies this idea of "making room for otherness" that is seen in the autonomy of complex systems and their ability of self-organization.[97] He notes that in our biblical story of creation, God does not create the plants directly but rather proclaims, "Let the *earth* bring forth vegetation."[98] In Gregersen's terms, God is the "creator of creativity."[99] Like a strange attractor, God invites creation to evolve into beautiful complex fractal patterns, not through coercion but through attraction.

What might we learn from the concept of fractals as strange attractors? Might it give us an image of how God works in our lives as well? Perhaps God does not micromanage our lives, controlling circumstances in a deterministic way. Perhaps God works through strange attractors, drawing us and attracting us to complex and intricate patterns. As John Haught points out, novelty is necessary for creativity and life. As was noted above, Haught argues that in order for novelty, and thus creativity, to enter a system, the old order must break down. We can recognize such symmetry-breaking in our own world as the way in which God breaks in to create something new.

[95] Ibid.

[96] Haught, "Chaos, Complexity, and Theology," 194. Cites Pierre Teilhard de Chardin, "The Prayer of the Universe," in *Writings in Time of War* (New York: Harper & Row, 1968), 121.

[97] Gregersen, *From Complexity to Life*, 207.

[98] Ibid., 213. Emphasis mine.

[99] Ibid., 217.

If we hold on to the old, rigid order, we constrain the potential for growth in our world and society.

Examples of this "symmetry-breaking" could be the role of the Second Vatican Council in the Roman Catholic Church or the introduction of civil rights in American society. The rigid way of doing things had to be broken, resulting in a certain amount of chaos, before new, richer, more complex forms of order evolved. As Haught noted, "If natural order were absolutely inflexible and resistant to processes like 'symmetry breaking,' there could be no emergent novelty, no growth, no life, no evolutionary adaptation, no new patterning."[100] Being open to the future and God's ongoing creative activity in our lives and in our world requires that we be a bit flexible and open to symmetry-breaking so that new patterns of complexity can emerge and then "the world will always become something more than what it is."[101] Haught concludes that "to the theologian, [chaos, nonlinearity, and chance] suggest a divine discontent with the status quo, a Creativity that is always fresh and that invites our own complicity in making the world new."[102]

Our lives often exist on this fine edge between chaos and complexity, but when we can trust God and surrender to that turbulence, trusting God to bring order out of the turbulence, we may find ourselves in an intricate and complex web of life and relationships that lends itself to a much richer and deeper experience of reality than if one held oneself aloof from the messy turbulence of life. As John Haught notes, the universe operates in precisely this way, demonstrating what he calls a "gracious habit of turning confusion into complexity and order."[103] George Coyne notes that "we do not need God to explain the universe as we see it today. But once I believe in God, the universe as I see it today says a great deal about that God in whom I believe."[104] When one believes in a Creator God, one can look at creation and ask what it might tell us about the God who is

---

[100] Haught, "Chaos, Complexity, and Theology," 191.

[101] Ibid., 191.

[102] Ibid.

[103] Ibid.

[104] George V. Coyne, "The Dance of the Fertile Universe," Universidad Interamericana de Puerto Rico, AAAS Dialogue on Science, Ethics, and Religion (DoSER), Public Lecture, March 27, 2006, http://www.metro.inter.edu/servicios/decanatos/academicos/documentos/HandoutCoyne.pdf.

Creator. Looking at this trend of cosmic reality, might it not offer a reason for our hope that God can turn that confusion in our own lives and in our own world into complexity and order? As such, one does not expect to necessarily find easy answers. Complexity is a part of the world and the cosmos in which we live. Perhaps, however, one can find a new and beautiful order emerging out of the complexity.

John Polkinghorne notes that chaos theory teaches us that we do not and cannot know all of the initial circumstances of a system, and therefore we cannot predict all of the consequences of our actions. One of the implications of this knowledge could be to engender in us much more humility in discourse and action. Humility in discourse is necessary because there is simply so much about the cosmos that we do not yet know or understand and because we must recognize the limitations of our ability to predict how circumstances, both on a personal, human level and on a cosmic level, will unfold. We can have certain statistically based hypotheses, but we cannot have certainty. Humility in action is necessary because of the fact that we simply cannot predict the consequences of our actions, therefore we must be cautious in action and open to discovering the consequences and adapting accordingly rather than presuming we understand the outcome.

Similarly, when we look at complexity in our human lives, we frequently cannot know enough about the initial conditions or background of a situation to fully understand it, and so we frequently end up responding or reacting in our interactions without adequate information, possibly leading to vast mistakes in judgment. This point is important in its implications for understanding the complexity of human relationships. Fractals such as the Peano curve or the Sierpinski gasket are wonderful analogies for the finite infinity of the human subject—an infinitely long line wrapped in a finite space that never repeats or crosses itself. The depths of being a human subject are something like this idea. We cannot be reproduced or repeated. Even with so-called doppelgangers or duplicates of ourselves in possible parallel universes, who a person is would be uniquely shaped by that person's relationships and experiences. We cannot even repeat pieces of our own lives. We have an infinite depth that cannot be captured in finite words or concepts, and yet we ourselves are finite, bounded by space-time, subject to death. Our infinite depth exists within a finite boundary.

Added to these circumstances is the fact that like a complex system, we live in a world that tends to be open to its environment. We are not a closed system. We have access to more information than we have ever had before in the history of humankind and have the potential for a greater breadth, if not always depth, of relationship across all of the world. Complexity arises out of this situation. Similar to the way the input of energy into a physical system creates complexity, the input of information can create complexity in human situations—hence, issues are rarely black and white. Likewise, it is the interactions between the component parts, in this case human beings, that give rise to such complexity. When people close themselves off from the world and associate only with people who think as they do out of fear of possible chaos, we end up with a stagnant equilibrium in that self-made, isolated system—no exchange of energy or ideas, no openness to new information, only a homogeneous steady state out of which nothing new is created. Peace that comes from exhausting one's energy or from a lack of engaged interaction with others in a "flee the world" mentality is a false peace. It is the equilibrium of stagnancy and death, the equilibrium of the cold, dark end of the universe. Isolated states stifle the ability of God's creative energy to do what it does in creation—hold systems in a beautiful, open state of complexity on the edge of chaos. We see narrative images of this creative energy in Scripture.

In our political climate, too, often we see individuals, political parties, and politicians who take absolutist views and are unwilling to engage those who think differently. This polarizing atmosphere tends to cement positions so that rather than looking at outcomes and adjusting terms to make society work better, an all or nothing mentality prevails. Whether addressing issues of healthcare, immigration, or the national budget, this mentality creates deadlock. Humility in our discourse and action would allow us to recognize that it is impossible to know the complete answer or all of the consequences of any proposed solution and help us to adjust our course of action in response to people's various and changing experiences.

Both the ecosystem and the earth as Gaia are complex systems. We do not know for sure the consequence of our actions, and so climate change skeptics will argue, despite the overwhelming evidence of scientific observation, that we cannot be certain that changes in the overall global temperature are due to human action as opposed to part of a larger cycle that preexists our measurement of the data. Nor can we know with certainty that the cataclysmic weather we have seen in recent years in the forms of more severe hurricanes, tornados, and fire-causing droughts are a result of that global temperature increase. Those who are skeptical must also admit that we do not and cannot know with certainty that we are not contributing to the rising global temperatures and cataclysmic weather events. One then must ask what prudent action entails, given that we cannot know for certain the consequences of our actions and our knowledge that very small triggers can have exponentially large consequences. What gamble, based on probabilities, do we want to make with the human race and the future of our very fragile yet resilient biosystem at stake? We can gamble that we are not the cause of climate change and continue on as we are, knowing the results of being wrong could mean the end of our existence. We can gamble that we are the cause and take action accordingly, knowing the result of being wrong could mean a continued rise in global temperature regardless of the actions we take. Which gamble is more prudent, and in which do we have more to lose, recognizing that in either option there are a multitude of other factors that could have completely unexpected results?

What might we learn from these cosmic observations about our own small, but not insignificant, part in the human and cosmic story? We might learn to value the complexity that comes from a system having a large number of parts as a reflection of the beauty of God's creation. In that lesson we see that the large number of parts is not about fragmentation but rather unity because the whole is more than simply the sum of the parts. We do not arrive at the whole by simply adding the fragments together. We only arrive at the whole through relationship and interaction among the parts. If we do not choose the false safety of homogeneity over diversity out of a fear of chaos, we can embrace the fractal beauty that comes out of the complexity of human life lived on the edge of chaos.

Chapter Five

Cosmology and the Big Bang

Scientific Developments—The Big Bang

We have made tremendous discoveries about the cosmos in the last century, and yet there is still so much that we do not and cannot yet know due to having no way to experimentally test many of the theories. At the Albertus Magnus lecture at Dominican University in Chicago, however, I heard the astrophysicist Fr. George Coyne, SJ, give the timeline of the cosmos,[1] and he reminded us that when we imagine the history of the cosmos as a twenty-four-hour day, humans only came into existence one second before midnight, and Galileo only invented the telescope milliseconds before midnight. So if we don't have all the answers about the universe yet, Fr. Coyne quipped, "Just give us another second or two."

The Big Bang (or "Everywhere Stretch")

Approximately 13.8 billion years ago, something happened that is commonly referred to as the big bang. Most people are familiar with the phrase, "the big bang" (if for no other reason than that it is

---

[1] George Coyne, "Children of a Fertile Universe: Chance, Destiny, and a Creator God" (Albertus Magnus Lecture, Siena Center at Dominican University, River Forest, IL, November 17, 2011). For a similar time schematic, see Ben Moore, *Elephants in Space: The Past, Present, and Future of Life and the Universe* (New York: Springer, 2014), 71–80.

currently the name of a very popular TV show!). As a video done by MinutePhysics on YouTube points out:

> "Big bang" is a horrible name—it would be much more accurate to call it "the everywhere stretch." Because one of the most common misconceptions about the big bang is that it implies that the entire universe was compressed into a single point from which it then somehow expanded into the surrounding . . . nothingness? . . . The event unfortunately known as the big bang was basically a time, long ago, when space was much more squeezed together, and the observable universe, that is, everything that we see from earth, was crammed into a very small piece of space. . . . And although people call this "the big bang," it wasn't just big, it was everywhere. And it wasn't really an explosion—it was space stretching out. It's really quite unfortunate that "the Everywhere Stretch" isn't nearly as catchy as "the Big Bang."[2]

Given that the "everywhere stretch" is neither as familiar nor as catchy as the "big bang," we will continue to use the phrase "big bang" with apologies to the folks at MinutePhysics. The important point highlighted by the term "the everywhere stretch" is that the big bang is the expansion of space itself.[3] In other words, it is not as if all of the matter of the universe is condensed into a small ball that explodes, thus propelling all of that matter out into the universe from a single, central point. Rather, the space itself is what expanded and continues to expand today at an accelerated rate. Two important points are a result of this knowledge. First, when we talk about observing galaxies "moving away from each other," the galaxies are not moving through space.[4] Rather, the space between the galaxies is continuing to stretch or expand creating more distance between them at an ever increasing rate.[5] Second, while objects cannot move through

---

[2] Henry Reich, "Science, Religion, and the Big Bang," *MinutePhysics*, YouTube video, 5:19 (see esp. 0:58–1:15; 2:09–2:46), August 19, 2013, http://youtu.be/q3MWRvLndzs.

[3] Note that whether or not it was the creation of space itself is a point debated.

[4] Common images to help us understand this notion are dots on the surface of a balloon as the balloon expands or raisins in a rising loaf of bread moving away from one another as the loaf expands. Both images still have the limitation of being objects that are in three-dimensional space and thus are expanding into something.

[5] Note that this point is not true for close neighboring galaxies, because gravity continues to pull these galaxies together, overcoming the expansion of space between

space faster than the speed of light, space itself can stretch or expand faster than the speed of light.

As we will see, the question about the observable universe and how it began, a state often referred to as "singularity"[6] or "t=0" is still an open question. When we ask questions about what happened at singularity or "what banged," so to speak, the answer is that we do not know. William Stoeger explains that in the standard models (those based on the Friedmann-Lemaître-Robertson-Walker or FLRW model), as scientists project calculations backward to the point they call singularity or the big bang, the universe is described "as having infinite temperature and infinite density," which Stoeger notes "serves as a warning that this did not actually happen."[7] The model breaks down at the Planck-era temperature, hence the calculations end up with results of infinity. Stoeger notes that while scientific models such as this are representative of certain aspects of reality, they are still models; it is important not to confuse the model with the reality.[8] I would point out that the same is true of our theological models of God. They represent a real aspect of our relationship with God, but the model should never be confused or identified with who God is in God's self. Our language falls short of capturing the mystery. One reason the standard models of the universe do not work to calculate prior to the Planck Era is that space-time does not exist in the form we understand it today when temperatures are as hot as they are during and prior to that point.

Given these limitations, when we try to figure out what is meant by singularity as the beginning of the universe, Paul Davies warns, "The finitude of time, in fact, need not imply that there was a first

---

them. See Charles H. Lineweaver and Tamara M. Davis, "Misconceptions about the Big Bang," *Scientific American* 292, no. 3 (March 2005): 40.

[6] Again the folks at MinutePhysics point out that this term, "singularity," is a misnomer and in fact just refers to " 'the part of the Everywhere Stretch where we don't know what we're talking about.' Basically, our current physical models for the universe are unable to properly explain and predict what was happening at the very very beginning when the universe was super SUPER scaled down. But rather than call it the 'time when we don't have a clue what was happening, ANYWHERE,' for some reason we call it a 'singularity.' " Reich, "Science, Religion, and the Big Bang," 3:00–3:19.

[7] William Stoeger, "The Big Bang, Quantum Cosmology, and *Creatio Ex Nihilo*," in *Creation and the God of Abraham*, ed. David B. Burrell, et al. (New York: Cambridge University Press, 2010), 158.

[8] Ibid., 160.

event. Imagine events labeled by numbers, with zero corresponding to the singularity. The singularity is not an event, it is a state of infinite density, or something like it, where spacetime has ceased. If one now asks, 'What is the first event after singularity?', this is the same as the question, 'What is the smallest number greater than zero?' There is no such number, for every fraction, however small, can always be halved. Likewise, there is no first event."[9] To turn once again to MinutePhysics for an example, they explain that at "singularity,"

> space was so incredibly compressed and everything was ridicu-lously hot and dense, our mathematical models of the universe break down SO MUCH that "time" doesn't even make sense. It's kind of like how at the north pole, the concept of "north" breaks down—I mean, what's north of the north pole? The only thing you can say is that everywhere on earth is south of the north pole, or similarly everywhen in the universe is after . . . the beginning.[10]

As scientists try to reconstruct what happened as close as they can speculatively get to the big bang, they come to 10^{-43} seconds, or less than a billionth of a second, after the big bang. At this time, referred to as the Planck Era,[11] scientists speculate that all of the known forces (gravity, electromagnetism, strong nuclear, weak nuclear) were possibly combined into one superforce. At this point our observable universe (which, remember, may be part of a larger whole) is approximately a "Planck length" of 10^{-35} meters and the "Planck temperature" of 10^{32} degrees kelvin.[12] The universe at this point is unimaginably dense and unimaginably hot. One of the reasons the standard models do not work at or before Planck time is that space and time do not exist in the same way at temperatures that high. Stoeger explains that what exists is a "highly energetic state with a

---

[9] Paul C. W. Davies, *God and the New Physics* (New York: Simon and Schuster, 1983), 19.

[10] Reich, "Science, Religion, and the Big Bang," 3:27–3:51.

[11] Ben Moore explains: "This timescale, called the Planck time, is the time taken for a photon to travel one Planck length, which is a natural distance that results from a simple combination of the fundamental constants of nature: the speed of light, the gravitational constant, and Planck's constant. Planck's constant is the size of a 'quantum' in quantum mechanics that describes the allowed energies that particles and photons can have." *Elephants in Space*, 49.

[12] Stoeger, "The Big Bang, Quantum Cosmology, and *Creatio Ex Nihilo*," 170.

discrete, broken-up, foam-like structure, which becomes space-time when the temperature falls below 10^{32}K, and the universe emerges from the Planck epoch."[13] Paul Davies looks at the question of the hotter and hotter temperatures of the very beginning and notes that "the trend is as the temperature is raised, so there is less and less structure, form and distinction among particles and forces. In the extreme high-energy limit, all of physics seems to dissolve away into some primitive abstract substratum. Some theorists have even gone further and suggested that the very laws of physics also dissolve away at ultra-high energies, leaving pure chaos to replace the rule of law."[14] Davies notes that some suggest that at the Planck value of 10^{32} degrees, matter may become a sea of strings existing in ten-dimensional space-time, and the distinction between matter and space-time becomes nebulous, a point to which we will return in the discussion of string theory in chapter 8.[15]

Stoeger further explains how the earliest eras of the universe, all of which take place in less than one second, correspond to the fundamental four interactions of all that exists: gravity, electromagnetism, the weak nuclear interaction, and the strong nuclear interaction.[16] Scientists propose that as the universe cooled below 10^{32}K, gravity separated from the other three, which in their combined state are known as the grand unified force.[17] Stoeger suggests that until we have gravity as a separate force, there is no space-time, as we understand it. We often tend to think of space and time coming into existence at the big bang; but in actuality, space-time, as we understand and experience them, did not come into existence until after the Planck Era. Thus, Stoeger concludes that there is no such thing as absolute time or space.[18] What does it mean for time not to be absolute? Stoeger explains that "in the Planck era, time may have been very much like space and that it only became what we identify as time once the universe cooled enough for space-time to enter the non-quantum, or smooth classical, regime."[19]

---

[13] Ibid., 160.
[14] Davies, *God and the New Physics*, 125.
[15] Ibid.
[16] Stoeger, "The Big Bang, Quantum Cosmology, and *Creatio Ex Nihilo*," 156.
[17] Ibid.
[18] Ibid., 162.
[19] Ibid., 163.

Returning to our cosmic timeline, from 10^{-36} to 10^{-32} (the Inflationary Era) the strong nuclear force separates from the still unified weak nuclear and electromagnetic force (referred to as the electroweak force). At this moment, scientists such as Alan Guth, Andre Linde, Andreas Albrecht, and Paul Steinhardt propose that there was a brief (10^{-35} seconds) period of exponential expansion (perhaps 10^{30}, 10^{50}, or 10^{100} times) called inflation.[20] As Brian Greene puts it, on the most conservative estimation (10^{30}), it "would be like scaling up a molecule of DNA to roughly the size of the Milky Way galaxy, and in a time interval that's much shorter than a billionth of a billionth of a billionth of a blink of an eye."[21] This period of inflation possibly locked in the uniformity of the universe and "relinquished its pent-up energy to the production of ordinary particles of matter and radiation."[22] This cosmological material is often referred to as quark soup—basically a plasma of quark and antiquark pairs and gluons,[23] the building

---

[20] Brian Greene, *The Fabric of the Cosmos: Space, Time, and the Texture of Reality* (New York: A. A. Knopf, 2004), 283–84. In the August 2014 Special Edition of *Scientific American*, Paul Steinhardt, one of the early theorists of inflationary cosmology, offers arguments both in favor and against the theory. He notes that while the theory is often taken for granted in cosmology today, there are still a lot of unresolved issues. See Paul Steinhardt, "The Inflation Debate," *Scientific American Special Editions* 23, no. 3 (August 2014): 70–75. Note that Steinhardt describes the time frame of inflation as within 10^{-30} second (71). He explains that "the volume of space we observe today was a quadrillionth the size of an atom when inflation began. During inflation it grew to the size of a dime (71)."

[21] Greene, *Fabric of the Cosmos*, 285.

[22] Ibid. See also Brian Greene, *The Hidden Reality: Parallel Universes and the Deep Laws of the Cosmos*, EPUB eBook ed. (New York: A. A. Knopf, 2011), loc. 60 of 347.

[23] For an overview of these particles, see Greene, *Fabric of the Cosmos*, 254–68; 345–50. As a basic summary, there are different types of fields with different types of particles associated with them. The messenger particles for forces are called bosons and those for matter are called fermions. For our purposes here, we are not going to delve into the other types of quarks, muons, taus, or neutrinos.

Force/Energy Fields and associated particles	Matter Fields (related to the probability wave of a particle) and particles	Higgs Fields (associated particles are Higgs bosons)
Electromagnetic—photons	Electron—leptons	Grand Unified Higgs
Gravitational—gravitons	Proton—two up quarks, one down quark	Electroweak Higgs
Strong nuclear—gluons	Neutron—two down quarks, one up quark	Inflaton
Weak nuclear—W and Z particles		

blocks of all that exists in our observable universe today. At the time of writing this book, great excitement had been generated over possible new evidence to support the theory of inflation, but then that evidence was negated by additional observational evidence. Nonetheless the search continues.[24]

During the next phase, the Electroweak Era from 10^{-32} to 10^{-6} seconds, as the temperature cooled to 10^{15} K (a million billion degrees Kelvin) at about 10^{-11} seconds, the electroweak force separated into the electromagnetic force and the weak nuclear force, leaving us with the four fundamental forces we experience today.[25] Brian Greene explains that it is also at this temperature that "the [electroweak] Higgs field condenses into a nonzero value" forming what he calls a "Higgs ocean" but is technically referred to as "a nonzero Higgs field vacuum expectation value."[26] One of the recent exciting scientific discoveries at CERN was evidence of the existence of the Higgs boson and thus the Higgs field.

From 10^{-6} to 10^1 seconds, the Hadron and Lepton Era, the temperature cools to a mere 10 billion degrees kelvin, and quarks begin to

[24] Moore, *Elephants in Space*, 50. For a thorough explanation of inflation, see Greene, *Fabric of the Cosmos*, 282–94, and *The Hidden Universe*, loc. 52–73 of 347. At the time of writing this book, the first evidence of inflation was discovered only to then be thrown into a sea of controversy over the results. The BICEP-Keck collaboration claimed to have discovered evidence of gravitational waves in the Cosmic Microwave Background Radiation. If their results were accurate, however, "hints of these waves should have been seen in the temperature fluctuations observed by the European Space Agency's Planck satellite. But they were not! Furthermore, microwave emission from dust in our galaxy tends to be polarized, which could confuse BICEP-Keck observations, at least to some extent." Niayesh Afshordi, Robert B. Mann, and Razieh Pourhasan, "The Black Hole at the Beginning of Time," *Scientific American* 311, no. 2 (August 2014): 42. Indeed, further analysis of the BICEP-Keck observations in conjunction with the Planck observations confirmed that the supposed waves were dust, but subsequently the two teams are now working together to adjust the telescope settings accordingly to distinguish the dust from the possible evidence of gravitational waves, and so the search will continue. See Elizabeth Gibney, "Gravitational-Wave Hunt Enters Next Phase," *Nature* 518 (February 5, 2015): 16–17.

[25] Note that at this point we have experimental evidence supporting the electroweak unification, but we do not yet have evidence supporting GUT. See William Stoeger, "The Big Bang, Quantum Cosmology, and *Creatio Ex Nihilo*," 157. The Large Hadron Collider at CERN near Geneva, Switzerland, has been able to re-create conditions similar to this Electroweak Era to investigate the behavior of particles at these high energies. See Moore, *Elephants in Space*, 51–52.

[26] Greene, *Fabric of the Cosmos*, 257–59.

combine to form protons and neutrons, while electrons and antielectrons form neutrinos and antineutrinos.[27] All of the above stages took place in a mere second. Ben Moore points out the amazing fact that just two seconds after the big bang, "the neutrinos were free to travel the universe in all directions and from all places. Today these relic neutrinos fill space—there are trillions of them passing through your bodies every second."[28] The Photon Era then takes over (10^1–10^{13} seconds) with photons "ruling the landscape," to use Moore's phrase.[29] Moore notes that after three minutes, "there was a brief 17-minute window where nuclear fusion occurred, resulting in the formation of the nuclei of hydrogen, helium, and a trace of lithium."[30] After this seventeen-minute interval, the temperature drops below the level at which nuclear fusion takes place, leaving a universe that is approximately 75% hydrogen and 25% helium.[31]

For some 377,000 years, the universe existed in this plasma state in which photons bounced off of electrons, thus capturing all of the light, but as the universe cooled and the electrons slowed down, they were able to join with protons to create hydrogen atoms.[32] At this point, the universe becomes transparent, in other words, the electrons become sparse enough that the photons are released to travel through space and the opaque plasma clears. Since there were not yet any

---

[27] Moore, *Elephants in Space*, 52.

[28] Ibid.

[29] Ibid., 53.

[30] Ibid.

[31] Matt Tweed succinctly describes these first seconds after the big bang as follows: "With the young universe cooling fast and space expanding at close to the speed of light, first photons, then quarks and leptons [electrons] condensed out of the fizzing quantum vacuum like mist on a cold window to form a quark-gluon plasma sea. Next, after one millionth of a second, the quarks combined into hadrons, primarily protons and neutrons, while vast amounts of matter and antimatter wiped each other out leaving only a billionth of the original material, along with vast quantities of gamma rays. Roughly a second after the birth of the universe its temperature dropped enough to crystallize whizzing neutrinos from the photons. Nucleosynthesis started around this time, with protons and neutrons joining to form the nuclei of helium, deuterium, and lithium." "The Compact Cosmos," in *Scientia: Mathematics, Physics, Chemistry, Biology, and Astronomy for All* (New York: Walker Publishing, 2005), 322. As a side note, Tweed reminds us that plasma is "a gaseous, high energy state of stuff where electrons are freed from their atoms" (364).

[32] Prior to capturing electrons, hydrogen existed in its ionized state of a single proton with no electrons.

stars to give light, this era is often referred to as "the dark ages." These photons have been traveling through the universe ever since that point; we can actually "see" them today in the cosmic microwave background radiation (CMBR).

MinutePhysics describes this development as follows:

> For a while, things would have been so sweltering that electrons didn't settle down as parts of atoms or molecules but instead roamed freely in a kind of red-hot cosmic soup. That soup would have had lots of light bouncing around it too, scattering off of electrons and protons like a hall of mirrors or the interior of the sun. . . . However, as the universe expanded, there was less and less energy to be had in any one place. And when things had cooled to just below the temperature of the sun, pairs of electrons and protons no longer had the energy to resist each other and they fell into the electromagnetic embrace we call the hydrogen atom. These electrons were so enamored by their new proton love interests that they effectively began to ignore all the light bouncing around them. So, with fewer free electrons for light to interact with, the universe suddenly became transparent, and all the pent-up light was sent forth in whatever direction it had been headed after its last scattering, doomed to travel alone and un-noticed through the cosmos. That is, until it bumps into some-thing solid. . . . When we finally see it here on earth, this light has been stretched so much by the thirteen-billion-year expan-sion of space, that, like a record slowing down, its frequency and color have shifted from the original sunlight-white all the way to cool microwaves. Thus, it's often called the "cosmic Micro-wave background radiation," or CMB. And just as we can tell the temperature of a red- or white-hot iron from its glow, this light tells us the temperature of empty space: currently around 2.725 degrees Kelvin, or minus 270 degrees Celsius.[33]

[33] "Picture of the Big Bang (A.K.A. The Oldest Light in the Universe)," *MinutePhysics*, YouTube video, 4:01 (see esp. 0:44–2:01), June 7, 2012, http://youtu.be/_mZQ-5-KYHw. Unlike other particles, photons do not slow down as the universe cools; they always travel at the constant speed of light. Their wavelengths, however, get longer, and so the photons that reach us today have wavelengths that are in the microwave portion of the spectrum and are no longer visible to our eyes, which can only see visible light. These are the wavelengths that fall between ultraviolet and infrared on the electro-magnetic spectrum.

Many people today watch the popular TV show *The Big Bang Theory*. Little do most people know that those of us who are old enough to have watched analog TV have watched the actual big bang on our TVs, or at least the remnants of it. Brian Greene explains that an old-fashioned television set picks up cosmic microwave background radiation: "About 1 percent of the snow on a television that's been disconnected from the cable signal and tuned to a station that's ceased broadcasting is due to reception of the big bang's photons."[34] We literally "see" the cosmic microwave background radiation from the big bang on our TV sets, or rather, we did before we had digital TV.

The Birth of the Stars

As we have noted, there is a remarkable uniformity to the temperature of the CMBR (2.725 K), but there are in fact very slight variations in the temperature. As MinutePhysics points out, these spots are "hotter or colder than their surroundings by a factor of about one in a hundred thousand—that's like noticing that a bacteria makes a beach ball bigger."[35] These very tiny fluctuations became the seeds of the first stars and galaxies.[36] The fluctuations in the CMBR were likely caused by random quantum effects during the Planck Era which were then stretched into larger fluctuations during the Inflationary Era.[37] Ben Moore points out that the result of this expansion was that some regions of space had more particles than others, and then gravity worked to pull the matter together until "within a billion years of the big bang, gravity began to assemble the first complex and massive structures in our galaxy—the dark matter and atomic particles collapsed into giant structures that are thousands of light years across. Gas accumulated at the centres of these structures and formed stars and eventually galaxies."[38] Moore goes on to explain

[34] Greene, *The Hidden Reality*, 42.

[35] "Picture of the Big Bang (A.K.A. The Oldest Light in the Universe)," *MinutePhysics*, http://youtu.be/_mZQ-5-KYHw, 2:29–2:36.

[36] As William Stoeger explains, these variations are "small density fluctuations in the ionized gas" (Stoeger, "The Big Bang, Quantum Cosmology, and *Creatio Ex Nihilo*," 157).

[37] Moore, *Elephants in Space*, 59.

[38] Ibid.

that turbulence initially increases the motion of the particles in the gas, causing the gas to radiate photons while gravity increasingly pulls the particles together as their density increases.[39] These areas, called nebulae, are basically star nurseries where thousands of stars are being born. Some of these stars will garner enough mass to begin nuclear fusion while others will not and will die out.[40]

Stars are born, and stars die. During their lives, they exist in a balance between the thermonuclear fusion that occurs in their core, initially transforming hydrogen into helium and then heavier elements, and gravity pushing inward on the star.[41] When a star has burned up much of its fuel and can no longer maintain this balance, the star dies in an explosion that expels all of its gaseous material back out into the universe, creating the raw material and the turbulence for the birth of new stars. George Coyne explains:

> The birth and death of stars is very important. If it were not happening, you and I would not be here, and that is a scientific fact. In order to get the chemical elements to make the human body, we had to have three generations of stars. A succeeding generation of stars is born out of the material that is spewed out by a previous generation. But now notice that the second generation of stars is born out of material that was made in a thermonuclear furnace. The star lived by converting hydrogen to helium, helium to carbon, and if it were massive enough, carbon to oxygen, to nitrogen, all the way up to iron. As a star lives, it converts the lighter elements into the heavier elements. That is the way we get carbon and silicon and the other elements to make human hair and toe nails and all of those things. To get the chemistry to make amoebas we had to have the stars regurgitating material to the universe.[42]

---

[39] Ibid., 61. Moore notes that one can view images of these nebulae taken by the Hubble Space Telescope. To see these images, visit http://hubblesite.org/gallery/album/.

[40] Ibid.

[41] George V. Coyne and Alessandro Omizzolo, *Wayfarers in the Cosmos: The Human Quest for Meaning* (New York: Crossroad, 2002), 117–18.

[42] George V. Coyne, "The Dance of the Fertile Universe," Universidad Interamericana de Puerto Rico, AAAS Dialogue on Science, Ethics, and Religion (DoSER), Public Lecture, March 27, 2006, http://www.metro.inter.edu/servicios/decanatos/academicos/documentos/HandoutCoyne.pdf.

Ben Moore similarly explains that we are made out of the big bang and stardust:

> Our bodies are made up from about 10^{28} different molecules which are themselves composed of individual atoms consisting by weight of 65 percent oxygen, 19 percent carbon, 10 percent hydrogen, 3 percent nitrogen and 3 percent everything else. Over half of our body weight is made up of water molecules (H^2O). . . . 60 percent of the particles in our bodies are actually hydrogen. The hydrogen atoms in the water were made just a few minutes after the beginning of the universe. Thus a large fraction of your body is 13.8 billion years old! The oxygen and the rest of the atoms in our bodies were forged in stars and not just one star—they originated from literally thousands of different stars from all over the galaxy. By mass, 90 percent of your body is made of stardust, elements created in the nuclear furnaces at the centres of stars that lived and died between 4.5 and 13.8 billion years ago.[43]

Coyne also points out that not even amoebas emerge (so far as we know, as we can't account for whether life may exist elsewhere in the universe nor, if it did, in what timeframe it may have emerged) until 12 billion (out of a total of 14 billion) years after the big bang, because it took three generations of stars to get the chemistry needed for the amoeba.[44] From the generation of galaxies and stars, we also get planets. Some material in the gaseous cloud remains in orbit around the star and continues to grow, collecting more and more molecules until solid material forms (the image of rolling a galactic snowball comes to mind).[45]

We can look at the night sky and be astounded by what we see and the extent to which we continue to make new discoveries. When we look up into the night sky in a remote location on a clear night, we can see more stars than we can possibly count with our naked eye. We can even see the cloudy arm of our edge of the Milky Way galaxy. We have also come to know that when we look into the sky, we are looking into the past. Light cannot travel faster than the speed of

---

[43] Moore, *Elephants in Space*, 58.
[44] Coyne, "Dance of the Fertile Universe."
[45] Ibid., 65.

light, so the light that we see takes time to reach us. George Coyne reminds us: "We see the moon as it was about one and one-half seconds ago, and the sun as it was about eight minutes ago. The light from the center of our galaxy took 30,000 years to reach us. Hubble Space Telescope has seen objects as they were ten billion years ago."[46] We literally look into the past.

When we think of the most distant images from the Hubble Space Telescope, we have to remember that in our solar system, the amoeba came into being only 2 billion years ago, so when we look at the most distant regions of space we are capable of seeing, we are seeing them as they were 8 billion years before life came to be in our own cosmic neighborhood. We have no way of knowing what they look like at this exact moment. As Richard Panek points out, prior to Galileo's telescope in 1610, we thought that we could see all that existed, "but then Galileo found mountains on the Moon, satellites of Jupiter, hundreds of stars. Suddenly we had a new universe to explore, one to which astronomers would add, over the next four centuries, new moons around other planets, new planets around our Sun, hundreds of planets around other stars, a hundred billion stars in our galaxy, hundreds of billions of galaxies beyond our own."[47]

Prior to 1919 and the discoveries of Edwin Hubble, we saw, even with telescopes, only the stars of our own galaxy. As Caleb Scharf puts it, "We all reside on a small planet orbiting a middle-aged star that is one of some 200 billion stars in the great swirl of matter that makes up the Milky Way galaxy. Our galaxy is but one of an estimated several hundred billion such structures in the observable universe— a volume that now stretches in all directions from us for more than 270,000,000,000,000,000,000,000 (2.7×10^{23}) miles."[48] As I have heard others state it, we live on a small speck of dust orbiting a star on the outer edges or boondocks of the Milky Way, one of hundreds of billions of galaxies. At the very least, these numbers should instill in us both awe and humility.

[46] Coyne, "Dance of the Fertile Universe," 3–4.

[47] Richard Panek, *The 4 Percent Universe: Dark Matter, Dark Energy, and the Race to Discover the Rest of Reality* (Boston: Houghton Mifflin Harcourt, 2011), xvi.

[48] Caleb Scharf, "Cosmic (in)Significance," *Scientific American* 311, no. 2 (August 2014): 74.

What makes these numbers truly amazing is the discovery of dark matter and dark energy. When scientists studied the mass and density of the universe, they ultimately discovered that everything we can see in the universe, all of the galaxies, stars, planets, everything that is on the planets, and all of the gaseous or plasma material in the universe only makes up 4.6% of the material of the universe.[49] Another 24% of it is dark matter. Dark matter is nonbaryonic matter, that is, matter that is not made up of protons, neutrons, and electrons. Scientists cannot see this dark matter, but they know that it exists due to its influence on the gravitational force. Current theories suggest that dark matter is made up of WIMPs or weakly interacting massive particles. These are particles that have a very large mass but little to no interaction with the baryonic particles (protons, neutrons, electrons) that we can observe. Therefore, we do not detect the WIMPs.[50] As will be seen in our discussion of string theory in chapter 8, if we do exist in an eleven dimension multiverse reality but can only detect that which exists within the three dimensions of our universe's brane, it is possible that dark matter is matter that exists in the other dimensions and is thus undetectable to us other than through the influence it has on gravity.[51]

The other 71.4% of the universe is thought to consist of dark energy.[52] When we talk about creation and the big bang, we are not talking about an event that happened in the past and is done. Rather,

[49] National Aeronautics and Space Administration, "What Is the Universe Made of?," *Universe 101: Our Universe*, http://map.gsfc.nasa.gov/universe/uni_matter.html.

[50] Michael Lemonick, "The Mystery of Dark Matter: WIMPs May Have the Answer," *Time*, April 8, 2014, http://time.com/54214/dark-matter-wimps-gravity-galaxy/; Clare Moskowitz, "Dark Matter May be Destroying Itself in Milky Way's Core," *Scientific American*, April 8, 2014, http://www.scientificamerican.com/article/dark-matter-wimps-fermi-milky-way/. Other theories suggest that dark matter might consist of black holes or brown dwarf stars. See NASA, "What Is the Universe Made of?"

[51] All baryonic matter and photons are open strings that are limited to the three dimensional brane of our universe according to this theory, whereas gravity is supposed to be a closed string and thus would interact with all eleven space-time dimensions of the multiverse.

[52] Ibid. Note that these numbers vary slightly among authors, so for example, Richard Panek uses 4% matter, 23% dark matter, and 73% dark energy (Panek, *The 4 Percent Universe*, xv). See also Matthew Chalmers, "Out of the Darkness," *Nature* 490 (October 2012): S2–S4.

we are talking about an event that is still happening. From the time of Edwin Hubble's discovery in 1919, we have known that the universe is still expanding from that initial moment referred to as the big bang or singularity. For a long time, scientists hypothesized that gravity would eventually slow down the force of that expansion, and perhaps the universe would even start to collapse back in upon itself. Instead, scientists have discovered that the universe continues to expand and that the acceleration of this expansion is actually speeding up. For the last 7 billion years, the expansion of the universe has been accelerating; scientists term the reason for this acceleration "dark energy." The problem is that they do not yet actually know the cause of the acceleration.[53] This dark energy acts as "antigravity" creating a repulsive force, but theorists disagree on whether, as Einstein predicted, it is a cosmological constant (maintaining a constant force) due to vacuum energy in space or it is a force such as a scalar quantum field that may evolve over time (referred to as "quintessence") or one of a hundred other theories.[54] Some even suggest that the theory of gravity as we currently understand it is simply incorrect. While gravity attracts matter at the distances at which we have been able to study it, perhaps it repels matter at further distances.[55] Future space probes will hopefully provide more data that will allow scientists to refine these theories. In fact, some of the most recent data seems to lean toward the idea of a cosmological constant.[56] For now, however, much of how the universe began, how and why it expands, and how it may come to an end simply remains a mystery beyond what can be scientifically tested. Theology, in dialogue with cosmology, must resist both the temptation to fill in these gaps of scientific

---

[53] Tamara M. Davis, "Cosmology: Hydrogen Wisps Reveal Dark Energy," *Nature* 498, no. 7453 (June 2013): 179.

[54] Chalmers, "Out of the Darkness," S3.

[55] Stephen Battersby, "Chasing Shadows," *New Scientist* 218, no. 2916 (May 2013): 32–35.

[56] The research into these topics is a continual waiting game, as getting the results that support or contradict a theory takes years and even decades. The European Space Agency is currently building a space probe, Euclid, to investigate the question of dark energy, and it is scheduled to be launched in 2020. See http://www.euclid-ec .org/. Note that Stephen Battersby ("Chasing Shadows," 32–33) explains that even if dark energy does seem to be constant, as recent data suggests, it will not rule out the idea of quintessence, which could be a field with a nearly constant density.

theory with God (a God-of-the-Gaps theology) as well as the temptation to take new theories that have not been experimentally confirmed as "proof" of creation by God.

Theological and Pastoral Implications

God, Creation, and Causality

When Fr. Georges Lemaître, a priest and astrophysicist, put forth the theory that became known as the big bang, many (including Pope Pius XII) took the thesis as proof of *creatio ex nihilo*, or the theological doctrine of creation from nothing.[57] Lemaître himself urged caution, making an excellent distinction between theology and scientific discovery, realizing that to link the two concepts endangers the theological concept should the day come when new scientific discoveries upend the old scientific theory. In a sense, that day is here. As was noted above, while the big bang is certainly accepted as the beginning of our observable universe and life as we know it, many scientists do not believe it was the absolute beginning, and the concept of a multiverse (which will be discussed further in chapter 6) is rapidly gaining ascendancy in scientific circles.

As was mentioned in chapter 4, the concept of *creatio ex nihilo* is not prevalent in Scripture. The concept developed in opposition to first-century philosophy which maintains that matter is eternal and that the world is created or shaped out of this preexisting matter. Having surveyed the references to creation in the Old and New Testaments, Ernan McMullin concludes, "It seems fair to conclude that the question of whether the work of cosmic creation had proceeded *ex nihilo* had not been of particular concern to the biblical writers generally."[58] He goes on to explain that the Platonists and Stoics

---

[57] Robert J. Russell, *Cosmology: From Alpha to Omega; The Creative Mutual Interaction of Theology and Science* (Minneapolis, MN: Fortress Press, 2008), 40.

[58] Ernan McMullin, "Creation *Ex Nihilo*: Early History," in *Creation and the God of Abraham*, ed. David B. Burrell, et al. (New York: Cambridge University Press, 2010), 16. Robert John Russell sums up the early development of this doctrine as follows: "In its contest with Greek culture, the church sought to reject both metaphysical dualism, in which the world was an eternal divine substance equal to and over against God; moral dualism, in which the world was an evil power resisting a good God;

understood matter as a principle over and against God and the Gnostics went even further to see matter as antithetical to God.[59] Theologically, the concept of *creatio ex nihilo* is not dependent on any scientific theory. Rather, what the concept expresses is the radical dependency of everything that exists on God. Creation from nothing expresses the belief the cosmos, whether it consists of our observable universe or something larger we are only part of, perhaps even an infinite multiverse, is dependent on God for its existence. William Stoeger explains:

> It seems highly unlikely that cosmology, or any physical science, will ever be able to unveil a point of *absolute* beginning—before which *nothing* existed, before which time of any sort was not—which would require the direct influence of God. That does not mean that such an event did not occur. It does mean that cosmology is *not* able to discover it and reveal it as the "Ur-event," the event needing other than secondary causes for its immediate explanation. Nor does it mean that miracles do not occur—just that science is incapable of revealing them as such, or of providing positive evidence of their occurrence.[60]

Stoeger follows Thomas Aquinas in understanding God's causality in terms of primary and secondary causes. Stoeger points out that the concept of God as Creator is utterly beyond us, and "when we talk about God 'causing' or 'acting' when God creates, we are speaking metaphorically or analogically. God acts or causes in a very different way from the way in which anything in our experience acts or causes."[61] Too many people have a Sistine Chapel image of God as Creator, where Michelangelo imaged God as an old man creating Adam. God is not an old man in the sky. When God creates, it is not

---

emanationism, in which the world emerged from and was the body or substance of God; and monism (or pantheism), in which the world was God. Hence the *ex nihilo* argument first of all affirms that God alone is the source of all that is, and God's creative activity is free and unconditioned." Russell, *Cosmology: From Alpha to Omega*, 34.

[59] McMullin, "Creation *Ex Nihilo*: Early History," 17–18.

[60] William Stoeger, "Contemporary Cosmology and Its Implications for the Science-Religion Dialogue," in *Physics, Philosophy, and Theology: A Common Quest for Understanding*, 3rd ed., ed. Robert J. Russell, William Stoeger, and George V. Coyne (Vatican City: Vatican Observatory, 1997), 240.

[61] Stoeger, "The Big Bang, Quantum Cosmology, and *Creatio Ex Nihilo*," 172.

like a person who is an artist or an architect or an engineer. We can say that our observable universe was created out of nothing as in no-thing. Theologian Ted Peters suggests that to be no-thing is to be indeterminate, whereas to be some-thing is to be determinate, to exist as determined in and by space-time.[62] We did not come to be through some previously existing material; material itself, as we experience it in this world, came to be in some sort of quantum fluctuation that we call the big bang. Time and space itself, as we experience it, came to be in the big bang, or perhaps in the process of inflation or the breaking of symmetry that resulted in the cooling and expanding universe. There is no "before creation," both because creation is eternal and because "such terms are already time-dependent."[63] One is reminded of the Buddhist notion of *sunyata* or emptiness or no-thing-ness which can also be understood as the openness or space or horizon that makes relation and thus existence possible. Creation out of nothing is not a doctrine about what caused the big bang; it is a doctrine about our radical relatedness. Existence is relation. To be is to be related.

Stoeger notes that creation participates in the being of the Creator and suggests "in this regard, it also seems clear that it is better to conceive of the Creator more like a verb than an entity."[64] While Stoeger suggests the traditional verbs of act or being, one of the most appropriate verbs that can be used (metaphorically) to describe God is Love.[65] The theologian and philosopher Jean-Luc Marion, in his book *God without Being*, purports that God as Love brings existence out of nonexistence.[66] God loving us is what creates, grounds, and sustains us out of the nothingness that continually threatens our existence. Peters reminds us that the idea of creation followed redemption.[67] The God who calls Israel into being out of the Exodus

---

[62] Ted Peters, "On Creating the Cosmos," in *Physics, Philosophy, and Theology: A Common Quest for Understanding*, 3rd ed., ed. Robert J. Russell, William Stoeger and George V. Coyne (Vatican City: Vatican Observatory, 1997), 280.

[63] Ibid., 281.

[64] Stoeger, "The Big Bang, Quantum Cosmology, and *Creatio Ex Nihilo*," 172.

[65] See Jean-Luc Marion, *God without Being: Hors-Texte* [Dieu sans l'être], 2nd ed., trans. Thomas A. Carlson (Chicago: The University of Chicago Press, 2012); see also Ilia Delio, *The Unbearable Wholeness of Being: God, Evolution, and the Power of Love* (Maryknoll, NY: Orbis Books, 2013).

[66] Marion, *God without Being*, 88.

[67] Ted Peters, "On Creating the Cosmos," 276.

and the God who brings life out of death is the God who creates out of nothing.

God as cause (in this case of creation) cannot be understood as another cause alongside the laws of nature. Stoeger explains, "The ultimate ground of being and order is not another entity or process in the universe, which can be discerned or isolated from other physical causal factors and entities. It is not scientifically accessible! And yet it is causally distinct from them because without it, nothing would exist. And yet it does not substitute for created causes—it endows them with existence and efficacy."[68] God is always the cause that underlies and grounds the laws of nature and the processes of the evolution of the cosmos. God and the laws of nature are both causes of creation, each working in the way proper to it so that God as primary cause works in and through the secondary causes. Stoeger warns that "God does not substitute for, interfere with, countermand or micro-manage the laws of nature."[69] Stoeger does point out the following:

> Physics can never tell us how we get from absolutely nothing—nothing like space or time, or matter or energy, wavefunction or field, nothing physical at all—to something that has a particular order. There is no physics of 'absolutely nothing.' . . . This is precisely why physics in general, and quantum cosmology in particular, do not provide an alternative account of the creation of the universe, philosophically or theologically speaking.[70]

The theological doctrine of creation is a statement of faith, not science. At the same time, the doctrine of faith does not contradict nor is it contradicted by any scientific discovery. Scientists such as Stephen Hawking or Lawrence Krauss, who proclaim that science has done away with the need for a Creator God, fundamentally misunderstand the idea of God as primary cause versus secondary cause.[71] The theology of creation does not propose that we need God

---

[68] Stoeger, "The Big Bang, Quantum Cosmology, and *Creatio Ex Nihilo*," 170.

[69] Ibid., 173.

[70] Ibid., 169.

[71] See Stephen Hawking and Leonard Mlodinow, *The Grand Design: New Answers to the Ultimate Question of Life* (New York: Bantam Books, 2010); see also Lawrence Krauss, *A Universe from Nothing* (New York: Simon and Schuster, 2012).

to explain some piece of the cosmos that cannot be explained by science. Nor does theology suggest that we will one day discover scientific proof of the point where God acted instead of the laws of nature. Stoeger explains that *creatio ex nihilo* expresses the belief that God is the ultimate ground of existence and order, whereas science looks to explain what Stoeger calls "the primordial originating processes and entities."[72] Stoeger suggests that science and philosophy or theology are different ways of knowing in the same way that intuition and common sense are different ways of knowing.[73]

Creatio ex nihilo is not endangered as a theological concept by scientific evidence that the universe may be infinite. Theologically, an infinite universe would still be understood to be radically dependent on God as the ground of its existence. Likewise, *creatio continua* can be understood as God's ongoing sustaining presence to all that exists. God is not the big watchmaker in the sky who set the cosmos ticking and left it to be. Rather, God's presence undergirds and pervades all that exists as the invitational force calling it to greater growth and depth of being. Stoeger points out that *creatio ex nihilo*, as a concept describing our ultimate dependence on God, "is not about a creation event, but about a *relationship* which everything that exists has with the Creator. So *creatio ex nihilo* is also *creatio continua*, continuing creation. The relationship between the Creator and created continues as long as something exists. The Creator sustains or conserves reality—and the universe—in existence."[74] God sustains creation, enabling and empowering it by endowing it with freedom, not by controlling it or intervening in it, hence as primary cause working through secondary causes.[75] *Creatio ex nihilo* can be thought of as describing God's transcendence, Creator as totally other than creation and creation as utterly dependent on Creator, whereas *creatio continua* can describe God's immanence, "deeply present and active, but present and active as Creator, not as another created cause—within all aspects of creation. Transcendence does not impede or contradict immanence—it enables it!"[76]

---

[72] Stoeger, "The Big Bang, Quantum Cosmology, and *Creatio Ex Nihilo*," 152–75.

[73] Ibid., 171. Stoeger points out that technically, *creatio ex nihilo* is a philosophical construct that is employed by theology (171).

[74] Ibid., 172.

[75] Ibid., 173.

[76] Ibid.

On a personal level, Stoeger references conversations he had with George Ellis in which they discussed the fact that complexity, life, consciousness, human values, and meanings are all things that cannot be explained by fundamental particles and forces, and perhaps there is room to talk about these factors of our existence as being created from nothing, though he notes that even these are not unmediated.[77] Likewise, when we think of the universe being given meaning and order, being grounded and sustained in its existence by the Creator God, one realizes that every aspect of our lives is likewise given meaning and order, grounded and sustained by the God who creates out of nothing. The very emptiness of our existence is given ultimate meaning and fulfillment in God. Karl Rahner calls this emptiness or openness our *capax infiniti* or *capax Dei*. Out of that no-thing-ness, God creates everything that is most human in us.

Similar to our understanding of creation on a cosmic level, *creatio ex nihilo*, on a personal level, is about our relationship to God as the ground of our very being. When we think of the absolute dependence on God of everything that exists, we come to a new and deeper understanding of Rahner's axiom that dependence on God and our own autonomy exist in direct, not indirect, proportion. In other words, the more we realize our absolute dependence on God, the more we become truly free, truly the unique and individual persons we were created to be. God does not micromanage the evolution of the cosmos, nor does God micromanage our lives, and yet, the God of *creatio continua* is intimately present to every aspect of our lives. This perspective can have a profound impact on our understanding of freedom and prayer. As was discussed in chapter 2, our freedom is grounded in God, and so every choice we make is always already part of the reality held in the heart of God. We cannot choose in such a way that puts us outside of God, because there is no outside of God. We may not always choose to be our best selves, as we often fall short of the potential that we could be, but the person we are in actuality through our choices and our becoming is the person who was created by God *ex nihilo* and is sustained by God *continua*. We are cocreators of our reality with the God who is our primary cause but endows us with the gift of freedom and marvels in the person we use that freedom to become.

---

[77] Ibid., 170.

Likewise, while God is intimately connected to every aspect of our lives through *creatio continua*, that relationship is one of presence and creative transformation rather than intervention and micromanagement. One significant challenge to our faith can be our desire for a God who intervenes to make everything turn out alright in the end. Reality too often teaches us that things do not always turn out alright in the end. How do we make sense of God at the times when we can make no sense of our world and our lives? It is at these times that Karl Rahner suggests we must let go of our image of God in order to discover the reality of God.[78] Doing so enables us to see the remarkable way in which God is present to us in the midst of our suffering, creating meaning and life out of the nothingness that threatens to envelop us and sustaining us when we cannot see a way through. Karl Rahner's understanding of grace defines the moment when we cannot think of a single reason to get out of bed in the morning and do so anyway. Grace is God's self-communicative presence to us in the everyday sustaining moments of our lives, our personal experiences of *creatio continua*.

[78] Karl Rahner, *The Content of Faith: The Best of Karl Rahner's Theological Writings* [Rechenschaft des Glaubens], ed. Karl Lehmann and Albert Raffelt, trans. Harvey D. Egan (New York: Crossroad, 1993), 216–20.

Chapter Six

The Possibility of a Multiverse

Scientific Developments—The Multiverse

One of the most publicized theories of recent decades is the idea of a multiverse. When the concept of a multiverse enters the conversation, the first question one must ask is what kind of multiverse is being discussed. Theorists generally designate four types of multiverse scenarios. The first type, designated a Level I multiverse, is the simplest idea and not so much a multiverse per se. Rather, it describes a really, really big universe. This model of the multiverse takes into account the fact that we can only see into space the distance that light has been able to travel since the big bang. Taking into account the expansion rate, the observable universe is 4×10^{26} meters or 42 billion light years, and it grows by a light year every year.[1] In the Level I multiverse, the assumption is that the laws of nature are the same in all parts of the multiverse, with the only real variation being the distribution of matter.[2] The question raised by the distribution of matter

[1] Max Tegmark, "Parallel Universes," *Scientific American* 288, no. 5 (May 2003): 41–42. While one might think that the furthest light should have been able to travel is 13.8 billion light years, since that is the age of the universe, one has to take into account that during the time that the light has been traveling to us, the source of the light has simultaneously been moving away from us due to the ongoing expansion of the space between us. Note that the light from our closest neighboring stars and galaxies do not demonstrate this gap, because gravity holds these clusters together and thus overcoming the effect of space expansion.

[2] George F. R. Ellis, "Does the Multiverse Really Exist?," *Scientific American* 305, no. 2 (August 2011): 40. This variation in the distribution of matter is also referred to as different initial conditions.

is whether or not the reaches of the multiverse beyond our observation also have matter. While many suggest that they do not, seeing our observable universe as an island universe, Max Tegmark suggests that recent observations suggest a uniformity to the distribution of matter that would suggest the existence of galaxies, stars, and planets beyond the area we can observe.[3] He goes on to explain that with an infinite amount of space, but universes with finite numbers of particles, every possible configuration of those particles would eventually have to repeat, thus mathematically estimating a possible identical parallel universe to our own at a distance of 10×10^{118} meters. Tegmark, however, suggests that "your nearest doppelganger is most likely to be much closer than these numbers suggest, given the processes for planet formation and biological evolution that tip the odds in your favor. Astronomers suspect that our Hubble volume has at least 10^{20} habitable planets; some might well look like Earth."[4]

The Level II multiverse goes one step further and predicts an infinite number of Level I multiverses, each with differing aspects such as different space-time dimensionalities, types of particles, and physical constants.[5] Tegmark describes the most popular Level II theory, chaotic inflation: "Space as a whole is stretching and will continue doing so forever, but some regions of space stop stretching and form distinct bubbles, like gas pockets in a loaf of rising bread. Infinitely many such bubbles emerge. Each is an embryonic Level I multiverse: infinite in size and filled with matter deposited by the energy field that drove inflation."[6] We would never have access to

[3] Tegmark, "Parallel Universes," 42. Note that there would be innumerable other parallel universes using the current vocabulary but only some of them would be "identical parallel" universes, meaning universes that are identical or nearly identical to the one we experience.

[4] Ibid., 42.

[5] Ibid., 44. E.g., a five-dimensional world with different strengths of electromagnetism and the strong nuclear force. Tegmark explains that many scientists believe that these aspects of our universe came to be through the process of symmetry-breaking due to the initial expansion of the universe. Therefore different bubbles would have different rates of expansion and different types of symmetry-breaking, resulting in these differing aspects in the various universes. Tegmark refers to these factors as the effective laws of nature, as opposed to the fundamental laws of nature that differ in a Level IV multiverse.

[6] Ibid., 44. "A quantum field known as the inflaton causes space to expand rapidly. In the bulk of space, random fluctuations prevent the field from decaying away. But

these other Level I multiverses because of the expansion of the space between us, in that they would be moving away from us (literally the space between us would be expanding) faster than we are able to travel. One of the scientific reasons for developing the idea of the Level II multiverse is the fact that the conditions for life to exist in our universe had to be so precise that it would be an incredible co-incidence for all of the factors to come together that needed to do so for life to exist, a fact referred to as fine tuning or the anthropic prin-ciple.[7] For example, if there were more than three space dimensions in our world, atoms would be unstable, but if there were less than three, complex structures could not exist.[8] In the Level II multiverse scenario, there can be an infinite number of possible combinations of those factors, making it statistically inevitable that in at least one universe, and more likely in multiple universes, life would develop.

Level III multiverses are based on the Many Worlds Interpretation (MWI) of quantum mechanics proposed by Hugh Everett III. As was briefly discussed in chapter 2, one interpretation of the wave function is not that it collapses into a particle when it is observed but rather the superposition of states is in fact a reality with each state corre-sponding to a different world or universe. Tegmark explains that with a Level III multiverse, one is no longer talking about parallel worlds that are unimaginable distances away from us. Rather, one is talking about parallel worlds that exist all around us in Hilbert space, an abstract infinite-dimensional space, as different quantum branches.[9] Either the parallel worlds exist in far-off regions of our

---

in certain regions, the field loses its strength and the expansion slows down. Those regions become bubbles" (45, box graphic explanation). Other examples of Level II multiverses include Paul Steinhardt and Neil Turok's idea of multiple branes (44) and Lee Smolin's idea of new universes developing through black holes (46).

[7] Tegmark explains, "If protons were 0.2 percent heavier, they could decay into neutrons, destabilizing atoms. If the electromagnetic force were 4 percent weaker, there would be no hydrogen and no normal stars. If the weak interaction were much weaker, hydrogen would not exist; if it were much stronger, supernovae would fail to seed interstellar space with heavy elements. If the cosmological constant were much larger, the universe would have blown itself apart before galaxies could form" (46). See also Martin J. Rees, *Just Six Numbers: The Deep Forces that Shape the Universe* (New York: Basic Books, 2000), 173. Tegmark also references an article by Martin Rees, "Exploring Our Universe and Others," *Scientific American* 281, no. 6 (December 1999): 78–83.

[8] Tegmark, "Parallel Universes," 45, box graphic.

[9] Ibid., 46.

three-dimensional space (Level I), or they exist as different bubbles separated by the inflation of space (Level II), or they exist as different quantum branches of Hilbert space (Level III). In any one of these theories, one has possibility of the existence of all possible conditions, so the fine-tuning we find in our universe that allows for life to exist is not an anomaly but just one numerical probability given the infinite number of worlds. Recalling our deck of cards example from chapter 4, while it is highly improbable to randomly shuffle a deck of cards and have them end up arranged in order by number and suit, if you shuffled them an infinite number of times, they would inevitably end up in order by number and suit at least once. If every possible configuration of the physical constants of a universe actually exists, then the existence of our universe with the exact parameters for life as we know it to exist is inevitable.

The final category of multiverse that Tegmark calls a Level IV multiverse has to do with the variance of not only the effective laws of nature (the physical constants, dimensionality, etc.) but also the variance of the fundamental laws of nature themselves.[10] Tegmark himself has proposed this fourth alternative in which "all mathematical structures exist physically as well [as theoretically]. Every mathematical structure corresponds to a parallel universe. The elements of this multiverse do not reside in the same space but exist outside of space and time."[11] Interestingly, Tegmark adds that it is "what the late Harvard University philosopher Robert Nozick called the principle of fecundity,"[12] a point to which we will return when talking about the prodigality of God.

Tegmark sums up these various theories of the multiverse as "a four-level hierarchy, in which universes become progressively more different from ours. They might have different initial conditions (Level I); different physical constants and particles (Level II); or different physical laws (Level IV). It is ironic that Level III is the one that has drawn the most fire in the past decades, because it is the only one that adds no qualitatively new types of universes."[13] George Ellis suggests that the first of these theories, in which there are many—perhaps even infinite—domains beyond our cosmic visual horizon

---

[10] Ibid., 49.
[11] Ibid., 50.
[12] Ibid., 50.
[13] Ibid., 51.

that operate with the same laws of physics as ours, is accepted by most cosmologists today.[14] He expresses extreme skepticism about the Levels II, III, and IV multiverses, however, primarily because he sees them as experimentally unverifiable.[15] While he explains that cosmologists do have some empirical tests they use to put forth their arguments, Ellis does not feel that any of the results have been or are likely to be conclusive.[16] Tegmark, alternatively, argues that there are more and more empirical discoveries occurring that will be able to confirm or deny the multiverse theories, and that in fact, like a set of numbers versus a single number or a set of solutions versus a specific solution, a multiverse is a simpler answer to the universe's mysteries than the singular existence of this universe alone.[17]

As mentioned above, the driving force for the multiverse theories is fine-tuning or the anthropic principle, the fact that things in our visible universe had to be precisely the way they are in order for life to emerge—not just human life but the galaxies of stars and planets as well. Ellis questions whether a multiverse is indeed the only explanation, arguing, "Other options exist, too. The universe might be pure happenstance—it just turned out that way. Or things might in some sense be meant to be the way they are—purpose or intent somehow underlies existence. Science cannot determine which is the case, because these are metaphysical issues."[18] Ellis concludes that we do not know whether or not parallel universes exist, stating, "We are going to have to live with that uncertainty. Nothing is wrong with scientifically based philosophical speculation, which is what

[14] Ellis, "Does the Multiverse Really Exist?," 38.

[15] Ibid., 41. Note that the Level I multiverse is also experimentally unverifiable, but Ellis accepts this possibility, because the theory says nothing more than that the universe doesn't end at our cosmic horizon. Ellis specifically outlines seven arguments proposed by multiverse theorists, specifically focusing on chaotic inflation, a Level II theory, and addresses why he feels each argument falls short (41).

[16] Ibid., 42–43. For a more technical argument, see G. F. R. Ellis, U. Kirchner, and W. R. Stoeger, "Multiverses and Physical Cosmology," *Monthly Notices of the Royal Astronomical Society* 347 (2004): 921–36.

[17] Tegmark, "Parallel Universes," 51.

[18] Ellis, "Does the Multiverse Really Exist?," 43. Ellis acknowledges that when an entity is "unobservable but absolutely essential for properties of other entities that are indeed verified, it can be taken as verified," but he then goes on to ask the multiverse proponents, "Can you prove that unseeable parallel universes are vital to explain the world we do see? And is the link essential and inescapable?" (43).

multiverse proposals are. But we should name it for what it is."[19] In both science and theology, there are questions to which we do not have answers.

Theological and Pastoral Implications

God of the Multiverse?

Over the course of human history, we have had to change our perspective on our place in the cosmos multiple times. Humans used to think that the earth was the center of the cosmos and that the sun revolved around the earth. This perspective was due to our observations; we saw the sun rise and set each day. This perspective also fit with a theology that understood humanity to be the center and high point of creation. In time, with the Copernican revolution, scientists learned that the earth revolved around the sun. As is clear from the Galileo affair, this new knowledge did not come without upheaval to our religious worldview. Theology had to reconfigure its way of thinking about creation and the place of humanity in a cosmos that no longer centered on us. We learned that our planet was one of several in our solar system that revolved around the sun. We eventually learned that our solar system was one of many in a gigantic galaxy that we call the Milky Way. Now we now know that our galaxy is one of hundreds of billions of galaxies in the universe. Each of these steps in our knowledge came as we were able to expand the boundaries of how far we could see into space. What if the discovery that we are just one more universe among billions in a multiverse is simply the next step? How might theology reconfigure itself in light of a multiverse? At the very least, we must think about what it means for space to extend far beyond our visible cosmic horizon.

Theology should not be too quick to dismiss the idea of the multiverse for the above reasons given by Ellis. Too often, the fine-tuning argument becomes material for a God-of-the-Gaps argument, where the narrow parameters allowing life in our universe are taken as evidence that God designed the universe in such a specifically detailed

---

[19] Ibid., 43.

way for the purpose of bringing life into existence. While not ruling out that possibility, those arguments present fuel to scientists like Stephan Hawking and Lawrence Krauss, not to mention Richard Dawkins, among others, who use the multiverse argument to state that we no longer need God to explain our universe. Such arguments miss the nuances of a theology of creation as discussed above in which creation is about dependence rather than direct causality, which is to say all that exists depends on God for its very being rather than saying that God is the chronologically first cause in a chain of other causes. Rather, one can believe that if we do live in a multiverse, God created the multiverse. God can create the conditions for life to exist in this universe in and through the secondary cause of the multiverse, because God as primary cause is not a cause alongside the natural causes. Rather, God grounds and undergirds the natural causes themselves. Creation, as noted in chapter 5, is about dependence and relationship, not direct causality or intervention in the laws of nature.

Discovering the mystery and prodigality of the cosmos helps us to better appreciate the mystery and prodigality of God. The parable often referred to as "the prodigal son" is actually about the prodigal Father. The word "prodigal" means to spend or give extravagantly and lavishly. The word not only describes the way in which the younger son wastes his inheritance but also (and more importantly) describes the way in which the Father loves his sons and the way God loves us. The existence of a multiverse need not threaten our concept of God, but rather, it could reinforce what we believe about God, that God's very being is prodigal, self-diffusive love that overflows into creative activity. God creates lavishly and extravagantly. God's creative love is the principle of fecundity. The idea that all possible universes that could exist do exist in Tegmark and Nozick's principle of fecundity just illustrates the unlimited and prodigal nature of God's creative love.

So what about the idea of doppelgangers? What if there is a world out there that is an almost exact copy of this one with an almost exact copy of me sitting on a couch in a room like this one, typing on a computer. First, there is no scientific evidence whatsoever to suggest this scenario is so. Second, I think it is a mistake to see such possibilities as threats. On the one hand, perhaps it is a way of saying, as we did in chapter 2 on quantum mechanics and the discussion of virtual reality, that there is no outside of God, that every possible choice I could make is always, already held in the reality of God. On the other hand, I think it leads us to a deeper discussion of what we mean by personal subjectivity and identity.

If there is another person or an infinity of persons out there who are just like me in every way, except in the choices they make, then perhaps they are not just like me, for who am I outside of the choices I make? Our ability to choose who we become is what makes us who we are. We are cocreators in and through our freedom, deciding at each and every moment who this person I call me will become. Those possible doppelgangers would not be loved any less by God, but they are not me. I am this person, sitting here, choosing to write this book. We often look back over our lives and wish we had made other choices at various points and times, but part of the recognition here is one of acceptance of our past and the dynamism of our future. If I had made other choices, good or bad, I would be a different person. An analogy can be seen in the questions regarding the possibility of human cloning. Were we ever to clone a human being, that clone would be a true human being and a unique individual, despite the replicated DNA, because that person would have the freedom to make his or her own choices. The identity and vocation that has been given to me in my creation, an act that was not completed at the moment of my conception, but one that is ongoing, must be lived out in time and space and freedom.

As Ellis highlights, we must live with uncertainty, with not knowing all the answers. Such a place of lived tension is also possible in our relationship with God, even while we profess our belief in God's prodigal love. Like other possible universes beyond our observation or experience, God is always beyond our direct observation and experience. All of our experience of God is mediated, if by nothing else, at least by our bodies, our brains, and our cognitive abilities to process experiences using the categories and concepts that are determined by our cultures. Just as the other possible universes may, however, have some tangible effects on the world in which we live, even if we are not entirely certain what those effects may be, we hope that God has a tangible, if indirect, effect on our lives. As noted previously, we often long for a God who directly intervenes, who makes things turn out alright in the end, but God doesn't micromanage our lives. A God who works through secondary causes, however, can still have that tangible effect on our lives, first and foremost in and through the ways in which our relationship with God makes us different than we might otherwise be, ideally more loving, more open, and more relational. Secondly, God can have that tangible effect on our lives in and through the network of relationships that forms us, upholds us, and nurtures us. We believe in the presence and the power of God's love in the world, but while love can be tangible, it cannot be proven.

Chosenness

In the stories of salvation history found in Scripture, God works through the small and insignificant, the weak and the vulnerable, the lowly and unexpected. God chooses Abram and Moses, David and Solomon, and prophets that protest that they are too young, too insignificant, and not well spoken enough. In the stories, these individuals are chosen not because they are special or significant but rather to serve.[20] The Christian tradition likewise begins with a young, unmarried peasant girl, Mary, who is chosen to be the bearer of the Christ. Jesus himself is born in the city of the smallest tribe and grows up in Nazareth, a town that is derided for its insignificance.[21] God works in history through humans who are insignificant, who are fallible and sinful. God is incarnate and dwells among these same humans in and through the humble person of Jesus, spreading the good news of unconditional love and significance not due to status but from being loved by God. God does not love us because we are significant; we are significant because we are loved by God. We are loved out of nothingness into something. We are loved into disciples and witnesses and those who have been chosen to be a symbol of God's love in the world. Jesus' message is solidarity with the least, the lowest, and the meek, those who have been cast off and despised by society.

The paradigmatic image of chosenness in Scripture and the image on which we base the idea of the church as people of God is Israel as the chosen people. The story of Israel is integrated into the story of

---

[20] George E. Okeke, "The Church as the Community of God's Chosen People," *Communio Viatorum* 30, nos. 3–4 (December 1987): 199–213.

[21] John 1:46: "Can anything good come from Nazareth?"

all humanity symbolized in God's covenant with Noah and the promise never again to destroy all living things (Gen 9:8-17). This covenant stands between God and all of living creation. As an interesting cosmological note, the covenant does not promise that the earth will exist forever, but rather, the covenant stands for "all the days of the earth." (8:22) The genealogy of Noah (Gen 11) describes all the nations of the known world at that time descending from him, so Noah and his descendants symbolize all of humankind after the flood. One of these descendants is Terah, the father of Abram. The theme of God working through the insignificant is evident in this biblical story. Terence Fretheim observes, "At the end of this short passage (Gen 11:27-31), the author reports Terah's death, his uncompleted journey to Canaan, the death of one of his sons, the barrenness of the wife of the other son, and an orphaned grandson (Lot). The word of God (vv. 1-3) enters into a point of great uncertainty for the future of this family."[22] Abram's story begins in this place of uncertainty and continues as one of faith in the promises of God.

Abram, in spite of this shaky lineage, is chosen by God. He is chosen not for his own sake but rather to mediate God's blessings to the world; hence in Genesis 12:3 God tells Abram, "All the families of the earth will find blessing in you." Fretheim suggests, "We do not know why God chose Abraham rather than another person or family. But we do know that God chose him so that the human and non-human creation might be reclaimed and live harmoniously with the original divine intention. God's choice of Abraham constitutes an initially exclusive move for the sake of a maximally inclusive end. Election serves mission."[23] He notes that God works in and through the chosen people to mediate blessing to the whole world.[24] Fretheim points out, "This family does not come onto the world scene out of the blue; it has deep familial connections to *all* the nations of the world. This family thereby enables God's cosmic purposes and activity."[25] Furthermore, Abram's family is not more perfect or better than other

---

[22] Terence Fretheim, "The Book of Genesis," in *The New Interpreter's Bible: A Commentary in Twelve Volumes*, ed. Leander Keck, David Petersen, et al., vol. 1 (Nashville, TN: Abingdon Press, 1994), 422.

[23] Ibid., 417.

[24] Ibid., 419.

[25] Ibid., 425.

people; there is no room for airs of superiority in the story. Rather, it is through all of their faults and failings that God's promise and blessing continues to prevail.[26]

Likewise in the cosmic perspective, we do not believe that humanity has a special relationship with God because we are so significant in and of ourselves. But we do profess to believe that because God chooses to be in relationship with humanity, we have a special role and mission to play in the history of the cosmos, even if we do not know precisely what that role will entail. Abram did not know either, but he trusted God, and it was credited to him as righteousness.[27] Like Abram, we have the potential of mediating God's blessing to others. That special relationship to God in no way excludes the possibility of God being in relationship with other life in the cosmos. On the contrary, all that exists is already in relationship to God as Creator.[28] Election by God is not indicative of exclusivity but rather brings the chosen one into God's plan of inclusivity. In Abraham's story, this inclusion is symbolized by his numerous descendants, not only from Sarah and Isaac, or even from Hagar and Ishmael, but also from the little known or mentioned Keturah and her descendants (Gen 25:1-6).[29]

Similarly, we live in a place of cosmic uncertainty. We do not know the future of the universe or the future of humanity. We can predict with pretty great certainty the ultimate destruction of earth and our solar system. Whether humanity will still exist at that point in cosmic history and/or whether we will have been able to discover a way to leave our solar system and make a home elsewhere in the universe is simply unknown at this point. We also live at a point of great uncertainty for the future of the human family, and so we also live on the hope engendered in the blessings and promises of God, promises that will not come to fruition in our own lifetimes. As Fretheim notes,

---

[26] Ibid., 425.

[27] Gen 15:6; Gal 3:6; Rom 4:3.

[28] Ibid., 425. Fretheim suggests, "Yet, the 'families of the earth' are *not* totally dependent on their relationship to the chosen for blessing; the blessings of God the creator (e.g., sun and rain) continue to flow to all independently of their relationship to Abraham's family. . . . The difference remains this: Blessings will be intensified or made more abundant (30:27–30) by this contact, made even more correspondent to God's intentions for the creation" (425).

[29] Ibid., 419.

"Promises do not result in certainty; certainty exists only in myth. Promises can only be trusted, believed in; the journey toward fulfillment of the promise involves faith, not sight (Hebrews 11)."[30] Nonetheless, our belief and action in the here and now have an impact on the future outcome of those promises, just as Abram's obedience had an impact on the future blessings and promises of Israel.[31] Fretheim warns:

> Human sin has negative creational effects. . . . Abram has committed no sin that led to this famine; this is the way things are in the land when God makes the promise. While the land is full of creational potential; presently it falls short of its promise and contributes to human suffering. So God's gift to Abram can fail, having been spoiled through what human beings have done (see Lev 26:18-20; Deut 11:13-17). The land needs healing, as it often does during Israel's history. In eschatological vision, when God's promises are fulfilled on a cosmic scale, famine will be no more (Isa 65:21; Amos 9:13-14).[32]

Hence our actions have an impact on the world that God created, as was discussed in chapters 3 and 4. In both our present ecological crisis and any future cosmic exploration, it is important to remember that while God's creation is overflowing with blessing, human abuse of that creation can negate that blessing. Nonetheless, our human actions do not annul God's promise.[33] As seen in the story of Israel, God's covenantal relationship must continually be renewed due to a human lack of fidelity and, in the case of the creation with which we have been entrusted, a lack of prudent stewardship. In the story of Abram, the covenant is made and renewed multiple times with a reiteration of God's promises and blessings.[34]

---

[30] Ibid., 430.

[31] Fretheim notes, "What Abraham does and says has an effect on what happens in the future beyond the promise" (419) and "although Abram will never see this future, his response will shape it" (422).

[32] Ibid., 430.

[33] Ibid., 419.

[34] Ibid. Fretheim notes that "the specific language of blessing appears nearly one hundred times in chaps. 12–50" (419). Fretheim sees the reiteration of the covenant in chap. 17 as more than a renewal. He sees it as a revision. See p. 457.

Being chosen, like being created, establishes an identity. We come to be who we are called to be by being loved and by being in relationship with God. Thus in our biblical stories, Abram becomes Abraham, Sarai becomes Sarah, Jacob becomes Israel; in our Christian tradition, Simon becomes Cephas/Peter and Saul becomes Paul. Of Abram's name change, Fretheim maintains, "A name change does not refer to a change in personality or character, but marks a new stage in his identification with the divine purpose. He must now live up to his new name, which focuses not on his personal relationship with God but on his relationship to the nations. The name looks outward, centered on the lives of others. Abraham's election involves mission."[35] The entire story of Abraham is an archetype that mirrors the story of Israel, and so in Abraham's election for mission, we see the greater story of Israel as a covenanted people, chosen for mission.[36] Note that all of the name changes above follow this pattern of receiving a new name in the context of being called to a greater role in God's mission.

Those who are so called are not called because of their greatness or their worthiness. Likewise, God does not choose Israel because Israel is the biggest, most powerful, and significant nation on earth. In fact, the opposite was true. Israel was a group of people enslaved by one of the most powerful nations in the ancient world, Egypt. God called this collection of tribes out of nothing and made them into something. Scripture describes this relationship as one of adoption in which God finds Israel, lost in the desert: "He found them in a wilderness, a wasteland of howling desert. He shielded them, cared for them, guarded them as the apple of his eye. As an eagle incites its nestlings, hovering over its young, so he spread his wings, took them, bore them upon his pinions" (Deut 32:10-11). The image of a lost orphan child is found in the prophet Hosea: "When Israel was a child I loved him out of Egypt, I called my son. . . . I drew them with human cords, with bands of love; I fostered them like those who raise an infant to their cheeks; I bent down to feed them" (Hos 11:1, 4).

The image of Israel as a small orphan child, vulnerable and needing protection, corresponds nicely to humankind lost amid the vast universe and/or multiverse, wandering on this speck of dust that is

---

[35] Ibid., 457.
[36] Ibid., 447.

orbiting a nonremarkable star in the outer edges of the Milky Way, one of hundreds of millions of galaxies in our observable universe, one of perhaps an infinite number of universes that may exist. The belief that God chooses to be in relationship with us is not surprising. Rather, it is precisely in line with the stories reflected in our salvation history. The God who creates the cosmos is moved by compassion and so makes this abandoned, lost child God's own. God's special care and adoption, however, comes with an expectation; Israel is to do as God has done and show care and compassion for the orphan and the stranger, those who are most vulnerable in society.

In the midst of this story of a chosen people is the story of their chosen leader, Moses. The story begins with the infant son of an enslaved people destined for infanticide. Scripture designates him a Hebrew, and Walter Brueggemann explains that in the ancient Near East, Hebrew "refers to any group of marginal people who have no social standing, own no land, and who endlessly disrupt ordered society. . . . They are 'low-class folks' who are feared, excluded, and despised."[37] When Moses is called by God to lead the Israelites, he is a fugitive known to have killed an Egyptian soldier. Moses' response to God is to ask, "Who am I that I should go to Pharaoh and bring the Israelites out of Egypt?" (Exod 3:11), highlighting, as Brueggemann notes, his own unimportance, insignificance, and lack of authority.[38] The God who calls Moses is YHWH, the Creator God who causes to exist that which did not exist, the God who makes the insignificant significant. This God Who Is "is the power for life, the power for being, the power for newness."[39] This God who will be

---

[37] Walter Brueggemann, "The Book of Exodus," in *The New Interpreter's Bible: A Commentary in Twelve Volumes*, ed. Leander Keck, David Peterson, et al., vol. 1 (Nashville, TN: Abingdon Press, 1994), 695.

[38] Ibid., 713. Brueggemann also notes the similarity of this response to that of Gideon in Judges 6:15.

[39] Ibid., 713. The Christian theologian and philosopher Jean-Luc Marion suggests that Exodus 3:14 must be read in light of 1 John 4:8, "God is love." Jean-Luc Marion, *God without Being: Hors-Texte* [Dieu sans l'être], 2nd ed., trans. Thomas A. Carlson (Chicago: The University of Chicago Press, 2012), 73–75; see also Heidi Russell, "From Being to Love: Reconceiving the Trinity in Light of Jean-Luc Marion's Phenomenological Shift," *Horizons* 41, no. 1 (June 2014): 22–48. In this sense, God as Creator, source, and ground of creation *ex nihilo* and *continua* is more intimately connected with the metaphor of God as Love than God as Being.

present, who will be faithful is the God of both *creatio ex nihilo* and *creatio continua*.

Brueggemann explains that the Exodus narrative is directly connected to God as Creator with the power to create and destroy. The plagues are an "undoing of creation," where we see chaos and darkness being unleashed on the Egyptians.[40] In darkness, the powerful become vulnerable, whereas the vulnerable are given light.[41] The narrative reminds us of our own vulnerability amid the powers of creation and the constant biblical message of reversal, the first shall be last and the mighty brought low, while the poor, the meek, and the lowly shall be blessed and raised.

This God of creation creates a people out of a collection of marginalized slaves, the Hebrews, the least significant within their society. In Brueggemann's words, they are an "amorphous group of marginated outsiders who have not yet become a real community" and "given Yahweh's special care for the marginated, all social relations are now to be transformed, so that the ones conventionally dismissed as unimportant become peculiarly important."[42] God did not call the Hebrews because they were the best, most upstanding of all people. The stories of the Hebrew Scriptures tell us that their leaders were as fallible as any other. Their struggle to be a nation that was just and upheld the law that had been given to them was very real. Nonetheless, they were called, not because they were loved more or were somehow better than all the rest, but because God chose the small and the insignificant to be a light to the nations.[43]

At the heart of this biblical narrative are the covenant and the meaning of being chosen. To be chosen is to be given a vocation. All of creation always already "belongs" to God ("the whole earth is mine"), but Israel is chosen to be a "priestly kingdom" and a "holy nation" (Exod 19:5). Brueggemann notes that this relationship is

---

[40] Brueggemann, "The Book of Exodus," 765.

[41] Ibid.

[42] Ibid., 750, 752. God is referred to as "God of the Hebrews" throughout the confrontations with Pharaoh in Exodus 9:1, 9:13, and 10:13.

[43] See Raphael Jospe, "The Concept of the Chosen People: An Interpretation," *Judaism* 43, no. 2 (March 1994): 127–48. Note that Jospe's perspective on the Christian interpretation of being chosen is not reflective of Roman Catholic theology but rather seems to reflect a more biblical literalist perspective. His understanding of the Jewish concept is, however, in line with the argument being put forth above.

conditional, dependent on the clause "if you keep my commands" (Exod 19:5). Israel's relationship with God is to be marked by Israel's ability to listen and obey. The obedience referred to here is not the blind obedience of a soldier obeying the commands of a dictator but rather the obedience of being true to oneself and becoming who one was created to be. It is the obedience of fulfilling the potential with which one was endowed by one's Creator. Brueggemann notes that "the community of faith (synagogue, church) is given a vocation to be a distinct presence in the world on behalf of the world. Specifically, the priestly vocation of this community is to ponder and mediate the presence of the holy God in the midst of the nations, acting to resist any profanation of life that dismisses and banishes the powerful inconvenience of God."[44]

God's ability to make a people and a covenant is tied to God's role as Creator.[45] Brueggemann notes that both creation and covenant are speech acts in Scripture; God's word creates and calls.[46] Creation is not a scientific account of how the world came to be; it is a theological doctrine about relationship. Brueggemann maintains, "It is not that this person belonging to God existed and then was claimed for God. Rather, the act of claiming is the act of giving life and identity to that person. Before being called and belonging to, the person was not. In the Bible, 'person' means to belong with and belong to and belong for. Covenant is thus deeply set against every notion of human autonomy."[47]

Brueggemann goes on to explain that covenant overcomes the contradiction between freedom and authority. Karl Rahner's axiom that God and humanity do not compete but rather enjoy a relationship of direct rather than inverse proportion maintains the same

---

[44] Brueggemann, "The Book of Exodus," 837. See also 1 Peter 2:9-10.

[45] Walter Brueggemann, "Covenanting as Human Vocation: A Discussion of the Relation of Bible and Pastoral Care," *Interpretation* 33, no. 2 (April 1979): 118. One can also look at this relationship between God and Israel in terms of God's roles. God roles, from Israel's perspective, first and foremost experienced in the exodus, are God as liberator, redeemer, and savior. It is the experience of their God acting in history that ultimately leads them to reflect on God's role as Creator, the one who grounds and sustains all existence. The two interpretations are not mutually exclusive but rather inform one another in a hermeneutical circle.

[46] Ibid., 119.

[47] Ibid., 120.

perspective on the divine-human relationship. Brueggemann sees the main elements of the human response to this covenantal relationship being hoping, listening, and answering.[48] To believe in a God who is Creator is to believe that one receives one's identity from another, to believe that one "is not self-grounded and therefore does not have within himself/herself the essentials for accepting or arriving at an identity. Rather, identity for a person is given in the call of the other One. It is the voice of the initiating One who calls human persons to a destiny. Maturation is coming to terms in free ways with that givenness of God's purpose in our lives."[49] Contrary to a popular viewpoint that associates the multiverse and the statistical probability of the occurrence of life in the cosmos with the meaninglessness and insignificance of our existence, the Judeo-Christian covenantal theology asserts that there is meaning and purpose to life and that humanity is called to be a part of God's plan for creation. Our smallness and insignificance (on a cosmic scale) are irrelevant in the face of that calling. Our belief in that grounding relationship does not solve the mysteries of the cosmos nor the precarious nature of human existence. As Brueggemann assures us, "The upshot of faithfulness then is not certitude, but precariousness—precariousness which requires a full repertoire of hoping, listening, and answering to live joyously. The Bible is realistic in knowing that life does not consist in pleasant growth to well-being, but it consists in painful wrenchings and surprising gifts. And over none of them do we preside."[50]

In the context of this identity-shaping narrative that is central to the Judeo-Christian faith, it is not peculiar to think that God is in relationship with this miniscule group of creatures, humanity, on this small planet in the outer obscure regions of the Milky Way. God finds us wandering in the desert, the howling wasteland and makes us God's own people, God's chosen ones. In recognizing our own cosmic insignificance and God's pattern of choice, we must ask ourselves

---

[48] Ibid., 122.

[49] Ibid., 123. Brueggemann makes this claim both for Israel, citing Exodus 4:22 and Hosea 11:1, and for the New Testament church, citing Romans 4:17, Galatians 5:13, and 2 Timothy 1:9.

[50] Ibid., 126. Brueggemann argues that the appropriate response to life's painful wrenchings and surprising gifts are grief rather than denial, rage rather than sulking, and praise rather than introspection, all of which evoke relationship rather than self-absorption.

who are the Hebrews in our society today, the feared, excluded, and despised, for that is where we should expect to find God. The Christian church itself as the Body of Christ and the people of God is chosen despite its tumultuous history of human scandals. How we understand the concept of chosenness has major significance for how we understand what it means to be Christian in a pluralistic world. It also has implications for how we understand ministry, both ordained and lay, within that Christian community, those who are called to be leaders of our communities and how the communities themselves are called by their baptismal vocation and confirmed in that vocation of discipleship.

On that individual level of discipleship, we can feel as small and insignificant as the earth in the vast cosmos, but our smallness does not make our calling any less real. God acts throughout biblical history through small and insignificant individuals. Just as we can gaze in awe at the vastness of the night sky and the stunning fact that earth and humanity came to be at all in this vast array, we can see our own individual existence as a similarly stunning fact in the vast array of humanity. We can sit and wonder at the fact that with all that exists in our world and in our cosmos, God chooses us. We can protest this choice, as do so many of the biblical characters in the stories of our faith, but our protest cannot annul God's choice, and so we are left simply to respond as best we can, trusting in God's fidelity to what has been promised.

Hopefully the realization that God does work through the insignificant and the impotent can free us from the paralyzing fear that there is nothing we can do to change the world. As we saw in the discussion of chaos, a very tiny change can have exponential effects. God can work through the smallest of responses to make significant changes in the world. Like the parables of yeast or the mustard seed, we are called to listen and respond and trust that the result can be far greater than what our own imaginations and abilities might suggest. We are called to go out beyond our comfort zones to the other, to the marginalized, to the poor, and there we discover who we are in the God who loved us into existence.

While this realization of God's choice can lead to a sense of wonder and awe, at the same time, our cosmological insignificance as well as our biblical history provide a powerful antidote to a sense of Christian superiority, the idea that we are somehow special or more loved because we are Christian, baptized, confirmed, or ordained. God's presence and action in one community do not imply God's absence in other communities. As noted in the discussion of creation, all that exists is grounded in and sustained by God's love. Thus as we think about the possibility of a multiverse, one more decentering paradigm shift in our cosmological understanding, the response should not be one of defensiveness but rather an increase in awe at the God of so vast and expansive a creation who nonetheless chooses us.

Might there be other intelligent life in our visible universe? Might there be parallel worlds in the multiverse? If so, why would that in any way negate God's love for us? Does a parent love a first child less in having a second child? Does God love Israel less after the new covenant in Jesus the Christ? The Jewish people are no less the chosen people today with the emergence of the Christian people. God's love does not have boundaries. We have come a long way (and perhaps still have a long way to go) in realizing that God's love is not bound by certain ethnic groups or certain religions or certain nations. Similarly, there is no reason to suppose that there are any cosmic boundaries to God's love. Part of recognizing a larger cosmic story is recognizing that we are part of a creation that is bigger than ourselves. The fecundity of the cosmos is a sign of God's creative love, not a sign of God's partisanship.

Chapter Seven

Cosmic Death and Resurrection

Scientific Developments—The Death of the Universe

When we think of life, death, and resurrection, we usually do so on an individual scale, but what about the death of the universe itself? There is an axiom in theology that "protology is eschatology," that our stories about the beginning (protology) tell us something about the end (eschatology). In other words, when we read the creation narratives of Genesis, these stories of paradise and the ideal relationship between humanity and God tell us something about our final destiny. In a serendipitous parallel, the end of the universe as it is pictured by science also seems to be a reflection of the beginning. Humanity will likely die off through a mass extinction caused by our own destruction of our fragile ecosystem or some cataclysmic event such as a collision with an asteroid. Our planet that was formed by dust being drawn into orbit around the sun will eventually be swallowed by that same sun. The sun that began as a combination of gases will eventually burn out and release gases back into the cosmos. Likewise, all of the other stars in the universe will burn out, and in some instances, their deaths will create black holes that will envelop entire galaxies. As the universe expands at an ever-accelerating rate, some theories suggest that matter itself will break down into its elementary particles, with even those particles themselves possibly dissolving in the end and leaving us with the unknown. As it was in the beginning is now and will be forever, Amen. So how do we maintain an attitude of hope if our ultimate fate is the entropic death of the universe? Is this a scenario against which our faithful response can only be Brueggemann's grief and rage, or is there also room here for praise, for awe at the wonder of God's creation?[1]

The astronomy journalist Gemma Lavender from SpaceAnswers .com describes the fate of the cosmos as follows:

> There's three possible fates for the universe, one is called the Big Crunch, where gravity takes over and begins to pull the cosmos back, compressing to one point. Another extreme is the Big Rip, where the expansion of the universe just gets faster until galaxies, stars, planets, atoms and space itself is ripped apart. Somewhere between these two extremes is what the now-defunct Wilkinson Microwave Anisotropy Probe (WMAP) mission's data showed to be the likely scenario where the expansion of the universe is not great enough for a big rip and gravity is not strong enough for a big crunch. Instead it will continue to expand, carrying everything we see today over the cosmic horizon where they will be so far away, that their light cannot reach us. The sky will be dark and all of the stars will begin to go out, the universe will grow, cold and lifeless in a so-called big freeze.[2]

Lavender goes on to explain that these scenarios depend on our understanding of whether the universe is closed, resulting in the big crunch, or open and curved or open and flat, both of which result in the big freeze or the big rip. Evidence seems to be that the universe is open and mostly flat, that is, not completely flat but also not curved like a saddle as some theories suggested. The other factor at play is the role of dark energy, which, according to Lavender, leads to indefinite expansion and the big freeze, if it proves to be a cosmological constant, or either the big crunch or big rip, if it proves to be quintessence which could either reverse or destabilize expansion.

Many cosmologists today, however, do not believe that our observable universe is all that exists. Therefore the big bang may not have been the beginning, and the death of our universe might not be

---

[1] Walter Brueggemann, "The Book of Exodus," in *The New Interpreter's Bible: A Commentary in Twelve Volumes,* ed. Leander Keck, David Peterson, et al., vol. 1 (Nashville, TN: Abingdon Press, 1994), 126.

[2] Gemma Lavender, "How Will the Universe End?," *Space Answers* (February 2014), http://www.spaceanswers.com/deep-space/how-will-the-universe-end/. The big freeze is also referred to as the big chill and sometimes as the heat death or entropic death of the universe, meaning that the universe will reach the state of maximum entropy and thermodynamic equilibrium.

the end. In other words, there might be life after death for the universe itself. Lee Smolin is one scientist who suggests that the history, or perhaps ancestry is a better word, of our universe extends back before the big bang and that the history will continue after its death. He explains the so-called fine-tuning of the universe (those necessary factors for life to exist in our universe) as the result of a type of cosmic evolution. He proposes that the universe has undergone a series of transitions (one of which is the big bang) and in the process of undergoing these transitions, the universe itself evolves, as do the laws of nature that govern it, through what he calls cosmological natural selection.[3] Smolin explains: "The basic hypothesis of cosmological natural selection is that universes reproduce by the creation of new universes inside black holes. Our universe is thus a descendant of another universe, born in one of its black holes, and every black hole in our universe is the seed of a new universe."[4] Our observable universe may come to an end, but not before it has given life to new universes. Smolin's controversial claim is that the laws of nature themselves, presumed by many to be immutable and constant, may evolve through a process similar to biological evolution.[5] Each new universe varies slightly, but not drastically, from its parent universe. Smolin suggests that these universes evolve toward greater self-organization and complexity, explaining that the very elements needed for the existence of black holes, carbon and oxygen, are also the necessary elements for the universe to have carbon-based life.[6] Therefore the existence of life in our universe is not improbable and does not require a vast multiverse in which most of the other universes are unlike our own in order to explain the statistical occurrence

---

[3] Lee Smolin, *Three Roads to Quantum Gravity* (New York: Basic Books, 2001), 200–201; see references also in *Time Reborn: From the Crisis in Physics to the Future of the Universe* (Boston: Houghton Mifflin Harcourt, 2013), 123–39; Lee Smolin and Roberto Mangabeira Unger, *The Singular Universe and the Reality of Time* (Cambridge, UK: Cambridge University Press, 2014); Lee Smolin, "Time, Laws, and the Future of Cosmology," *Physics Today* 67, no. 3 (March 2014): 38–43; for Smolin's earlier book-length study on this topic, see Lee Smolin, *The Life of the Cosmos* (New York: Oxford University Press, 1997).

[4] Smolin, *Time Reborn*, 124; see also Niayesh Afshordi, Robert B. Mann, and Razieh Pourhasan, "The Black Hole at the Beginning of Time," *Scientific American* 311, no. 2 (August 2014): 36–43; see also Jacob D. Bekenstein and Alfred T. Kamajian, "Information in the Holographic Universe," *Scientific American* 15, no. 3 (March 2006): 74–81.

[5] Smolin, "Time, Laws, and the Future of Cosmology," 38–43.

[6] Smolin, *Time Reborn*, 126.

of our own finely tuned laws of nature.[7] On the contrary, in Smolin's model, life becomes probable, and other existing universes would be very similar to our own.

Andrew Linde's theory of a self-reproducing universe offers another possible theory about the universe in which the universe as a whole does not end with the death of our observable universe. Linde proposes that a self-reproducing universe solves several problems inherent in the standard big bang theory, namely, where and when it all began, the flatness of space, why the universe is so big, the timing of the expansion, the uniform distribution of matter in the universe, and the uniqueness problem, or why the universe is the way it is.[8] For our purposes, what is important about his model is that it begins with symmetry-breaking, a concept involved in the rise of complexity from chaos discussed in chapter 4, in which patterns form spontaneously in the process of self-organization in nonlinear systems. Linde explains that at the beginning of the universe, all particles are light, and so the fundamental forces are united.[9] As the universe expands, scalar fields develop, and as particles interact with these fields, they become heavy, and the fundamental forces separate through symmetry-breaking.[10] The energy of the scalar field is what caused the rapid expansion referred to as inflation in the beginning of universe, and then when the energy of the field declined, the expansion slowed down.[11] Linde uses the image of a ball that rolls down the side of a bowl. What happens when it reaches the bottom? It rolls back and forth until it settles. Linde states that

> like the ball as it reaches the bottom of the bowl, the scalar field began to oscillate near the minimum of its potential energy. As the scalar field oscillated, it lost energy, giving it up in the form

---

[7] Recall that Tegmark's Level II multiverse, which is congruent with string theory, suggests that if every possible type of universe—each with its own distinct laws of nature—exists, statistically one universe that has our specific laws leading to the emergence of life is bound to occur. Smolin takes a different approach by noting a possible evolution of universes in which life emerges through cosmic natural selection as the laws of each universe successively moved toward the emergence of complexity, self-organization, and in our universe, life.

[8] Andre Linde, "The Self-Reproducing Inflationary Universe," *Scientific American* 271, no. 5 (November 1994): 48–49.

[9] Ibid., 50.

[10] Ibid.

[11] Ibid.

of elementary particles. These particles interacted with one another and eventually settled down to some equilibrium temperature. From this time on, the standard big bang theory can describe the evolution of the universe.[12]

Linde goes on to explain how this model solves the problems listed above (though we are not going to address those issues here) and argues that the model produces testable predictions such as the evidence of gravitational waves in the cosmic microwave radiation background that were claimed to be found in March 2014, albeit a claim later qualified as not being definitive. Again, without going into all of the details of Linde's theory, he ultimately hypothesizes:

> If the universe contains at least one inflationary domain of a sufficiently large size, it begins unceasingly producing new inflationary domains. . . . In essence, one inflationary universe sprouts other inflationary bubbles, which in turn produce other inflationary bubbles. This process, which I have called eternal inflation, keeps going as a chain reaction, producing a fractallike pattern of universes. In this scenario the universe as a whole is immortal. Each particular part of the universe may stem from a singularity somewhere in the past, and it may end up in a singularity somewhere in the future. There is, however, no end for the evolution of the entire universe.[13]

Linde notes that the question of whether or not there was an initial big bang that started the entire process becomes irrelevant, but one can consider each bubble its own big bang, so that rather than inflation being a stage in the big bang, the big bang is a stage of inflation.[14] Linde goes on to speculate, in an almost theological fashion:

> In thinking about the process of self-reproduction of the universe, one cannot avoid drawing analogies, however superficial they may be. One may wonder, Is not this process similar to what happens with all of us? Some time ago we were born. Eventually we will die, and the entire world of our thoughts, feelings and memories will disappear. But there were those who lived before us, there will be those who will live after, and humanity as a

---

[12] Ibid., 50–51.
[13] Ibid., 54.
[14] Ibid., 55.

whole, if it is clever enough, may live for a long time. Inflationary theory suggests that a similar process may occur with the universe. One can draw some optimism from knowing that even if our civilization dies, there will be other places in the universe where life will emerge again and again, in all its possible forms.[15]

While Smolin's and Linde's theories differ scientifically, they share a couple of ideas in common. Both theories hold that our observable universe came from some form of universe that existed before us, and both claim that our observable universe will give rise to new universes that come after us. Likewise, both understand part of this process to be an evolution toward self-organization and greater complexity, a pattern that seems inherent in creation as observed in our own universe and discussed in chapter 4. We speak theologically of the end times and scripturally of a new heavens and a new earth. What do these concepts mean in light of the possibility that the universe itself may be re-created after its demise, the idea that out of the death of our observable universe comes new life? Might we speak of the resurrection of the cosmos itself?

Theological and Pastoral Implications

The End Times

First and foremost, we must take into consideration Jürgen Moltmann's caveat, "Theology does not acquire its eschatological horizons from the general observation of the world, neither the observation of the stars in the universe nor a contemplation of the events of world history; it acquires them from its particular experience of God. We call this 'root experience,' because here are experienced events in which God 'reveals' himself, and from which human communities acquire their identity."[16] Moltmann names these "root experiences"

---

[15] Ibid.

[16] Jürgen Moltmann, "Cosmos and Theosis: Eschatological Perspectives on the Future of the Universe," in *The Far-Future Universe: Eschatology from a Cosmic Perspective*, ed. George F. R. Ellis (Philadelphia, PA: Templeton Foundation Press, 2002), 250. For further reflections on eschatology and cosmology, see John Polkinghorne and Michael Welker, eds., *The End of the World and the Ends of God: Science and Theology on Eschatology* (Harrisburg, PA: Trinity Press International, 2000).

as the Exodus for Israel and Judaism and the Christ event for Christianity.[17] From these experiences we first come to an understanding of God and our relationship to God, and within that context, we contemplate eschatology or the end times.

Theologically, when we think about the end of time, we use the image of a new creation—a new heavens and a new earth—but we do not imagine that there is literally going to be a new planet created on which we start over. Through space exploration, it is possible that humanity will inhabit some other part of space or planet before the "end times," but that new habitation would still be part of the currently existing creation. The biblical concept of the idea of a new heavens and a new earth is primarily drawn from Isaiah 65, in which the creation of a new heavens and a new earth in verse 17 is part of God's promise to humanity. The image is not meant to be taken literally, but rather it represents God's promise for an end to suffering and for future harmony described in idyllic images such as the wolf lying down with the lamb. Herein we also see the concept that protology (the beginning) is eschatology (the end) in the way these garden images mirror the Garden of Eden in Genesis. A similar theme of an end to suffering and a renewed relationship between God and God's people is seen in the image of a new heaven and earth in Revelation 21.

A New Heavens and a New Earth

Second Peter, chapter 3 also uses this image of a new heavens and earth, stating in verse 13, "But according to his promise we await new heavens and a new earth in which righteousness dwells." Here the context is the delay of the second coming of Christ, which the early Christians had expected to happen in their lifetime. The author connects the creation and destruction of the world through water and uses the Day of the Lord imagery from the prophets to predict a final destruction in which the heavens are dissolved in flames and the earth or elements melted in fire. The author concludes with the point of his exhortation, namely, that Christians should live their lives so as to be found without spot or blemish at that time. Again, this imagery of destruction should not be taken literally and correlated

[17] Moltmann, "Cosmos and Theosis," 250–51.

with possible scientific images of the earth's ultimate demise by the sun nor with the ultimate cosmological destruction of the universe through the fry scenario, another term for the big crunch in which a closed universe collapses back into the immeasurably hot density of the big bang conditions, a scenario that is no longer widely held by scientists, at any rate. The imagery is symbolic, drawing on images familiar within the tradition. Likewise, the re-creation imagery should not be taken literally either. The theological point of this Scripture passage is a promise of the ultimate triumph of righteousness and an exhortation to be steadfast in one's own path of righteous living. The imagery is about God's faithfulness and the fulfillment of that promise of righteousness; it is not a scientific theory about the end of the universe.

Another passage often highlighted in this discussion is Romans 8 with its reference to the redemption of creation itself. Romans is a bit more complicated because it has to do with the concept of corruption and death being a consequence of the sin of Adam. Paul's point is that the created world itself is subject to corruption because it is caught up in the destiny of sinful humankind, and so it will also be freed from that corruption and share in the redemption that is now the destiny of humankind through the grace of Christ.

Biblical exegesis cautions us against taking any of these images literally in terms of connecting them to scientific cosmology, whether trying to correlate the end of the earth in fire with the passages in Second Peter or the literal re-creation of the cosmos with the passages in Romans. What we can take from these passages is the point that because creation involves more than just humanity, humans are connected to a larger story of the cosmos.

Resurrection from the Dead

Moltmann explains that in the Christ event, Christians experienced God "not only as the Creator of all things but also as the one who brings all things to completion."[18] The end times for the early Christians involved an "already-not yet" aspect. The end has been ushered in by the death and resurrection of Christ. Moltmann suggests that

[18] Ibid., 251.

"from the moment when the disciples called that which happened to the dead Christ 'resurrection from the dead,' the universal eschatological horizon was already present in the understanding of this unique historical event."[19] This eschatological horizon goes beyond humanity to encompass all creation. Moltmann warns, "Without an eschatology of the universe, Christian eschatology cripples the Godness of its God."[20] Just as the early Hebrew people had to move from an understanding of God as a tribal God to a God of all creation, if we do not want to cripple the Godness of God, we must move beyond an anthropocentric (human-centered) God to a God of the whole cosmos. If resurrection is ultimately about continued existence, relationship, and meaningfulness of creation, we can see ourselves as part of a resurrection story that is much larger than just the resurrection of humankind.

The question of eschatology that is connected to our understanding of the end of our universe is whether the framework of our existence is one of meaningful complexity or absurd chaos. Recall from chapter 4 that the creation narratives involve an ordering of chaos. The promise of a new heavens and a new earth is the continuation of that creative process, a promise of a continued framework of meaning and relationship beyond the existence of this world. Chaos abounds in the human experiences of the Israelites being forced into exile or in the death of early Christians before the promised second coming of Christ, events Moltmann would call catastrophic. The assurance given to these communities in the imagery of a new heavens and earth is that God continually creates anew. God holds back the chaos and brings meaning and life out of the darkness. Out of what seems like random chaos to us, deep, fractal layers of meaningful complexity emerge.

Death is part of creation. We can look at the correlation between death and the individual, mass extinction and the species, solar death and the planet, and, ultimately, entropy and the observable universe in order to see this. How do we respond? On the one hand, we ask ourselves why the fact that our observable universe is going to end leads us to think it would be meaningless if this fate came to pass. A flower blooms and dies, and yet we do not find it meaningless.

[19] Ibid.
[20] Ibid., 252.

Is there not simply a beauty to existence in itself? Is not that beauty at times enhanced by its fleeting nature? Why must we believe that our universe must have a continued existence in order to have eternal significance? On the other hand, our framework of meaning in the Christian context is the concept that out of death comes resurrection, whether on an individual scale, a conceptual scale (in the sense of the death of old ideas and misconceptions), or on a cosmic scale. Both Smolin and Linde suggest that the entire universe may be an inter-dependent, self-regulating, and self-organizing system, such as we discussed in chapter 4.

As such, what Christian theology adds to this story for believers is our interpretive lens of death and resurrection. Jürgen Moltmann notes:

> In Christian eschatology we always find a combination of the two ideas: an end and a beginning, a catastrophe and a new start, farewell and greeting; for eschatology can only be called Christian if it takes its bearings from Israel's Exodus and the Christ event. Israel's bondage and the death of Christ are primal images of catastrophe. The Exodus into the liberty of the promised land, and the resurrection into the eternal life of the future world are primal images of the new beginning.[21]

Resurrection is about what comes after death. There is continuity but also unexpectedness and transformation. God affirms and makes valid who we became in life through resurrection.

Such a position is congruent with the possibility of the death of our observable universe into the possible resurrection/birth of a new universe in Lee Smolin's idea of cosmic natural selection or Andre Linde's idea of eternal inflation. Note the need for caution in taking either theory too literally, as neither has been able to produce conclusive supporting evidence yet and may never be able to do so. Considering these perspectives from a theological standpoint, however, connects the concept of death and resurrection to the end of our observable universe through whatever means it comes to an end.

Linde's suggestion of a complex, fractal universe has a resonance with the image of creation as continually evolving toward complexity

---

[21] Ibid.

while on the edge of chaos. The fractal nature of the self-reproducing universe is attractive because of its synchronicity with the way in which we see a pattern through all of existence in which complexity arises out of simplicity and order comes to be out of disorder as was discussed in chapter 4. The pattern of complexity repeats itself in the evolution of the cosmos: from the initial birth of stars, to successive generations of stars and planets forming into solar systems and galaxies, to the complexity of our own planetary system enabling life, to the ecosystem that sustains humanity, and to the complexity of the human body and our individual cells. Wonder and awe can emerge from contemplating what might come next, what might come after us. The theme of creation as an ordering of chaos and bringing meaningful complexity out of the chaos repeats itself in Linde's theory whereby the universe is re-created in fractal patterns of ever greater complexity and self-organization. Moltmann suggests that a universe that is an open, complex system both demonstrates congruence with the systems of matter and life that we know and would be most congruent with a theological eschatology that follows this model of life from death and new beginnings from catastrophe revealed in the Exodus and the Christ event.[22]

In Lee Smolin's model of the universe, the births of new universes come from black holes, which involve the death of massive galactic systems. In the big freeze or heat death of the universe, the stars will eventually all die, leaving nothing but black holes prior to the possible dissolution of matter itself. While the image painted seems to be an endless cold landscape of death, what if out of each of those black holes new life is being formed? Our galaxy may collapse into a black hole, but perhaps a new universe will be born out of our cosmic death. We can see the death of our own galaxy similar to the death of an individual in human civilization. The world goes on, but we also believe it is different due to the existence of that one person. There can be great hope in thinking that the end of our observable universe may not be the end but may simply be the next step of God's creative act.

Moltmann notes that the cosmic story is much larger than humanity, pointing out that "it is impossible to shift human protology back

---

[22] Ibid., 264.

to the big bang, and to extend human eschatology to the death of the universe through heat or cold."[23] Caleb Scharf puts it another way stating, "Our species has sprung into existence within the barest instant of this universe's enormously long span of history, and it looks like there will be an even longer future that may or may not contain us. The quest to try to find our place, to discover our relevance, can seem like a monumental joke."[24] When we think of the brevity of human existence on a cosmic scale, we need not conclude that our existence is meaningless in the face of such vastness. Brevity is not equivalent with meaninglessness, particularly in a Gospel perspective.

Look at the short and insignificant period of time Christ lived and ministered, and yet look at the impact of that one life on the world. Our scriptural narrative tells us that God works in exactly this way, using the small, brief, and insignificant to have a very big impact. Chaos theory, as we saw in chapter 4, tells us that small triggers can have an exponentially large impact. Humanity and our universe existing for such a short space of time and perhaps being such an infinitesimally small part of cosmic history does not make our existence meaningless. Perhaps we can be both very small and insignificant on a cosmic scale and have an extraordinary impact on the cosmic system. (I would add, given humanity's proclivities toward destruction, hopefully a positive rather than negative impact.) Ask anyone who has lost a loved one at too young an age, and many, if not most, will tell you that the brevity of that person's life did not make their existence any less meaningful. The fact that life in the world continues after an individual's death does not make the individual any less significant in the eyes of loved ones. That person may have existed for one brief moment in the history of the world, but the world has forever been changed by the existence of that person. In Smolin's theory, the new universes that come into existence evolve. They take the advances toward complexity and self-organization made in our own universe and become something more, just as we hope that the world becomes more because of our existence and the person we become during our lives in that world.

[23] Ibid., 252.
[24] Caleb Scharf, "Cosmic (in)Significance," *Scientific American* 311, no. 2 (August 2014): 74.

Moltmann suggests that rather than reading the cosmic story in light of humanity, perhaps we should read the human story in light of the cosmos. In doing so, Moltmann concludes, "The future of the universe would then not be bound to the future of human beings; instead the future of the human being would be integrated into the future of the universe. Just as there are an inexhaustible number of thoughts and ideas in the human mind, there can similarly be an inexhaustible number of conditions in the universe. Just as the human mind regulates its potentialities according to its constructive hopes and its destructive fears, the continual appearance of new possibilities can similarly constitute the universe's openness to the future."[25] Similarly, Keith Ward warns against the assumption that humans are the center of the universe. Like Moltmann, he holds out hope that humans have a vocation and "positive responsibility to shape the material universe so that it is productive and protective of personal life, whatever its form. The human responsibility is not merely to leave things as they are, but to change them so that the personal, in all its forms, can flourish."[26] Andre Linde suggests that through a self-reproducing universe, life will emerge again and again. Ward sees humanity's role in that cosmic story as a vocation to contribute in whatever way possible to the potential flourishing of life beyond our own existence.

We don't get to see the whole picture, and so what looks like random points to us could be some stunningly beautiful geometric pattern from a different perspective, similar to the way in which individual points of a fractal tend to look completely random. Such interplay between randomness and order/pattern/beauty is built into creation itself. Perhaps part of our eternal significance consists in being part of the evolution of something bigger than ourselves. Perhaps that evolution into complexity can put our own pettiness into perspective. Our great hope in God can be that we are *not* the end of the story of creation, that creation continues after the extinction of humanity, after the death of our sun and solar system, after our galaxy becomes a black hole, perhaps giving life to a new universe

---

[25] Moltmann, "Cosmos and Theosis," 253.

[26] Keith Ward, "Cosmology and Religious Ideas about the End of the World," in *The Far-Future Universe: Eschatology from a Cosmic Perspective*, ed. George F. R. Ellis (Philadelphia, PA: Templeton Foundation Press, 2002), 247.

in the process, and after our universe itself comes to an end. Just because we are not the end of the creation story does not mean that we are unimportant or insignificant. Herein lies the revelation of God in Christ—that God is in union with us and our cosmos, connecting us into that fractal pattern we cannot see.

Chapter Eight

Strings or Loops?

Scientific Developments—
String Theory and Loop Quantum Gravity

Lee Smolin, in his book *Three Roads to Quantum Gravity*, explains that the irreconcilable nature of quantum mechanics and general relativity has to do with the way each disagrees with Newtonian physics. While Newtonian physics explains the world we can observe and in which we interact with a great deal of success, general relativity describes the world of the very large on a cosmic scale, and quantum theory describes the world of the very small on an atomic level. In doing so, general relativity accepts the assumptions that Newton made about the relationship between observers and the system they observe but altered Newton's understanding of time and space. Quantum mechanics alternatively accepted Newton's understanding of time and space as an unchanging background but altered Newton's understanding of the relationship between the observer and the observed.[1] Consequently, one of the great issues that faces science today is the fact that these two theories which have been so successful in describing and explaining the way things work on their respective levels do not agree with one another. Scientists from the time of Einstein on have been searching for one unified theory that will explain all aspects of reality from the cosmic large to the quantum small. Two theories have proven vastly successful, namely, loop quantum gravity, which begins from the perspective of relativity, and

---

[1] Lee Smolin, *Three Roads to Quantum Gravity* (New York: Basic Books, 2001), 3–5.

string theory, which begins from the perspective of quantum theory.[2] Smolin describes the main difference between the two as the fact that loop quantum theory is background independent, whereas string theory is background dependent, concepts that will be explained in more detail below but, in short, have to do with how each understands the nature of time and space.

One huge problem in this field is that experimental evidence for any theory is at best tangential, as direct observation is not currently possible on the scale at which quantum gravity has an effect. No evidence exists for any of the current competing theories; it is hard to judge between them due to our inability to make observations of any kind on such a small scale. Brian Greene notes that this scale is "a million billion times beyond the scales we can probe with the world's most powerful accelerators."[3] Scientists in the fields that study the issue of quantum gravity, however, are quick to point out that the existence of atoms was theorized centuries (even millennia, if we consider that the idea was first suggested by Democritus in the fourth or fifth century BCE) before we had any experimental evidence of their existence.[4] Furthermore, the first evidence of atoms, that of Brownian motion, was not direct observation of the atoms themselves but rather the effect of the movement of the atoms on dust grains. Similarly, the evidence we currently look for in string theory or loop gravity is indirect evidence, evidence of the effects of these theories rather than direct observation. Smolin suggests the possibility that

[2] Ibid., 9–10. Note that Smolin also includes a third path (his third of three roads) that is more conceptual and theoretical, abandoning both relativity and quantum theory for completely new starting points. He sees this third road as not only being included in any final unifying theory but also what will most likely provide the conceptual framework that will make such unification possible (10–11). Due to the limits of this chapter, we will explore only string theory and loop gravity. For a sampling of other theories, such as geometry theory and causal dynamical triangulations, see A. Garrett Lisi and James Owen Weatherall, "A Geometric Theory of Everything," *Scientific American* 303, no. 6 (December 2010): 54–61; Jan Ambjørn, Jerzy Jurkiewicz, and Renate Loll, "The Self-Organizing Quantum Universe," *Scientific American* 299, no. 1 (July 2008): 42–49.

[3] Brian Greene, *The Hidden Reality: Parallel Universes and the Deep Laws of the Cosmos*, EPUB eBook ed. (New York: A. A. Knopf, 2011), loc. 81–82 of 347.

[4] See Martin Bojowald, "Follow the Bouncing Universe," *Scientific American* 299, no. 4 (October 2008): 44–51; Cliff Burgess and Fernando Quevedo, "The Great Cosmic Roller-Coaster Ride," *Scientific American* 297, no. 5 (November 2007): 52–59. Note that these two articles provide good, concise overviews of loop gravity and string theory respectively.

scientists will eventually discover a way in which these two theories, both incomplete in themselves, may eventually come together to be understood as two perspectives looking at the same reality.[5]

Hyung Choi refers to this issue as the legend of the tangibility of matter.[6] He breaks down the issue into an ontological, epistemological, and methodological problem. In other words, when we start to talk about reality as we experience it, we run into problems with what really *is* or what really exists (ontology), what we can know (epistemology), and how we test either (methodology).[7] One of the issues that physics has run into today as it attempts to reconcile relativity and quantum mechanics is the issue of methodology and how to test new theories. String theory, for example, has provided beautiful mathematical solutions to this problem of reconciling relativity and quantum mechanics, but it is as yet unable to be experimentally tested—and may prove to ultimately be untestable—and thus unknowable.

String Theory

Starting from the perspective of relativity, superstring theory, or M-theory as it is also called, seeks to unify the four forces: electromagnetism, strong nuclear, weak nuclear, and gravity. The first three had been successfully unified in quantum mechanics and quantum field theory, but gravity was the outlier, unable to be reconciled with the other three. String theory has demonstrated remarkable mathematical success in uniting all four forces. It has done so by once again

---

[5] Note that Smolin is more optimistic in this regard in his earlier book, *Three Roads to Quantum Gravity* (2001). In his later books he seems more skeptical of string theory and makes a case concerning the fact that science and the resources that support scientific research have overwhelmingly and mistakenly backed string theory, and that such a single-minded concentration of effort and resources in the face of a lack of experimental evidence is a huge mistake. See Lee Smolin, *The Trouble with Physics: The Rise of String Theory, the Fall of a Science, and What Comes Next* (Boston: Houghton Mifflin, 2006). For a scientifically detailed analysis of these theories and their current status, see Abhay Ashtekar, et al., "General Relativity and Gravitation: A Centennial Perspective," *arXiv Preprint arXiv:1409.5823* (2014). Accessed at http://arxiv.org/pdf/1409.5823v1.pdf.

[6] Hyung Choi, "Knowledge of the Unseen: A New Vision for Science and Religion Dialogue," in *Expanding Humanity's Vision of God: New Thoughts on Science and Religion*, ed. Robert Hermann (Philadelphia, PA: Templeton Foundation, 2001), 3.

[7] Ibid.

changing the way we think of particles. Rather than picturing particles as a point, string theory suggests that particles (each associated with a certain field) are "tiny, stringlike, vibrating filaments" and that "the strings within different kinds of particles are identical, the leitmotif of string unification, but vibrate in different patterns."[8] The common analogy used to explain string theory are the strings of a musical instrument. Greene illustrates, "Much as different vibrational patterns of strings on a guitar produce different musical notes, different vibrational patterns of the filaments in string theory produce different particle properties."[9] String theory has been extremely successful in explaining the properties of elementary particles, most importantly accounting for the properties of the hypothetical graviton, the particle associated with the gravitational field on the quantum level, thus unifying gravity with quantum mechanics.[10]

The problem, as Greene explains, is that

> because of the string's infinitesimal size, on the order of the Planck length—10^{-33} centimeters—even today's most refined experiments cannot resolve the string's extended structure. The Large Hadron Collider, which slams particles together with energies just beyond 10 trillion times that embodied by a single proton at rest, can probe to scales of about 10^{-19} centimeters; that's a millionth of a billionth of the width of a strand of hair, but still orders of magnitude too *large* to resolve phenomena at the Planck length.[11]

So while string theory has offered some very exciting possibilities in terms of solving some of the most pressing issues in physics, no one has ever actually seen a string or proven that strings actually exist. While the idea that all that exists is made of tiny vibrating strings does not seem to take a huge leap of the imagination, given that most of us were brought up to think of everything that exists is made of tiny particles, in order for the mathematics of string theory to work, there are a couple of other necessary elements to the theory: extra dimensions and branes.

[8] Greene, *The Hidden Reality*, loc. 82 of 347.
[9] Ibid., loc. 82–83 of 347.
[10] Ibid., loc. 84 of 347.
[11] Ibid., loc. 83 of 347.

Figure 8.1

Calabi-yau

A shape representing the possible folded up nature of the extra dimensions of string theory.[12]

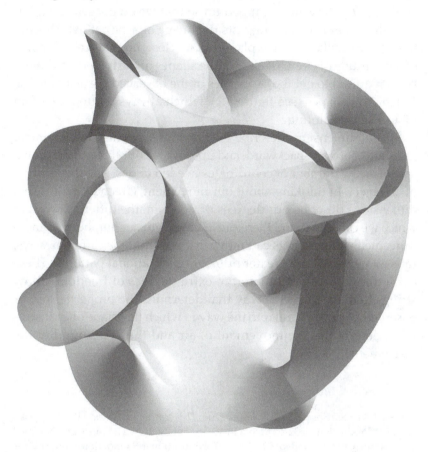

String theory posits the existence of eleven dimensions—ten spatial dimensions and the additional dimension of time. While these extra dimensions are basically impossible to visualize, given that we can only visualize things in one, two, or three dimensions, certainly analogies do exist to help us understand. Brian Greene's famous example

[12] Image created by Jbourjai (Mathematica output) [Public domain], via Wikimedia Commons, http://commons.wikimedia.org/wiki/File:Calabi_yau.jpg.

is that of an electrical cable stretched between two poles. When we look at it from a distance, it looks like a one-dimensional line. To an ant crawling on the wire, however, it is two-dimensional; in addition to being able to walk horizontally across the wire, the ant can circumnavigate it as well.[13] Similarly, the extra dimensions of string theory could be very tiny and wrapped up so that we do not see or experience them. Greene also suggests the image of a carpet, which from the distance looks like a flat plane, but up close, one realizes it is made of a multitude of circular loops.[14] The shapes of the folded up dimensions required to get the properties of the observed particles are the Calabi-Yau shapes (see figure 8.1), which always remind me of an M. C. Escher painting.[15]

Spatial dimensions describe the directions in which we can move (left-right, forward-backward, and up-down in our three-dimensional space) or the number of coordinates needed to describe the location of an object. In thinking about our movement, Greene explains that dimensions describe our degrees of freedom, the different ways in which we can move, and therefore having a greater number of dimensions means that strings can move in a multitude of different ways, thus allowing them a greater number of vibrational patterns. These extra dimensions, and therefore extra degrees of freedom, allow strings to move in such a way that determine the properties of our observed particles, similar to the way in which the shape of an instrument determines the movement of air and thus the sound of the instrument.[16]

---

[13] See PBS *Nova* Special with Brian Greene, *The Fabric of the Cosmos: What Is Space?* A NOVA Production by 32-12 Media in association with ARTE France and National Geographic Channel, video, 52:52, WGBH Educational Foundation, PBS Airdate: Nov. 2, 2011, http://www.pbs.org/wgbh/nova/physics/fabric-of-cosmos.html#fabric -space.

[14] Ibid., loc. 87–88 of 347.

[15] For a wonderful Escher-like drawing suggesting these dimensions in a Calabi-yau shape as a roller coaster, see the image in *Scientific American* by Jean Francois Podevin on the opening pages of the article, Burgess and Quevedo, "The Great Cosmic Roller-Coaster Ride," 52–59. See http://www.scientificamerican.com/article/the-great -cosmic-roller-coaster-ride/.

[16] Greene, *The Hidden Reality*, loc. 91 of 347. Note that one issue with string theory is the inability to determine exactly what the Calabi-Yau shape of space might be, as there are a massive number of possible Calabi-Yau shapes. For this reason among

Furthermore, string theory (or M-theory as it came to be known) suggests the existence not only of strings but also branes or membranes. A membrane is a surface, such as we would picture with a two-dimensional membrane, but these branes can come in any number of dimensions and may be very large or on a similar Planck scale size as the strings. The strings interact with the branes. Strings can be open, as you might picture a snippet of actual string with two loose ends, or, similar to a rubber band, closed. Open strings can have their ends attached to a brane and thus not be able to leave a brane, whereas closed strings would be able to move freely. Why is this information relevant? Greene explains: "Theorists think that the space in our universe once had nine dimensions, all on equal footing. Early in cosmic history, three of them partook in the cosmic expansion and became the three dimensions we now observe. The other six are now unobservable, either because they have stayed microscopic with a doughnut-like topology or because all matter is confined to a three-dimensional surface (a membrane, or simply 'brane') in the nine-dimensional space."[17] In other words, it is possible that what we know of the universe is a three-dimensional brane existing in a larger dimensional space. One possible explanation for the big bang offered by string theory is that it was caused by the collision of our brane with a parallel brane, and that these collisions happen in a cyclic pattern.[18] Likewise, the interactions between neighboring branes and what theorists call antibranes may account for inflation.[19] Because all of our known particles are open strings, we can only interact with and observe our three-dimensional brane. For example, we are only able to see because of light. Light is made up of photons. Greene explains that it is possibly because certain strings such as photons "stick" to our three-dimensional brane that we are not able to see the other dimensions.[20] Likewise, everything we experience with the exception of gravity, which according to string theory is a closed

others, scientists such as Lee Smolin are critical of string theory for being a solution without an actual theory to unify the different possible solutions.

[17] Max Tegmark, "Parallel Universes," *Scientific American* 288, no. 5 (May 2003): 44.

[18] Gabriele Veneziano, "The Myth of the Beginning of Time," *Scientific American* 16, no. 1 (January 2006): 72–81; see also Greene, *The Hidden Reality*, loc. 118–19 of 347.

[19] Burgess and Quevedo, "The Great Cosmic Roller-Coaster Ride," 58.

[20] Brian Greene, *The Fabric of the Cosmos: Space, Time, and the Texture of Reality* (New York: A. A. Knopf, 2004), 393.

string rather than an open string, would be confined to this three-dimensional brane.[21] As Burgess and Quevedo explain,

> [Membranes] act like slippery sheets of flypaper: the ends of open strings move on them but cannot be pulled off. Subatomic particles such as electrons and protons may be nothing more than open strings and, if so, are stuck to a brane. Only a few hypothetical particles, such as the graviton (which transmits the force of gravity), must be closed strings and are thus able to move completely freely through the extra dimensions. This distinction offers a second reason not to see the extra dimensions: our instruments may be built of particles that are trapped on a brane. If so, future instruments might be able to use gravitons to reach out into the extra dimensions.[22]

The fact that gravity would not be so confined might also account for dark matter. In other words, it is possible that the effects of dark matter are from interactions with the dimensions beyond the three we see and/or our interactions with other universes existing on other branes. The problem in proving the theory is that the graviton has such weak energy, we have not yet been able to detect its existence, let alone garner information from it about the possible existence of other branes. Greene suggests that the energy of gravity may be weak due to the fact that the extra dimensions posited by string theory are not tiny, wrapped up dimensions but in fact are very large yet undetectable dimensions accessible to gravity, therefore diluting the energy of gravity in the same way that larger pipes would weaken water pressure.[23]

One result of string theory is that it implies a multiverse. One understanding of this multiverse was mentioned above, in which other universes exist on other branes. Some theorists go even further and suggest that string theory solves the issue of the cosmological constant in that the 10^{500} possible forms that the shape of the extra dimensions in string theory can take each correspond to a universe,

---

[21] Ibid., 394.

[22] Burgess and Quevedo, "The Great Cosmic Roller-Coaster Ride," 57.

[23] Greene, *The Fabric of the Cosmos*, 401; Greene, *The Hidden Reality*, loc. 94–95 of 347.

resulting in one universe that produces the cosmological constant and laws of our own universe and hence life as we know it.[24]

Greene notes that while direct evidence for string theory, that is, being able to directly observe strings themselves, is unlikely any time in the near future, there are a number of ways we might find indirect evidence. No one piece of indirect evidence would be the "smoking gun," but a combination of them could build strong support for the case of string theory.[25] Greene provides a very positive outlook in his status report in *The Hidden Reality*, outlining the many successes of string theory and the potential for further confirmation.[26] Critics, however, remain skeptical, particularly in the face of several decades of research turning up no evidence to support string theory.[27]

Loop Quantum Gravity

While Lee Smolin does not advocate abandoning string theory altogether and still feels that it may in time yield further results that prove to be part of a larger solution, he makes a strong case for not putting all of our eggs in one basket, suggesting it would be prudent to invest more time and resources in other directions at this point in time, particularly loop quantum gravity (LQG).[28] Smolin's main argument is that string theory is background dependent, which is to say that it depends on Newton's idea of time and space as an unchanging scaffolding upon which reality is built. Starting from the perspective

---

[24] Ibid., loc. 148–51 of 347. See also R. Bousso and J. Polchinski, "The String Theory Landscape," *Scientific American* 291, no. 3 (Sep, 2004): 78–87. Note that Lee Smolin sees this issue of 10^{500} possible shapes to the extra dimensions as a reason to question string theory's utility. See Smolin, *The Trouble with Physics*.

[25] Greene, *The Hidden Reality*, loc. 94 of 347. In table 4.1, Greene outlines each of the possible pieces of experimental evidence that would move us in the direction of confirming string theory.

[26] See Table 4.2. Ibid., loc. 102–3 of 347.

[27] See Smolin, *The Trouble with Physics*, 183–94; Joseph Lykken and Maria Spiropulu, "Supersymmetry and the Crisis in Physics," *Scientific American* 310, no. 5 (2014): 34–39.

[28] Smolin, *The Trouble with Physics*, 198–99. For a technical assessment of the current state of the field, see Abhay Ashtekar, Martin Reuter, and Carlo Rovelli, "From General Relativity to Quantum Gravity," *arXiv Preprint arXiv:1408.4336* (2014). Accessed at http://arxiv.org/pdf/1408.4336v1.pdf.

of Einstein's theory of relativity, Smolin suggests that space is an emergent property, and unlike proponents of the block universe, argues for the fundamental reality of time.[29] Smolin explains: "Relativity theory merged space with time, leading to the block-universe picture, in which both space and time are understood to be subjective ways of dividing up a four-dimensional reality. The hypothesis of the reality of time frees time from the false constraints of this unification. We can develop our ideas of time with the understanding that time is very different from space. This separation of time from space liberates space, too, opening a door to a greater understanding of its nature."[30]

Smolin defines time as the fundamental element of reality describing change, whereas space is an emergent property of the relationships that are evolving in time. He argues that we live in a world of illusion. When we look around, we see individual objects existing in something we call space. Many of us probably picture "space" as this vast, perhaps endless, container that holds all of the objects that exist. Such a concept, however, begs the very question, because it leads one to ask what is outside of space. We can only envision space as being in some larger space. In his book *Three Roads to Quantum Gravity*, Smolin explains that these fundamental questions about space and time are difficult to think about, "because they are the backdrop to all human experience. Everything that exists exists somewhere, and nothing happens that does not happen at some time."[31]

From a philosophical perspective, space makes relationship possible.[32] For you and me to be in relationship, there must be some

---

[29] Note that in his latest book, authored with Roberto Mangabeira Unger, Unger disagrees with Smolin that the universe is eternal. Unger argues that the eternality of the world is a metaphysical assertion that cannot be proved as opposed to a scientific assertion: "We could never know the world to be eternal. It does not become eternal by growing older or by having a more ancient history than we supposed" (518). Lee Smolin and Roberto Mangabeira Unger, *The Singular Universe and the Reality of Time* (Cambridge, UK: Cambridge University Press, 2014).

[30] Lee Smolin, *Time Reborn: From the Crisis in Physics to the Future of the Universe* (Boston: Houghton Mifflin Harcourt, 2013), 172.

[31] Smolin, *Three Roads to Quantum Gravity*, 1.

[32] See Andrew Tallon, *Head and Heart: Affection, Cognition, Volition as Triune Consciousness* (New York: Fordham University Press, 1997), 39. Tallon, building on Martin Buber's concept of the between, explains that relationship requires there to be some distance or space between two subjects.

distance or space between us. Smolin, however, turns that proposition around and suggests that relationship is literally what makes space possible. Smolin argues that there is no such thing as empty space. Rather, space is nothing other than relationship between objects.[33] He uses the analogy of a sentence. Just as you cannot have a sentence without words, and a sentence is nothing other than the relationship between the words, you cannot have space without objects (or more precisely, as we will see below, processes or events).[34] Space is the relationship between objects. Smolin notes that we cannot even have space with just one object; we must have at least two objects, or we have no relationship by which to define where the one object is located.[35] Likewise, time is not a thing in and of itself; it is simply a way to describe changes in a network of relationships.[36] Smolin summarizes: "Neither space nor time has any existence outside the system of evolving relationships that comprises the universe," a concept called "background independence."[37]

For Smolin, a successful approach to quantum gravity includes three hallmark ideas: "that space is *emergent*, that the more fundamental description is *discrete*, and that this description involves *causality* in a fundamental way."[38] The key insight of Einstein's concept of relativity is that space is dynamic and evolves; it can curve and change as a result of the mass of objects and the movement of objects. The concepts of emergence and discreteness are related in that what is meant by space being "emergent is that the continuum of space is an illusion. Just as the apparent smoothness of water or silk hides the fact that matter is made of discrete atoms, we suspect that the smoothness of space is not real and that space emerges as an approximation of something consisting of building blocks that we can count."[39]

---

[33] Smolin, *Three Roads to Quantum Gravity*, 18.

[34] Ibid.

[35] Ibid.

[36] Ibid., 22.

[37] Ibid.

[38] Smolin, *The Trouble with Physics*, 141. While Smolin's approach focuses on loop quantum gravity, he notes that there are other approaches to quantum gravity that also address these three aspects of emergence, discreteness, and causality. Two examples Smolin gives are causal dynamical triangulations and quantum graphity. See Smolin, *Time Reborn*, 175.

[39] Smolin, *The Trouble with Physics*, 240.

Recall that the word quantum comes from the idea of quanta, initially referring to small packets or quantities or amounts of energy. In this sense, space comes in quanta—small, discrete quantities. In other words, rather than being infinitely divisible, eventually space hits a point where it cannot be divided again. There is a limit to how small small is. That smallest possible size is: a Planck length of 10^{-33} cm, a smallest area of Planck length squared, which is 10^{-66} cm, and a smallest Planck volume of Planck length cubed, which is 10^{-99} cm.[40] Not only does space come in discrete quanta, but time does as well. Smolin describes time as flowing "not like a river but like the ticking of a clock, with 'ticks' that are about as long as Planck time: 10^{-43} second. Or, more precisely, time in our universe flows by the ticking of innumerable clocks—in a sense, at every location in the spin foam where a quantum 'move' takes place, a clock at that location has ticked once."[41]

The third important element, causality, is what connects space and time. When we speak of these discrete quanta of space emerging, one must ask from what do they emerge, and the answer is causality, which implies time. In other words, when space is understood as relationship, and reality is understood as process, what becomes measurable is the change in the relationships between events. Causality is the most important relationship between two events in which one event causes the other.[42]

So what exactly does LQG tell us? Most importantly, it tells us that space is discrete, that it has a smallest possible volume. Smolin explains, "If you tried to halve a region of this volume, the result would not be two regions each with half that volume. Instead, the process would create two new regions which together would have more volume than you started with."[43] Without getting too deeply into the technical details, LQG uses a type of graph called a spin network to describe space, in which "there are quanta of volume associated with the nodes [where the edges meet] and quanta of area associated with

[40] Lee Smolin, "Atoms of Space and Time," *Scientific American* 290, no. 1 (January 2004): 71.

[41] Ibid., 72.

[42] Smolin, *Three Roads to Quantum Gravity*, 53.

[43] Ibid., 106.

the edges."[44] Smolin explains that even with the graphs, this concept of space is hard to conceptualize, because we tend to picture the graph situated *in space*, whereas in reality, "the spin networks do not live in space; their structure generates space. And they are nothing but a structure of relations, governed by how the edges are tied together at the nodes."[45] The key insight of LQG is the idea that these connections between the lines and the nodes change in time. In other words, space itself evolves over time as the relationships between processes and events change.

Smolin argues that since the time of Newton, we have mistakenly understood our world as a collection of objects first and foremost with change being something secondary that happens to those objects. Smolin asserts that "relativity and quantum theory each tell us that this is not how the world is. They tell us—no, better, they scream at us—that our world is a history of processes. Motion and change are primary. Nothing *is*, except in a very approximate and temporary sense. How something is, or what its state is, is an illusion. . . . Process is more important than, and prior to, stasis."[46] Even what appear to be objects to us are actually processes; they are just incredibly slow processes on our timescale.[47] Any object we encounter actually changes over time. Smolin would therefore say "it" is a process, not an object. We can understand this concept when we think of something like the Grand Canyon as a geological process.

Herein lies a fundamental truth of how we understand human reality and the process of becoming. Smolin uses the example of story to explain causality. He suggests that a story is not a list of events, which would be rather boring in the telling, but rather "what makes a story a story is the connections between events."[48] He notes that "what happens to a person as they grow up has an effect on who they are."[49] While we tend to objectify people, a person, in fact, is always in the process of becoming; we believe in possibilities like conversion

---

[44] Smolin, *The Trouble with Physics*, 248, Fig. 15.

[45] Smolin, *Three Roads to Quantum Gravity*, 138; see also Smolin, "Atoms of Space and Time," 71.

[46] Smolin, *Three Roads to Quantum Gravity*, 53.

[47] Ibid., 52.

[48] Ibid., 50.

[49] Ibid.

and reconciliation. Smolin states that we live in a relational universe. The most fundamental reality of our human lives is also the most fundamental reality of the universe in which we live.

Another consequence of LQG has to do with the way in which information travels. In a low-dimensional world, space can be thought of as a lattice with nodes at each vertice, and particles move by hopping from one node to the next. Smolin uses the image of an apartment building to explain our low-dimensional space, in which you are limited to how many neighbors you can have—six total with neighbors on either side of you, above you and below you, and in front and in back of you (picture across the hall and across the alley).[50] If you want to visit someone down the hall, or down the street, across town, or on the other side of the world, for that matter, it will take you time to get from your apartment to theirs. Similarly Smolin explains, "It takes time for a particle, or a quantum carrying information, to go a long way. Hence there emerges a description of the world with a finite speed of light."[51] Smolin suggests, however, that one can "disorder locality" by adding one "nonlocal" link, something like a cell phone connection that connects two people who had previously been separated by great distance.[52]

LQG suggests the existence of such nonlocal links. Smolin suggests that it is much easier and more probable to add a nonlocal link than a local link. There are very few ways to add a local link (there are a limited number of routes from my apartment to the apartment down the hall) because there are a limited number of ways in which a node can be connected to its neighboring nodes. There are, however, many more ways to add a nonlocal node, since it can conceivably be connected to any other node in the universe.[53] For this reason, Smolin suggests that there must be a reason why we live in a universe where

---

[50] Smolin, *Time Reborn*, 173.

[51] Ibid., 181.

[52] Ibid., 182.

[53] Ibid. Smolin explains that within a universe in which there are perhaps 10^{180} nodes, there would be 10^{360} places to insert a nonlocal link, but 10^{100} such links could be added before being noticed in the macro world, despite the fact that they would be quite common averaging one per cubic nanometer in space (182). He also posits the existence of very social nodes with many nonlocal connections which would act as gossips do in human communication systems, transmitting a great amount of information to many locations (182–83).

most connections are "turned off," leaving us with only our local neighbors and connections.[54]

Smolin uses the idea of a cell phone network to explain again. He invites us to imagine that space as we know it does not exist and distance is defined by how often you talk to someone, with the more often you talk making you closer neighbors and the less often you talk making you more distant neighbors. "Now," Smolin says, "notice how different and more flexible this notion of distance is than distance in space. In space, as we saw, everyone has the same number of potential nearest-neighbors [6]. . . . In a cell-phone network, you are also free to be as near or far as you like from any other user in the network. If I know how far you are from, say, 50,000 other users, that tells me nothing about how far you might be from the 50,001st."[55] In other words, your relationship to the 50,000 does not tell me about your relationship to the 50,001st, because your ability to have a close or distant relationship with the 50,001st is not impacted by your relationship to the rest of the network. Smolin goes on: "But in space, proximities are rigid. Once you tell me who your nearest neighbors are, I know where you live. I can tell how far away you are from everybody else."[56] Smolin, drawing on concepts from quantum-graphity, suggests that in the beginning of our universe, all of these networks were turned on. But as the universe cooled, there was less energy for creating and maintaining these connections; most of them turned off, leaving only the few connections of our three-dimensional world, and space as we know it emerged.[57]

In talking about space as relationship, Smolin explains that only things that are close to us can affect us (can be a cause of an event), noting that we do not worry about a tiger that is on another continent being a danger to us, because it is too far away to affect us.[58] Loop quantum gravity understands space as this type of causal network,

[54] Ibid., 186.

[55] Ibid., 187.

[56] Ibid.

[57] Ibid., 187–88. Smolin explains that this process of space emerging in the early universe has been called *geometrogenesis* and can explain features such as the universal temperature of CMB radiation, giving an alternative explanation to inflation (188).

[58] Ibid., 173. This concept is called locality in physics. Recall the issue of nonlocality in EPR has to do with an electron being affected by another distant but entangled electron.

so Smolin uses this image of a cell phone or internet-connected world in which we are able to have much more interaction with people who are large distances away from us. If the network fails, however, that access suddenly disappears, and suddenly we only have access to those in our immediate proximity.[59] Smolin suggests "that space is an illusion and that the real relationships that form the world are a dynamical network a bit like the Internet or cell-phone networks. We experience the illusion of space because most of the possible connections are off, pushing everything far away."[60] Smolin posits "an image of a physical world not so different from our interconnected human world. The world is a dynamical network of relationships; whatever lives on the network and the structure of the network itself are both subject to evolution."[61] Smolin summarizes this view of reality:

> Elementary particles are not static objects just sitting there, but processes carrying little bits of information between events at which they interact, giving rise to new processes. . . . Look around and imagine that you see each object as a consequence of photons having just travelled from it to you. Each object you see is the result of a process by which information travelled to you in the shape of a collection of photons. The farther away the object is, the longer it took the photons to travel to you. So when you look around you do not see space—instead, you are looking back through the history of the universe. What you are seeing is a slice through the history of the world. Everything you see is a bit of information brought to you by a process which is a small part of that history. The whole history of the world is then nothing but the story of huge numbers of these processes, whose relationships are continually evolving. We cannot understand the world we see around us as something static. We must see it as something created, and under continual recreation, by an enormous number of processes acting together. The world we see around us is the collective result of all those processes.[62]

The connection between causality and discreteness has to do with the issue of infinity (and remember that in scientific calculations, an answer of infinity usually indicates a problem in the theory). If space

---

[59] Ibid., 174–75.
[60] Ibid., 175.
[61] Ibid., 177.
[62] Smolin, *Three Roads to Quantum Gravity*, 64.

is continuous, that would mean that there is an infinite number of relationships between events, whereas space being discrete means that there is only a finite number of relationships possible between events. Note that Smolin specifically argues that this vision is not "mystical" but rather rational and scientific (in a move that I would argue falsely opposes the two), so when he speaks of creation and re-creation, he is not speaking of creation in a theological sense, but rather he is referring to a universe that is self-creating and re-creating. When one believes in a God who is Creator, however, believing that the world is created and re-created in and through this process of causality and becoming has profound implications for how we understand God and the world we believe God created.

Theological and Pastoral Implications

Certainty vs. Uncertainty

String theory and loop quantum gravity offer us new images of reality. The way we thought things were and the way in which we experience reality on a day to day basis is perhaps misleading. "The discovery of exotic dimensions [in string theory] would show that the entirety of human experience had left us completely unaware of a basic and essential aspect of the universe."[63] String theory tells us of a "hidden reality," a whole world of other dimensions, other branes, and other universes that we cannot see but that scientists believe exist and believe have influenced and perhaps continue to influence our observable universe. Such a scientific theory offers a wonderful metaphor for our relationship with God. To be very clear, I am not equating the two. In other words, I am not suggesting that God exists in these higher dimensions and from those extra dimensions influences our three-dimensional world.

What I am suggesting is that God is an infinite mystery of a different kind. If the extra dimensions of string theory exist, scientists hope that one day they will be able to prove their existence, and if we can develop technology that could use gravitons (which, remember, have themselves not yet been proven to exist) to interact with

---

[63] Greene, *Fabric of the Cosmos*, 19.

those dimensions, perhaps even be able to explore their existence. When we talk about God as mystery, we are not talking about something unknown that we hope to fully know or eventually discover. We are talking about a mystery whose depths we can never exhaust or comprehend. We are talking about incomprehensible mystery. If God were comprehensible, God would not fill the capacity for the infinite that each of us not only has but also is at the very core of our existence. As discussed in chapter 2, we would then be able to transcend God. God is that which can never be transcended. Karl Rahner suggests that this God of incomprehensible mystery is incomprehensible even in the beatific vision, the theological term for when we see God "face to face" after death.[64] Rahner argues that what happens to us at death does not involve *knowledge* of God but rather *union* with God, so that we do not grasp God in death, but rather, we are grasped by God in death. Rather than "solve" the mystery, we surrender to the mystery and let ourselves be enveloped in God's absolute love.

The incomprehensible mystery of God has been richly explored in the Christian tradition of apophaticism, or negative theology, the idea that God is beyond any of our human words or concepts. In acknowledging our limited knowledge of God, Lawler and Salzman quote two famous passages, the first one by Augustine and the second by Aquinas: "*Si comprehendis non est Deus*" (if you have understood, what you have understood is not God). Aquinas agrees: "Now we cannot know what God is, but only what God is not."[65] Of course, in our tradition, we acknowledge not only God's incomprehensibility but also our human need to put words and concepts to God, to talk about our experience of God and the ways in which God has been revealed in Scripture, tradition, and our own lives. We call that aspect of theology the cataphatic tradition, referring to affirmative or positive speech about God. The issue is when we start to take our words and concepts literally. At that point, our words and concepts become false idols, closing us off to the mystery that is God. Lee Smolin makes

---

[64] Karl Rahner, "The Hiddenness of God," in *Theological Investigations*, vol. 16, *Experience of the Spirit: Source of Theology*, trans. David Morland (London: Darton, Longman & Todd London, 1979), 230.

[65] Todd A. Salzman and Michael G. Lawler, "Method and Catholic Theological Ethics in the Twenty-First Century," *Theological Studies* 74, no. 4 (December 2013): 910–11. Cites Augustine, *Sermo* 52.16 and Aquinas, *Summa Theologiae* 1, q. 3, preface. Translations by the authors.

a similar case against taking string theory too literally before it has been proven experimentally. He warns that science closes itself off to other fruitful avenues of theoretical possibility in limiting itself to the unproven hypotheses of string theory. When we cling to certain concrete images of God, we close ourselves off to other fruitful ways in which God could reveal God's self in our lives.

Science has shown us time and again throughout history that presupposing one worldview or asking a question in such a way that presumes a certain type of answer limits us from allowing reality to reveal itself to us. In string theory, scientists had to get beyond the assumptions that only three dimensions exist in order for the theory to be mathematically workable. Once they let go of that assumption, a whole new universe of possibilities opened up. Similarly, when we limit our image of God, we run the danger of missing the ways in which God does reveal God's self to us because we are not asking the right questions—or we are presuming the wrong answers.

The questions we ask about God predetermine our answers. For example, to ask, "Why does God allow suffering?" presupposes that God can prevent suffering and that God is a being with intention who makes choices about what occurs in the world. If we start with our experience instead, that is, that there is suffering, that experience can lead us to new questions. What do I believe about God in light of that experience? God is presence. God is Love. God does not "cause" or "allow" suffering. New questions emerge such as, what is love in the face of suffering? Love is the antidote to evil. Love stands in the midst of suffering and suffers with—*compassio*. C. S. Lewis notes that our questions about suffering can be misleading in this sense. In the journal he wrote after the death of his wife, he asks, "Can a mortal ask questions which God finds unanswerable? Quite easily, I should think. All nonsense questions are unanswerable. How many hours are there in a mile? Is yellow square or round? Probably half the questions we ask—half our great theological and metaphysical problems—are like that."[66]

Often in life the moment our certainties disappear is the first time we face the reality of our lives torn apart by unbearable grief. Nothing makes sense anymore, and the more others try to assert that solid

[66] C. S. Lewis, *A Grief Observed* (New York: Bantam Books, 1976), 81.

scaffolding that makes them feel so secure in their own faith, the more people lost in grief know the curve and warp of reality in which the ground is constantly shifting under their feet. In those moments, they know reality not as a solid scaffolding but rather that network of relationships and processes that changes and evolves over the course of events in one's life. In moments of great suffering, one of the hardest realities we can face is the incomprehensibility of God, the fact that we can ask questions of God to which there simply are no answers. In talking about his own grief and image of the Holy, Lewis says, "My idea of God is not a divine idea. It has to be shattered time after time. He shatters it himself. He is the great iconoclast. Could we not almost say that this shattering is one of the marks of his presence?"[67]

There is great comfort in certainty, in definitive information. The modern mindset reveled in such certainty and determinism. People seek guarantees, but that same certainty, determinism, and guarantee that gives so much comfort at a time in one's life when things are going well can devastate one when tragedy hits. Often during this time of grief, those who seek to comfort the grieving person end up spouting religious and biblical platitudes in an unconscious effort to shore up their own certainty. Such platitudes can discomfort the grieving person for whom there no longer is certainty. William Sloane Coffin speaks to this situation in a famous sermon given after his twenty-four-year-old son died in a car crash: "The one thing that should never be said when someone dies is 'It is the will of God.' Never do we know enough to say that. My own consolation lies in knowing that it was not the will of God that Alex die; that when the waves closed over the sinking car, God's heart was the first of all our hearts to break."[68] He goes on to speak of those who tried to comfort him with Scripture passages:

> While the words of the Bible are true, grief renders them unreal. The reality of grief is the absence of God—"My God, my God, why hast thou forsaken me?" The reality of grief is the solitude

---

[67] Ibid., 76.

[68] William Sloane Coffin, "Transcript—William Sloane Coffin's Eulogy for Alex," Public Affairs Television, http://www.pbs.org/now/printable/transcript_eulogy_print.html. A digital recording of this sermon, "Alex's Death 1-23-1983," can be downloaded at http://williamsloanecoffin.org/index.php?page=download-sermons.

of pain, the feeling that your heart is in pieces, your mind's a blank, that "there is no joy the world can give like that it takes away" (Lord Byron). . . . In other words, in my intense grief I felt some of my fellow reverends—not many, and none of you, thank God—were using comforting words of Scripture for self-protection, to pretty up a situation whose bleakness they simply couldn't face.[69]

Karl Rahner suggests that when the experience of unbearable grief makes us feel that God is not present, what has most likely happened is that our image of God is no longer working. He speaks to the experience of unanswered prayer, in which God suddenly seems unreal and inaccessible and makes our suffering even worse, "because it leads us to the extravagance of a yearning that we can never fulfill, and that even [God] does not seem to fulfill."[70] It seems that at the moment we need God the most, in the depths of grief and sorrow and suffering, God is most absent. To the person grieving, what was once certain can feel like a lie at best or intentional cruelty at worst. Lewis describes this experience bluntly:

Meanwhile, where is God? This is one of the most disquieting symptoms. When you are happy, so happy that you have no sense of needing Him . . . you will be—or so it feels—welcomed with open arms. But go to Him when your need is desperate, when all other help is vain, and what do you find? A door slammed in your face, and a sound of bolting and double bolting on the inside. After that, silence. You may as well turn away. The longer you wait, the more emphatic the silence will become. . . . The conclusion I dread is not, "So there's no God after all," but, "So this is what God's really like."[71]

God becomes as inaccessible as another dimension we cannot experience because all of our ways of seeing are limited to our three dimensions. Many grow up believing in a God who makes everything okay, and then one day, everything is not okay, and that God is gone.

[69] Ibid.

[70] Karl Rahner, *The Content of Faith: The Best of Karl Rahner's Theological Writings* [Rechenschaft des Glaubens], ed. Karl Lehmann and Albert Raffelt, trans. Harvey D. Egan (New York: Crossroad, 1993), 216–17.

[71] Lewis, *A Grief Observed*, 4–5.

We are left with silence and questions to which there are no answers. Rahner states:

> The first thing we have to do is this: stand up and face this God-distance of a choked up heart. . . . We have to endure it without the narcotic of the world, without the narcotic of sin or of obstinate despair. What God is really far away from you in this emptiness of the heart? Not the true and living God; for he is precisely the intangible God, the nameless God; and that is why he can really be the God of your measureless heart. Distant from you is only a God who does not exist: a tangible God, a God of a human being's small thoughts and his cheap timid feelings, a God of earthly security, a God whose concern is that the children don't cry and that philanthropy doesn't fall into disillusion, a very venerable—idol! That is what has become distant.[72]

For Rahner, it is only in this enduring the silence and letting go of the idol that we discover the God who "has been waiting for you in the deepest dungeon of your blocked-up heart, and that for a long time he has been quietly listening to you, even though you, after all the busy noise that we call our life, do not even let him get a word in edgewise."[73] The God we discover in the silence, however, can no longer be the God of certainty but rather the God of uncertainty and unknowing. As C. S. Lewis moves on his own journey of grief, he notes that at points when he holds least tightly to his grief for his wife, he remembers her most clearly, and he ponders, "And so, perhaps, with God. I have gradually been coming to feel that the door is no longer shut and bolted. Was it my own frantic need that slammed it in my face? The time when there is nothing at all in your soul except a cry for help may be just the time when God can't give it: you are like the drowning man who can't be helped because he clutches and grabs. Perhaps your own reiterated cries deafen you to the voice you hoped to hear."[74] When we seek certainty, we find silence; when we embrace the uncertainty, we find hidden depths in both ourselves and God.

---

[72] Rahner, *The Content of Faith*, 217–18.
[73] Ibid., 218.
[74] Lewis, *A Grief Observed*, 53–54.

The loss of certainty is a common phenomenon in our scientific and religious worldviews. In the modern era, science thought everything was explicable and predictable. The twenty-first century is the dawning of the age of uncertainty. People today often experience life as more complicated than that, greyer and less black and white. And yet some cling to the desire for certainty, the longing for the clarity of black and white. Sometimes the pastoral approach is to challenge certainty. Science can help us do so, giving us a model for moving from the known into the unknown, from certainty into mystery, and delighting in that mystery. Science challenges us to surrender our need for absolutes and accept that the world is built much more on probability and openness to possibility than on that which is certain. Humility is a religious virtue and yet one we so often see lacking in religious discourse. History should teach us to be less certain that we are right.

As was seen above, Lee Smolin argues that change and motion are primary, that they have priority over stasis.[75] We tend to seek out calm and stability, and yet chaos and upheaval are so often the hallmarks of our lives. Change is hard. We tend to want to hold on, to grasp. We do so with people, with experiences, with feelings, and yes, with our images of God. Think of the compelling image of Mary Magdalene clinging to the resurrected Christ only to be compassionately told to stop holding on so that her life could take on a new meaning and a new mission now (John 20:16-18). As Smolin's understanding of process and event describes, everything is changing all of the time. The question becomes one of how we respond to and live into that change. Smolin suggests that "people's characteristics are best revealed in how they react to situations, both propitious and adverse, and in what they have sought to do and become."[76] Who do we choose to become in the face of our own personal triumphs and tragedies?

As time-bound beings, we are story and process. There is no certainty in being story and process—only trust, hope, and faith. We do not get guarantees. Things do not always turn out alright or the way we had hoped, wanted, and prayed. But can we live into the future? Can we choose life and resurrection in the face of death, shattered

[75] Smolin, *Three Roads to Quantum Gravity*, 53.
[76] Ibid., 50.

dreams, and failed love? That trust in life is what it means to be Christian. Being Christian does not mean that the story ends the way we choose. In the iconic 1970s film *Jesus Christ Superstar*, Mary Magdalene, Peter, and the other followers of Christ sing "Could We Start Again, Please?" after Jesus is arrested. The story did not go the way they had expected. The song speaks to their confusion, fear, and uncertainty in the face of these unexpected events. In the gospel stories, the disciples are paralyzed by fear and grief after these events. They flee the scene. They hide in the upper room, unsure of what to do next until they encounter the risen Lord, until the Spirit fills them with hope and new life. Then they are able to go out and live trans-formed lives, to live bravely into death. Their lives take on new shapes and possibilities. Peter, who denied Christ and fled in the face of Jesus' arrest, is suddenly standing in the streets boldly preaching the resurrection, leading the community of believers, healing the sick, and raising the dead. Peter's response is to choose life and resurrection.

We face this same choice all the time in our own lives. People we love die—tragically and unexpectedly. We face a world filled with violence and war. We face disappointment and disillusionment in our careers, in our families, in our governments, and even in our churches. We have to decide how we go forward from our shattered places because stasis is not an option. Change is the only real option. We do not get guarantees or easy answers. We find ourselves in a place where there is no longer a comfortable assurance that every-thing will be okay, and like Jesus on the cross, we pray both "My God, my God, why have you forsaken me" and "into your hands I com-mend my spirit." To whom else shall we go? The Christian promise in a life of change and uncertainty was never that things would turn out as we had hoped. The Christian promise is that God, Emmanuel, is with us always, until the end of the age (Matt 28:20). God is with us in our darkest moments of despair and God-forsakenness. The Christian promise is connectedness and relationality, or in a simple word, love.

Smolin explains that reality at its very beginning was perhaps total interconnectedness. Somehow most of those connections have been turned off. Here is a wonderful metaphor for the fall of humanity. At our core, we are interconnected with one another and God, and yet somehow we find ourselves limited in our relationality, finite in our

capacities to connect. Love provides us with a nonlocal spatial connection. Once again, I am not equating God or love with the nonlocal
network of Smolin's loop quantum gravity. I am suggesting that
the possibility that the reality of space itself is as Smolin describes
gives us a wonderful metaphor or analogy for how we think about
the God we believe created that reality. God is Love, and that Love
that is God creates a web that connects all of our life stories to one
another. That connectedness that is God is what has the potential to
hold us together in times of unspeakable grief and tragedy. William
Sloane Coffin, after talking about his grief and the discomforting
things people said to him after the death of his son, says to his
congregation,

> My own broken heart is mending, and largely thanks to so many
> of you, my dear parishioners; for if in the last week I have re-
> learned one lesson, it is that love not only begets love, it transmits
> strength. . . . That's why immediately after such a tragedy
> people must come to your rescue, people who only want to hold
> your hand, not to quote anybody or even say anything, people
> who simply bring food and flowers—the basics of beauty and
> life—people who sign letters simply, "Your brokenhearted sister."
> . . . And that's what hundreds of you understood so beautifully.
> You gave me what God gives all of us—minimum protection,
> maximum support. I swear to you, I wouldn't be standing here
> were I not upheld.[77]

In my own parish community some years ago, one of the families
experienced the death of their infant child. Upon arriving at the
funeral, each of us was asked to take a piece of a puzzle from a box.
During his homily, the priest told us that when he visited the family
in the hospital, the father told him he could not find God in this
horrible, tragic experience. Later, he told the priest of the way in
which the community had come, bringing food and love, bringing a
hand-knitted baby blanket for the burial. The priest then told us that
if we put all of our puzzle pieces together, the image that we would
see was the face of Christ, because the father of the baby told him
that it was in those gestures of love from the community that he was

---

[77] Coffin, "Transcript—William Sloane Coffin's Eulogy for Alex."

able to feel the love of Christ at a time when God seemed so distant. Our priest retold this story during his homily on Christmas Eve that year, for herein lies the mystery of the incarnation, of God being made flesh. Love can form a nonlocal spatial network that connects us, holds us, and supports us. That interconnection of relationship that forms and evolves through the events of our lives is what can enable us to find life and meaning, to experience resurrection in the midst of tragedy and grief. Another word for it is grace.

As Smolin highlights in loop quantum gravity, the relationships themselves evolve and change. Analogously, we are not the same after such events; our relationship with God—and one another—is no longer the same. That change can be discomfiting in itself. There can be a longing for the old, easier relationship, but the new, evolved relationship is truer and more real.

Despite all of our discoveries into the possibilities of reality on a Planck level, we continue to live our lives according to classical physics, because while we know that the laws of classical physics are inaccurate to describe what is occurring on a level smaller than Planck's constant, those incongruencies are not noticeable in our day to day lives. Likewise we can continue to use our words, concepts, and images of God, our cataphatic or positive theology, as a guide for the way we confidently live our lives but do so in a manner that does not make the presumption that these images give us an accurate picture of the reality of God. We can judge our religious principles on their utility. Do they make us better, more loving persons? Do they harm others? Do they help us make meaning of our lives? Do they inspire us to make the world a better place? Such a perspective requires humility and an openness to change when what was once held as true no longer works. "Newtonian physics is still accurate and useful in many circumstances, but utility and reality are very different standards."[78] We can accept the utility of our religious perspectives while maintaining a modicum of humility regarding their ability to access the reality that we call God and/or God's will. As William Sloane Coffin states, "Never do we know enough to say that."[79]

---

[78] Greene, *Fabric of the Cosmos*, 10.
[79] Coffin, "Transcript—William Sloane Coffin's Eulogy for Alex."

Bibliography

Afshordi, Niayesh, Robert B. Mann, and Razieh Pourhasan. "The Black Hole at the Beginning of Time." *Scientific American* 311, no. 2 (August 2014): 36–43.

Ambjørn, Jan, Jerzy Jurkiewicz, and Renate Loll. "The Self-Organizing Quantum Universe." *Scientific American* 299, no. 1 (July 2008): 42–49.

Ashtekar, Abhay. "Gravity and the Quantum." *New Journal of Physics* 7 (September 2005): 198.

Ashtekar, Abhay, Beverly K. Berger, James Isenberg, and Malcolm A. H. MacCallum. "General Relativity and Gravitation: A Centennial Perspective." *ArXiv Preprint arXiv:1409.5823* (2014).

Ashtekar, Abhay, Martin Reuter, and Carlo Rovelli. "From General Relativity to Quantum Gravity." *ArXiv Preprint arXiv:1408.4336* (2014).

Augustine. *Confessions.* Translated by Henry Chadwick. Oxford: Oxford University Press, 1991.

Barbour, Ian G. *Religion and Science: Historical and Contemporary Issues.* San Francisco: HarperOne, 1997.

———. *When Science Meets Religion: Enemies, Strangers, or Partners?* New York: HarperCollins, 2000.

Barr, Stephen M. "Theology after Newton." *First Things* no. 187 (November 2008): 29–33.

Barrow, John D., Paul C. W. Davies, and Charles L. Harper. *Science and Ultimate Reality: Quantum Theory, Cosmology, and Complexity.* Cambridge, UK: Cambridge University Press, 2004.

Battersby, Stephen. "Chasing Shadows." *New Scientist* 218, no. 2916 (May 2013): 32–35.

Bekenstein, Jacob D. and Alfred T. Kamajian. "Information in the Holographic Universe." *Scientific American* 15, no. 3 (March 2006): 74–81.

Bentley, Philip J. "Uncertainty and Unity: Paradox and Truth." *Judaism* 33, no. 2 (March 1984): 191–201.

Bojowald, Martin. "Follow the Bouncing Universe." *Scientific American* 299, no. 4 (October 2008): 44–51.

Bracken, Joseph A. "The Body of Christ: An Intersubjective Interpretation." *Horizons* 31, no. 1 (Spring 2004): 7–21.

Briggs, John, and F. David Peat. *Turbulent Mirror: An Illustrated Guide to Chaos Theory and the Science of Wholeness*. New York: Harper & Row, 1989.

Brueggemann, Walter. "The Book of Exodus." In *The New Interpreter's Bible: A Commentary in Twelve Volumes*, edited by Leander Keck, David Peterson, et al. Vol. 1, 675–981. Nashville, TN: Abingdon Press, 1994.

———. "Covenanting as Human Vocation: A Discussion of the Relation of Bible and Pastoral Care." *Interpretation* 33, no. 2 (April 1979): 115–29.

Bub, Jeffrey. "The Entangled World: How Can It Be Like That?" In *The Trinity and an Entangled World: Relationality in Physical Science and Theology*, edited by John C. Polkinghorne, 15–31. Grand Rapids, MI: W. B. Eerdmans Publishing, 2010.

Burgess, Cliff, and Fernando Quevedo. "The Great Cosmic Roller-Coaster Ride." *Scientific American* 297, no. 5 (November 2007): 52–59.

Callender, Craig. "Is Time an Illusion?" *Scientific American* 302, no. 6 (June 2010): 58–65.

Carroll, Sean M. *From Eternity to Here: The Quest for the Ultimate Theory of Time*. New York: Dutton, 2010.

———. *The Particle at the End of the Universe: How the Hunt for the Higgs Boson Leads Us to the Edge of a New World*. New York: Dutton, 2012.

———. *Mysteries of Modern Physics: Time*. Great Courses. Course No. 1257. Chantilly, VA: Teaching Company, 2012.

Cavanaugh, William T. "The Body of Christ: The Eucharist and Politics." *Word & World* 22, no. 2 (March 2002): 170–77.

Chalmers, Matthew. "Out of the Darkness." *Nature* 490 (October 2012): S2–S4.

Choi, Hyung. "Knowledge of the Unseen: A New Vision for Science and Religion Dialogue." In *Expanding Humanity's Vision of God: New Thoughts on Science and Religion*, edited by Robert Hermann, 3–22. Philadelphia, PA: Templeton Foundation, 2001.

Clayton, Philip. "Unsolved Dilemmas: The Concept of Matter in the History of Philosophy and in Contemporary Physics." In *Information and the Nature of Reality: From Physics to Metaphysics*, edited by Paul Davies and Niels Henrik Gregersen, 38–62. New York: Cambridge University Press, 2010.

Clifford, Richard, and Roland Murphy. "Genesis." In *The New Jerome Biblical Commentary*, edited by Raymond Brown, Joseph Fitzmyer and Roland Murphy, 8–43. Englewood Cliffs, NJ: Prentice Hall, 1990.

Cox, Brian, and Jeff Forshaw. *The Quantum Universe: And Why Anything That Can Happen, Does*. Boston, MA: Da Capo Press, 2012.

Coyne, George V. "Children of a Fertile Universe: Chance, Destiny, and a Creator God." Albertus Magnus Lecture, Siena Center at Dominican University, River Forest, IL, November 17, 2011.

———. "The Dance of the Fertile Universe." http://www.metro.inter.edu /servicios/decanatos/academicos/documentos/HandoutCoyne.pdf.

Coyne, George V. and Alessandro Omizzolo. *Wayfarers in the Cosmos: The Human Quest for Meaning*. New York: Crossroad, 2002.

Davies, Paul. "Complexity and the Arrow of Time." In *From Complexity to Life: On the Emergence of Life and Meaning*, edited by Niels Henrik Gregersen, 72–92. New York: Oxford University Press, 2003.

———. *The Cosmic Blueprint: New Discoveries in Nature's Creative Ability to Order the Universe*. Philadelphia, PA: Templeton Foundation Press, 2004.

———. "That Mysterious Flow." *Scientific American* 15, no. 3 (February 2006): 82–88.

Davies, P. C. W., and John Gribbin. *The Matter Myth: Dramatic Discoveries that Challenge Our Understanding of Physical Reality*. New York: Simon & Schuster, 2007.

Davis, Tamara M. "Cosmology: Hydrogen Wisps Reveal Dark Energy." *Nature* 498, no. 7453 (June 2013): 179–80.

Delio, Ilia. *From Teilhard to Omega: Co-Creating and Unfinished Universe*. Maryknoll, NY: Orbis Books, 2014.

———. *The Unbearable Wholeness of Being: God, Evolution, and the Power of Love*. Maryknoll, NY: Orbis Books, 2013.

DeWitt, Calvin B. "Contemporary Missiology and the Biosphere." In *The Antioch Agenda: Essays on the Restorative Church in Honor of Orlando E. Costas*, edited by D. Jeyaraj, R. Pazmino and R. Peterson, 305–28. Delhi: ISPCK, 2007.

———. "Three Biblical Principles for Environmental Stewardship." Au Sable Institute of Environmental Studies. http://www.leaderu.com/ theology/environment.html.

Drees, Willem B. *Beyond the Big Bang: Quantum Cosmologies and God*. La Salle, IL: Open Court Publishing, 1990.

Edmondson, Stephen. "Opening the Table: The Body of Christ and God's Prodigal Grace." *Anglican Theological Review* 91, no. 2 (March 2009): 213–34.

Edwards, Denis. *Jesus and the Cosmos*. New York: Paulist Press, 1991.

The Elegant Universe. Directed by Joseph McMaster, Julia Cort, B. Greene, et al. Boston: WGBH Boston Video, 2003.

Ellis, George F. R., "Does the Multiverse Really Exist?" *Scientific American* 305, no. 2 (August 2011): 38–43.

———. "Physics in the Real Universe: Time and Space-Time." In *Relativity and the Dimensionality of the World*, edited by Vesselin Petkov, 49–79. Dordrecht, The Netherlands: Springer, 2007.

Ellis, George F. R., U. Kirchner, and William R. Stoeger. "Multiverses and Physical Cosmology." *Monthly Notices of the Royal Astronomical Society* 347, no. 3 (2004): 921–36.

Ellis, George F. R., and William R. Stoeger. "Introduction to General Relativity and Cosmology." In *Quantum Cosmology and the Laws of Nature*, edited by Robert J. Russell, Nancey C. Murphy and Chris J. Isham, 33–48. Vatican City: Vatican Observatory, 1993.

Ferris, Timothy. *The Whole Shebang: A State-of-the-Universe(s) Report*. New York: Simon & Schuster, 1997.

Feynman, Richard P. *The Character of Physical Law*. Cambridge, MA: MIT Press, 1965.

———. *QED: The Strange Theory of Light and Matter*. Princeton, NJ: Princeton University Press, 1985.

Feynman, Richard P., Robert B. Leighton, and Matthew L. Sands. *The Feynman Lectures on Physics*. Vol. 3. Reading, MA: Addison-Wesley Pub. Co., 1963.

Ford, Joseph. "How Random Is a Coin Toss?" *Scientific American* 36, no. 4 (April 1983): 40–47.

Fretheim, Terence. "The Book of Genesis." In *The New Interpreter's Bible: A Commentary in Twelve Volumes*, edited by Leander Keck, David Petersen, et al. Vol. 1, 321–674. Nashville, TN: Abingdon Press, 1994.

Fritz, Peter Joseph. *Karl Rahner's Theological Aesthetics*. Washington, DC: The Catholic University of America Press, 2014.

Gleick, James. *Chaos: Making a New Science*. New York: Viking Books, 1987.

Goodenough, Ursula. *The Sacred Depths of Nature*. New York: Oxford University Press, 1998.

Greene, Brian. *The Elegant Universe: Superstrings, Hidden Dimensions, and the Quest for the Ultimate Theory*. New York: W. W. Norton, 1999.

———. *The Fabric of the Cosmos: Space, Time, and the Texture of Reality*. New York: Alfred A. Knopf, 2004.

———. *The Hidden Reality: Parallel Universes and the Deep Laws of the Cosmos*. EPUB eBook ed. New York: Alfred A. Knopf, 2011.

Greenlee, Thomas. "General Relativity, the Cosmic Microwave Background, and Moral Relativism." In *Science and Religion in Dialogue*, Vol. 1, 93–96. Oxford: Wiley-Blackwell, 2010.

Gregersen, Niels Henrik, ed. *From Complexity to Life: On the Emergence of Life and Meaning*. New York: Oxford University Press, 2003.

Gribbin, John. *Almost Everyone's Guide to Science: The Universe, Life, and Everything*. New Haven, CT: Yale University Press, 1999.

———. *Alone in the Universe: Why Our Planet Is Unique*. Hoboken, NJ: Wiley, 2011.

———. *Deep Simplicity: Bringing Order to Chaos and Complexity*. New York: Random House, 2004.

———. *In Search of Schrödinger's Cat: Quantum Physics and Reality*. New York: Bantam Books, 1984.

———. *Schrödinger's Kittens and the Search for Reality: Solving the Quantum Mysteries*. Boston: Little, Brown & Co., 1995.

Grieb, A. K. "People of God, Body of Christ, Koinonia of Spirit: The Role of Ethical Ecclesiology in Paul's 'Trinitarian' Language." *Anglican Theological Review* 87, no. 2 (Spring 2005): 225–52.

Hauerwas, Stanley. "Bearing Reality: A Christian Meditation." *Journal of the Society of Christian Ethics* 33, no. 1 (March 2013): 3–20.

Haught, John. "Chaos, Complexity, and Theology." In *Teilhard in the 21st Century: The Emerging Spirit of Earth*, edited by Arthur Fabel and Donald P. St. John, 181–94. Maryknoll, NY: Orbis Books, 2003.

Hawking, Stephen, and Leonard Mlodinow. *The Grand Design: New Answers to the Ultimate Question of Life*. New York: Bantam Books, 2010.

Heisenberg, Werner. *Physik Und Philosophie*. Stuttgart: S. Hirzel, 2000.

Helrich, Carl S. "On the Limitations and Promise of Quantum Theory for Comprehension of Human Knowledge and Consciousness." *Zygon* 41, no. 3 (September 2006): 543–66.

Hermann, Robert, ed. *Expanding Humanity's Vision of God: New Thoughts on Science and Religion*. Philadelphia, PA: Templeton Foundation, 2001.

Holland, John H. *Emergence: From Chaos to Order*. Reading, MA: Addison-Wesley, 1998.

Hughes, Daniel A. and Jonathan Baylin. *Brain-Based Parenting: The Neuroscience of Caregiving for Healthy Attachment*. New York: W. W. Norton & Company, 2012.

Hultgren, Arland J. "The Church as the Body of Christ: Engaging an Image in the New Testament." *Word & World* 22, no. 2 (March 2002): 124–32.

Isham, Chris J., and John C. Polkinghorne. "The Debate over the Block Universe." In *Quantum Cosmology and the Laws of Nature*, edited by Robert

J. Russell, Nancey C. Murphy, and Chris J. Isham, 135–44. Vatican City: Vatican Observatory, 1993.

Johnson, SueAnn. "How Is the Body of Christ a Meaningful Symbol for the Contemporary Christian Community?" *Feminist Theology* 17, no. 2 (January 2009): 210–28.

Jospe, Raphael. "The Concept of the Chosen People: An Interpretation." *Judaism* 43, no. 2 (March 1994): 127–48.

Kelly, Anthony J. "'The Body of Christ: Amen!': The Expanding Incarnation." *Theological Studies* 71, no. 4 (December 2010): 792–816.

Kohut, A., Keeter, S., Doherty, C. and Dimock, M. "Scientific Achievements Less Prominent Than a Decade Ago: Public Praises Science; Scientists Fault Public, Media." Washington, DC: The Pew Research Center for the People & the Press. http://www.people-press.org/files/legacy -pdf/528.pdf.

Krauss, Lawrence. *A Universe from Nothing*. New York: Simon and Schuster, 2012.

Krishnamurti, Jiddu and David Bohm. *The Limits of Thought: Discussions*. New York: Routledge, 1999.

Kselman, John and Michael Barré. "Psalms." In *The New Jerome Biblical Commentary*, edited by Raymond Brown, Joseph Fitzmyer and Roland Murphy, 523–52. Englewood Cliffs, NJ: Prentice Hall, 1990.

Kumar, Manjit. *Quantum: Einstein, Bohr, and the Great Debate about the Nature of Reality*. New York: London: W. W. Norton, 2009.

Küng, Hans. *The Beginning of All Things: Science and Religion*. Translated by John Bowden. Grand Rapids, MI: W. B. Eerdmans Publishing, 2007.

Laszlo, Ervin. "Quantum and Consciousness: In Search of a New Paradigm." *Zygon* 41, no. 3 (September 2006): 533–41.

Lemonick, Michael. "The Mystery of Dark Matter: WIMPs May Have the Answer." *Time*, April 8, 2014. http://time.com/54214/dark-matter -wimps-gravity-galaxy/.

Lewis, C. S. *A Grief Observed*. New York: Bantam Books, 1976.

Ligomenides, Panos. "Scientific Knowledge as a Bridge to the Mind of God." In *The Trinity and an Entangled World: Relationality in Physical Science and Theology*, edited by John C. Polkinghorne, 74–92. Grand Rapids, MI: W. B. Eerdmans Publishing, 2010.

Linde, Andre. "The Self-Reproducing Inflationary Universe." *Scientific American* 271, no. 5 (November 1994): 48–55.

Lindley, David. *Uncertainty: Einstein, Heisenberg, Bohr, and the Struggle for the Soul of Science*. New York: Doubleday, 2007.

Lineweaver, Charles H. and Tamara M. Davis. "Misconceptions about the Big Bang." *Scientific American* 292, no. 3 (March 2005): 36–45.

Lisi, A. Garrett, and James Owen Weatherall. "A Geometric Theory of Everything." *Scientific American* 303, no. 6 (December 2010): 54–61.

Lorenz, Edward N. *The Essence of Chaos*. Seattle: University of Washington Press, 1993.

Lykken, Joseph and Maria Spiropulu. "Supersymmetry and the Crisis in Physics." *Scientific American* 310, no. 5 (May 2014): 34–39.

Malcolm, Lois. "Body of Christ: Our Diversity in Him." *Word & World* 22, no. 2 (March 2002): 187–318.

Masci, David. "Public Opinion on Religion and Science in the United States." Pew Research Center. http://www.pewforum.org/2009/11/05/public -opinion-on-religion-and-science-in-the-united-states/.

McClean, John. "A Search for the Body: Is There Space for Christ's Body in Pannenberg's Eschatology?" *International Journal of Systematic Theology* 14, no. 1 (January 2012): 91–108.

McFarland, Ian A. "The Body of Christ: Rethinking a Classic Ecclesiological Model." *International Journal of Systematic Theology* 7, no. 3 (July 2005): 225–45.

McMullin, Ernan. "From Matter to Materialism . . . and (Almost) Back." In *Information and the Nature of Reality: From Physics to Metaphysics*, edited by Paul Davies and Niels Henrik Gregersen, 13–37. New York: Cambridge University Press, 2010.

———. "Creation *Ex Nihilo*: Early History." In *Creation and the God of Abraham*, edited by David Burrell, Carlo Cogliati, Janet Soskice, and William Stoeger, 11–23. Cambridge, UK: Cambridge University Press, 2010.

Moltmann, Jürgen. "Cosmos and Theosis: Eschatological Perspectives on the Future of the Universe." In *The Far-Future Universe: Eschatology from a Cosmic Perspective*, edited by George F. R. Ellis, 249–65. Philadelphia, PA: Templeton Foundation Press, 2002.

Moore, Ben. *Elephants in Space: The Past, Present, and Future of Life and the Universe*. New York: Springer, 2014.

Moskowitz, Clare. "Dark Matter May Be Destroying Itself in Milky Way's Core." *Scientific American*, April 8, 2014. http://www.scientificamerican .com/article/dark-matter-wimps-fermi-milky-way/.

Murphy, Nancey C., Robert J. Russell, William R. Stoeger, and International Society for Science and Religion. *Physics and Cosmology*. Vatican City: Vatican Observatory Publications, 2007.

Neville, Graham. "Sinlessness and Uncertainty in Jesus." *Expository Times* 116, no. 11 (August 2005): 361–65.

Newport, Frank. "In U.S., 46% Hold Creationist View of Human Origins." *Gallup*, June 1, 2012. http://www.gallup.com/poll/155003/hold -creationist-view-human-origins.aspx.

Nichol, Lee. *The Essential David Bohm*. New York: Routledge, 2003.

Nürnberger, Klaus. "Eschatology and Entropy: An Alternative to Robert John Russell's Proposal." *Zygon* 47, no. 4 (December 2012): 970–96.

O'Collins, Gerald. "Cosmological Christology: Arthur Peacocke, John Polkinghorne, and Pierre Teilhard De Chardin in Dialogue." *New Blackfriars* 93, no. 1047 (December 2012): 516–23.

Okeke, George E. "The Church as the Community of God's Chosen People." *Communio Viatorum* 30, nos. 3–4 (December 1987): 199–213.

O'Murchu, Diarmuid. *In the Beginning Was the Spirit: Science, Religion, and Indigenous Spirituality*. Maryknoll, NY: Orbis Books, 2012.

———. *Quantum Theology*. New York: Crossroad Publishing Company, 1997.

Osborne, Kenan B. *Christian Sacraments in a Postmodern World: A Theology for the Third Millennium*. New York: Paulist Press, 1999.

Ostriker, J. P. and P. J. Steinhardt. "The Quintessential Universe." *Scientific American* 284, no. 1 (January 2001): 46–53.

Page, Scott E. *Diversity and Complexity*. Princeton, NJ: Princeton University Press, 2011.

Panek, Richard. *The 4 Percent Universe: Dark Matter, Dark Energy, and the Race to Discover the Rest of Reality*. Boston: Houghton Mifflin Harcourt, 2011.

Pannenberg, Wolfhart. "Eternity, Time, and Space." *Zygon* 40, no. 1 (March 2005): 97–106.

———. "God as Spirit—and Natural Science." *Zygon* 36, no. 4 (December 2001): 783–94.

Payne, Daniel. "Radical Atonement and the Cosmic Body of Christ." *Journal of Ecumenical Studies* 47, no. 2 (2012): 288–94.

Peters, Ted. "On Creating the Cosmos." In *Physics, Philosophy, and Theology: A Common Quest for Understanding*. 3rd ed. Edited by Robert John Russell, William Stoeger and George Coyne, 273–96. Vatican City: Vatican Observatory, 1997.

Peters, Ted, Robert J. Russell, and Michael Welker. *Resurrection: Theological and Scientific Assessments*. Grand Rapids, MI: W. B. Eerdmans Publishing, 2002.

Philip, Mary, John Arthur Nunes, and Charles M. Collier, eds. *Churrasco: A Theological Feast in Honor of Vítor Westhelle*. Eugene, Oregon: Pickwick Publications, 2013.

Polkinghorne, John C. *Belief in God in an Age of Science*. The Terry Lectures. New Haven: Yale University Press, 1998.

———. "The Demise of Democritus." In *The Trinity and an Entangled World: Relationality in Physical Science and Theology*, edited by John C. Polkinghorne, 1–14. Grand Rapids, MI: W. B. Eerdmans Publishing, 2010.

———. *The Faith of a Physicist: Reflections of a Bottom-Up Thinker*. Theology and the Sciences. Minneapolis, MN: Fortress Press, 1996.

———. *Faith, Science, and Understanding*. New Haven, CT: Yale University Press, 2000.

———. *Quantum Physics and Theology: An Unexpected Kinship*. New Haven, CT: Yale University Press, 2007.

———. *Quantum Theory: A Very Short Introduction*. Oxford: Oxford University Press, 2002.

———. *Quarks, Chaos & Christianity: Questions to Science and Religion*. New York: Crossroad, 2005.

———. *Reason and Reality: The Relationship between Science and Theology*. Philadelphia, PA: Trinity Press International, 1991.

———. *Science and Theology: An Introduction*. Minneapolis, MN: Fortress Press, 1998.

———. *Science and the Trinity: The Christian Encounter with Reality*. New Haven, CT: Yale University Press, 2006.

———. *The Trinity and an Entangled World: Relationality in Physical Science and Theology*. Grand Rapids, MI: W. B. Eerdmans Publishing, 2010.

Polkinghorne, John, and Michael Welker, eds. *The End of the World and the Ends of God: Science and Theology on Eschatology*. Theology for the Twenty-First Century. Harrisburg, PA: Trinity Press International, 2000.

Pontificia Commissio Biblica. *The Interpretation of the Bible in the Church*. Vatican City, Vatican: Libreria Editrice Vaticana, 1993.

Porter, Jean. "Divine Commands, Natural Law, and the Authority of God." *Journal of the Society of Christian Ethics* 34, no. 1 (March 2014): 3–20.

———. "The Natural Law and Innovative Forms of Marriage: A Reconsideration." *Journal of the Society of Christian Ethics* 30, no. 2 (September 2010): 79–97.

Rahner, Karl. "Christian Dying." In *Theological Investigations*. Vol. 18, *God and Revelation*, 226–56. Translated by Edward Quinn. Vol. 18. New York: Crossroad, 1983.

———. "Concerning the Relationship between Nature and Grace." In *Theological Investigations*. Vol. 1, *God, Christ, Mary, and Grace*, 297–318. Translated by Cornelius Ernst. Baltimore: Helicon Press, 1961.

———. *The Content of Faith: The Best of Karl Rahner's Theological Writings* [Rechenschaft des Glaubens]. Translated by Harvey D. Egan. Edited by Karl Lehmann and Albert Raffelt. New York: Crossroad, 1993.

———. "Dogmatic Questions on Easter." In *Theological Investigations*. Vol. 4, *More Recent Writings*, 121–33. Baltimore: Helicon Press, 1961.

———. "Eternity from Time." In *Theological Investigations*. Vol. 19, *Faith and Ministry*, 169–77. Translated by Edward Quinn. London: Darton, Longman & Todd, 1984.

———. *Foundations of Christian Faith: An Introduction to the Idea of Christianity* [Grundkurs des Glaubens]. Translated by William Dych. New York: Crossroad, 1978.

———. "The Hiddenness of God." In *Theological Investigations*. Vol. 16, *Experience of the Spirit: Source of Theology*, 237–46. Translated by David Morland. London: Darton, Longman & Todd, 1979.

———. *Hominisation: The Evolutionary Origin of Man as a Theological Problem*. New York: Herder and Herder, 1965.

———. "Ideas for a Theology of Death." In *Theological Investigations*. Vol. 13, *Theology, Anthropology, Christology*, 169–86. Translated by David Bourke. New York: Seabury, 1975.

———. "Nature and Grace." In *Theological Investigations*. Vol. 4, *More Recent Writings*, 165–88. Translated by Kevin Smyth. Baltimore: Helicon Press, 1961.

———. "On Christian Dying." In *Theological Investigations*. Vol. 7, *Further Theology of the Spiritual Life*, 285–93. Translated by David Bourke. Baltimore: Helicon Press, 1961.

———. *The Practice of Faith: A Handbook of Contemporary Spirituality* [Praxis des Glaubens]. Edited by Karl Lehmann and Albert Raffelt. New York: Crossroad, 1983.

———. "The Resurrection of the Body." In *Theological Investigations*. Vol. 2, *Man in the Church*, 203–16. Translated by Karl-H. Kruger. Baltimore: Helicon Press, 1963.

———. "The Theology of the Symbol." In *Theological Investigations*. Vol. 4, *More Recent Writings*. Translated by Kevin Smyth. Baltimore: Helicon Press, 1961.

———. "The Unity of Spirit and Matter in the Christian Understanding of Faith." In *Theological Investigations*. Vol. 6, *Concerning Vatican Council II*, 153–77. Translated by Boniface Kruger and Karl-H. Kruger. Baltimore: Helicon Press, 1969.

Rees, Martin J. "Exploring our Universe and Others." *Scientific American* 281, no. 6 (December 1999): 78–83.

———. *Just Six Numbers: The Deep Forces that Shape the Universe*. New York: Basic Books, 2000.

Reich, Henry. "Science, Religion, and the Big Bang." *MinutePhysics*. YouTube video, 5:19. August 19, 2013. http://youtu.be/q3MWRvLndzs.

Rovelli, Carlo. "Loop Quantum Gravity." *Physics World* 16 (November 2003): 37–42.

———. *Quantum Gravity*. Cambridge Monographs on Mathematical Physics. New York: Cambridge University Press, 2004.

Rozema, Lee A., Ardavan Darabi, Dylan H. Mahler, Alex Hayat, Yasaman Soudagar, and Aephraim M. Steinberg. "Violation of Heisenberg's Measurement-Disturbance Relationship by Weak Measurements." *Physical Review Letters* 109, no. 10 (2012): 100404-1–100404-5.

Russell, Heidi. "From Being to Love: Reconceiving the Trinity in Light of Jean-Luc Marion's Phenomenological Shift." *Horizons* 41, no. 1 (June 2014): 22–48.

———. *The Heart of Rahner: The Theological Implications of Andrew Tallon's Theory of Triune Consciousness*. Marquette Studies in Theology, Vol. 64. Milwaukee, WI: Marquette University Press, 2009.

———. "Quantum Anthropology: Reimaging the Human Person as Body/Spirit." *Theological Studies* 74, no. 4 (December 2013): 934–59.

Russell, Robert J. *Cosmology: From Alpha to Omega; The Creative Mutual Interaction of Theology and Science*. Minneapolis, MN: Fortress Press, 2008.

———. *Time in Eternity: Pannenberg, Physics, and Eschatology in Creative Mutual Interaction*. Notre Dame, IN: University of Notre Dame Press, 2012.

Russell, Robert J., Philip Clayton, Kirk Wegter-McNelly, and John C. Polkinghorne. *Quantum Mechanics*. Series on Scientific Perspectives on Divine Action, Vol. 5. Vatican City: Vatican Observatory and Berkeley, CA: Center for Theology and the Natural Sciences, 2001.

Russell, Robert J., Nancey C. Murphy, and Arthur Robert Peacocke. *Chaos and Complexity*. Series on Scientific Perspectives on Divine Action, Vol. 2. Vatican City: Vatican Observatory and Berkeley, CA: Center for Theology and the Natural Sciences, 1997.

Russell, Robert J., Nancey C. Murphy, and C. J. Isham. *Quantum Cosmology and the Laws of Nature*. Series on Scientific Perspectives on Divine Action, Vol. 1. Vatican City: Vatican Observatory & Berkeley, CA: Center for Theology and the Natural Sciences, 1993.

Salzman, Todd A., and Michael G. Lawler. "Method and Catholic Theological Ethics in the Twenty-First Century." *Theological Studies* 74, no. 4 (December 2013): 903–33.

Schäfer, Lothar. "Nonempirical Reality: Transcending the Physical and Spiritual in the Order of the One." *Zygon* 43, no. 2 (May 2008): 329–52.

———. "Quantum Reality and the Consciousness of the Universe: Quantum Reality, the Emergence of Complex Order from Virtual States, and the Importance of Consciousness in the Universe." *Zygon* 41, no. 3 (September 2006): 505–32.

———. "A Response to Carl Helrich: The Limitations and Promise of Quantum Theory." *Zygon* 41, no. 3 (September 2006): 583–92.

Scharf, Caleb. "Cosmic (in)Significance." *Scientific American* 311, no. 2 (August 2014): 74–77.

Segal, Robert A. "What is 'Mythic Reality'?" *Zygon* 46, no. 3 (September 2011): 588–92.

Siegel, Ethan. "A Tale of Two Slits." *Starts with a Bang!* June 1, 2009. Science Blogs. http://scienceblogs.com/startswithabang/2009/06/01/a-tale-of-two-slits/.

Silverman, Mark. *Quantum Superposition: Counterintuitive Consequences of Coherence, Entanglement, and Interference.* Berlin: Springer, 2008.

Smolin, Lee. "Atoms of Space and Time." *Scientific American* 290, no. 1 (January 2004): 66–75.

———. *The Life of the Cosmos.* New York: Oxford University Press, 1997.

———. *Three Roads to Quantum Gravity.* New York: Basic Books, 2001.

———. "Time, Laws, and the Future of Cosmology." *Physics Today* 67, no. 3 (March 2014): 38–43.

———. *Time Reborn: From the Crisis in Physics to the Future of the Universe.* Boston: Houghton Mifflin Harcourt, 2013.

———. *The Trouble with Physics: The Rise of String Theory, the Fall of a Science, and What Comes Next.* Boston: Houghton Mifflin, 2006.

Smolin, Lee and Roberto Mangabeira Unger. *The Singular Universe and the Reality of Time.* Cambridge, UK: Cambridge University Press, 2014.

Steinhardt, Paul. "The Inflation Debate." *Scientific American Special Editions* 23, no. 3 (2014): 70–75.

Stenger, Victor J. *God: The Failed Hypothesis: How Science Shows that God Does Not Exist.* Amherst, NY: Prometheus Books, 2010.

Stoeger, William R. "Contemporary Cosmology and Its Implications for the Science-Religion Dialogue." In *Physics, Philosophy, and Theology: A Common Quest for Understanding.* 3rd ed. Edited by Robert J. Russell, William Stoeger and George V. Coyne, 219–47. Vatican City: Vatican Observatory, 1997.

———. "Epistemological and Ontological Issues Arising from Quantum Theory." In *Quantum Mechanics: Scientific Perspectives on Divine Action*, edited by Robert John Russell, Philip Clayton, Kirk Wegter-McNelly, and John Polkinghorne, 81–98. Vatican City: Vatican Observatory, 2001.

Stortz, Martha Ellen. "Indwelling Christ, Indwelling Christians: Living as Marked." *Currents in Theology and Mission* 34, no. 3 (June 2007): 165–78.

Strogatz, Steven H. *Nonlinear Dynamics and Chaos: With Applications to Physics, Biology, Chemistry, and Engineering.* Studies in Nonlinearity. Reading, MA: Addison-Wesley, 1994.

———. *Sync: The Emerging Science of Spontaneous Order.* New York: Hyperion, 2003.

Susskind, Leonard. *The Cosmic Landscape: String Theory and the Illusion of Intelligent Design*. New York: Back Bay Books, 2006.

Swidler, Leonard. " 'Naming' Ultimate Reality." *Journal of Ecumenical Studies* 48, no. 1 (December 2013): 1–4.

Tallon, Andrew. *Head and Heart: Affection, Cognition, Volition as Triune Consciousness*. New York: Fordham University Press, 1997.

Taylor, Mark Lewis. "Torture and the Body of Christ." *Touchstone* 24, no. 3 (September 2006): 5–20.

Tegmark, Max. "Parallel Universes." *Scientific American* 288, no. 5 (May 2003): 40–51.

———. "The Interpretation of Quantum Mechanics: Many Worlds or Many Words?" *Fortschritte Der Physik* 46, nos. 6–8 (November 1998): 855–62.

Teilhard de Chardin, Pierre. *Hymn of the Universe*. Translated by Simon Bartholomew. New York: Harper & Row, 1965.

———. *Science and Christ*. Translated by René Hague. London: Collins, 1968.

Thiel, John E. "The Aesthetics of Tradition and the Styles of Theology." *Theological Studies* 75, no. 4 (December 2014): 795–815.

Tweed, Matt. "The Compact Cosmos." In *Scientia: Mathematics, Physics, Chemistry, Biology, and Astronomy for All*, edited by John Martineau, 317–80. New York: Walker Publishing, 2005.

Veneziano, Gabriele. "The Myth of the Beginning of Time." *Scientific American* 16, no. 1 (January 2006): 72–81.

Villars, C. N. "Microphysical Objects as 'Potentiality Waves.' " *European Journal of Physics* 8, no. 2 (April 1987): 148–49.

———. "Observables, States and Measurements in Quantum Physics." *European Journal of Physics* 5, no. 3 (July 1984): 177–83.

Walls, Jerry L. *The Oxford Handbook of Eschatology*. New York: Oxford University Press, 2008.

Ward, Keith. "Cosmology and Religious Ideas about the End of the World." In *The Far-Future Universe: Eschatology from a Cosmic Perspective*, edited by George F. R. Ellis, 235–48. Philadelphia, PA: Templeton Foundation Press, 2002.

Wilczek, Frank. *The Lightness of Being: Mass, Ether, and the Unification of Forces*. New York: Basic Books, 2008.

Winfield, Flora. " 'For Nothing Can Separate Us from the Love of Christ': Who Does Belong to the Body of Christ?" *Ecumenical Review* 47, no. 3 (July 1995): 364–72.

Wood, Susan K. "Body of Christ: Our Unity with Him." *Word & World* 22, no. 2 (March 2002): 186–318.

Wooddell, Joseph D. "Truth with a Capital T: Does It Really Matter? Public Discussion of Social and Economic Questions in a Relativistic Age." *Criswell Theological Review* 11, no. 2 (Spring 2014): 3–16.

Zeilinger, Anton. "Quantum Physics: Ontology or Epistomology?" In *The Trinity and an Entangled World: Relationality in Physical Science and Theology,* edited by John C. Polkinghorne, 32–40. Grand Rapids, MI: W. B. Eerdmans Publishing, 2010.

Index